EAT DAT

NEW ORLEANS

EAT DAT

NEW ORLEANS

*A Guide to the Unique Food Culture
of the Crescent City*

MICHAEL MURPHY

PHOTOGRAPHS BY RICK OLIVIER

COUNTRYMAN PRESS
WOODSTOCK, VERMONT

Published by The Countryman Press, P.O. Box 748, Woodstock, VT 05091
Distributed by W. W. Norton & Company, Inc., 500 Fifth Avenue, New York, NY 10110
Printed in the U.S.

10 9 8 7 6 5 4 3 2 1

Dedicated to the spirit of New Orleans,
which feeds me every day

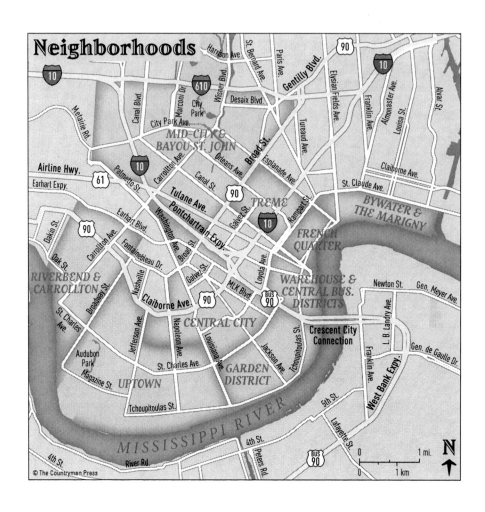

CONTENTS

Maryjane Rosas, chef at the Country Club, and Rik Slave, Cochon Butcher, wielding sharp instruments

INTRODUCTION

To get to New Orleans, you don't pass through anywhere else.
—Allen Toussaint

At the risk of annoying every potential reader who doesn't live in or currently love New Orleans, I'm going to open by stating when it comes to food, New Orleans is the greatest city in America. My provincial claim was recently echoed in *Saveur* magazine. Their cover and the issue's theme was, "New Orleans, the Best Food City in the Nation." The same month *Bon Appétit* had a one-page Q&A profile of Mario Batali. When asked to name his favorite food cities, he responded, "I love Sydney, Melbourne, and Shanghai right now, and what's going on in Peru and on the Chilean coast. In the U.S., it's New Orleans, hands down."

New York, San Francisco, Toronto—many cities have great restaurants and big-name chefs, but New Orleans is a food culture. The people here will argue over where to get the best gumbo or the best po' boy the way other cities will argue about the best sports teams. Just as you cannot be both a Yankees and Mets fan or a Carolina and Duke fan, you can't use Tabasco Pepper Sauce and Crystal Hot Sauce indiscriminately here. You have to choose sides.

While taping in New Orleans for his new TV show, *The Layover*, Anthony Bourdain said, "There is no other place on earth even remotely like New Orleans. Don't even try to compare it to anywhere else."

Chicago has a style of pizza, Philadelphia has cheese steaks, New England has its chowda, but no other city has such a wealth of indigenous dishes, like gumbo, beignets, jambalaya, Bananas Foster, étouffée, pralines, po' boys, muffuletta, Doberge cake, Oysters Rockefeller, bread pudding, crawfish pie, king cake, and red beans and rice (every Monday night).

There are food festivals in New Orleans practically every month—Wine & Food Experience (May), Creole Tomato Festival (June), Louisiana Seafood Festival (October), Food Fest (March), Coolinary New Orleans (August), Oyster Festival (June), Po' Boy Festival (October), Tales of the Cocktail (July), Roadfood Festival, Ponchatoula Strawberry Festival, Treme Creole Gumbo Festival, Crawfish Festival.

The food tents are an integral part of the annual Jazz Fest, where there are long lines for crawfish Monica, cochon de lait po' boys, and mango freezes. The French Quarter Fest is a music festival with $5 samplings from the great restaurants like Galatoire's and K-Paul's. It also features a signature and award-winning "dough boy" by a local donut shop, Blue Dot Donuts. The Thai-style pulled pork dough boy is served only one weekend each year, after smoking for twelve hours in the Blue Dot owner's backyard—never in the shop.

There are at least five cooking schools—Crescent City Cooks, Langlois Culinary Crossroads, New Orleans Cooking Experience, New Orleans School of Cooking, and the Mardi Gras School of Cooking—and each summer the one-hundred-year-old New Orleans Museum of Art offers cooking classes with name chefs included with the price of museum admission.

Tastebud Tours, Langlois Culinary Crossroads, Culinary History Tours, and Destination Kitchen are four of the growing number of food tours for visitors to the city. Clandestine New Orleans is my personal favorite because they create customized experiences.

New Orleans has nationally known TV chefs like Emeril "BAM" Lagasse, Paul Prudhomme, John Besh, and the late Justin "I gar-own-tee" Wilson plus two local radio shows devoted to food. Poppy Tooker has her twice-weekly *Louisiana Eats*, and Tom Fitzmorris's *The Food Show* breaks into ESPN for three hours each Monday through Friday.

Eat Dat will reveal the very unique food culture of New Orleans through its story-filled culinary history. There will be profiles of key restaurants, not *all* restaurants. There are 1,359 restaurants in New Orleans this week. I'm pretty sure we are the only city that counts our restaurants each week. You can get the latest tally at Tom Fitzmorris's www.nomenu.com. To include all restaurants would require a book the size of the old two-volume *Oxford English Dictionary*.

Choices had to be made. I have chosen not to include any restaurants outside the city limits. There are many fine restaurants in Abita Springs, Bucktown, and Old Metarie. Mosca's in Westego and Middendorf's Seafood in Akers definitely deserve mention.

Mosca's was awarded the '99 James Beard Award as an "American Classic." Chef and co-owner Mary Jo Mosca refused to go to New York to accept the award, saying "We'd have to close the restaurant." But, alas, Mosca's sits on the wrong side of the Huey Long Bridge to be included in *Eat Dat*. In Appendix A of this book, local experts have chosen their "Best of;" Middendorf's was chosen by two noted food writers as among the best in the area, but is just outside the area within *Eat Dat's* scope.

There are many restaurants in the heart of New Orleans where you can have a very decent meal, but (in my mind) neither their food nor their stories were rich enough to be included. Sorry, Rum House, getting on a Food Network show is not enough of a story to overcome your jerk chicken. Chain restaurants are automatically jettisoned. If you come to New Orleans and seek out the packaged blandness of a Subway or Papa John's, I ask you to put this book down immediately. No, I mean *now*! I don't want you as a reader. I don't think I even want you as an acquaintance.

As much as for the long-standing pillars of fine dining, such as Antoine's (1840), Tujague's (1856), and Galatoire's (1905), New Orleans is equally well known for her neighborhood holes-in-the-wall and juke joints. Elizabeth's in Bywater is locally famous for praline bacon. Camellia Grill battles Port of Call, Clover Grill, and now Company Burger for the title of best burger joint. Fights can break out deciding if Parkway Bakery, Johnny's, Domilise's, or Guy's serves the best po' boys.

In addition to name chefs like Emeril Lagasse, John Besh, and Leah Chase, *Eat Dat* will profile players who are lesser known but every bit as important. The photograph at the beginning of the introduction shows Maryjane Rosas and Rik Slave. Maryjane (with knife) is the self-taught but sensational chef for the Country Club, a GLBT restaurant with swimming pool (bathing suits optional). Rik Slave (with scissors and looking like a late-night horror host) is the lead singer in two bands, Rock City Morgue and Rik Slave & The Phantoms, but he's also classically trained by two James Beard Award–winning chefs, Susan Spicer and Donald Link. The Okra Man is a local icon, driving around in his beat-up, hand-painted truck, singing over a PA system what he has to sell each day: "I got baa-naa-naas . . . I got ohhhh-kraaa."

The aim of *Eat Dat* is to provide a deeper appreciation of our absolutely unique culture through our stories, and to encourage you to come savor (or fondly remember) our food.

We got Parkway Bakerrrreeee! We got Hansen's Snooo-Blizzzz!

AUTHOR'S NOTE

I am at this moment writing a lengthy indictment against our century. When my brain begins to reel from my literary labors, I make an occasional cheese dip.

—From A Confederacy of Dunces by John Kennedy Toole

Normally an author bio belongs at the end of the book. I place mine here because I feel that prior to being asked to wade through three hundred pages of my thoughts and opinions, you deserve to get a grasp of just who is doing the opinionating.

The first thing you may note is that I used "who" rather than "whom." It's not that I'm trying not to turn off readers by seeming too hoity-toity. The real reason is that I still don't get when to use "whom" so I tend to avoid it altogether. I agree with Calvin Trillin's statement, "As far as I'm concerned, 'whom' is a word that was invented to make everyone sound like a butler." I make no guarantee there will not be other grammatical errors over the course of this narrative.

When Ann Treistman, the talented senior editor with W. W. Norton, approached me to write a book about New Orleans food culture, I was both pleased and uncertain. Does the world need another book about New Orleans and food? I went to Amazon.com, brought up the books category, typed in "New Orleans food," and stared at 1,544 entries. Would there be anyone left to read my 1,545th entry? Then I typed in "Vampires" and saw 35,604 entries. Maybe.

I envision *Eat Dat* as fitting squarely in the middle of the 1,544 existing New Orleans food books. It will not be as comprehensive as *New Orleans Food* and *Hungry Town*, by our local food expert Tom Fitzmorris. He's been writing restaurant reviews and providing recipes since 1977. Tom now has a newsletter; a website, nomenu.com; and, one of my favorite testaments to New Orleans's obsession with food, his five-days-a-week, three-hour radio broadcast on ESPN radio. Only in New Orleans does ESPN, the Worldwide Leader in Sports, have coverage that is not 24/7. Monday through Friday here, it's 21/5.

Eat Dat will not stand as a historically exhaustive document, as does Liz Williams's *New Orleans: A Food Biography.* Liz is the founder and president of the Southern Museum of Food & Beverage and knows more about food history and food law than anyone I've ever met. Over lunch one day, she got me deeply involved in the foie gras debate.

My bigger concern was, *Who am I to write a food book in this city of so many superior chefs, restaurants, and critics of those restaurants?* I hardly have the pedigree of an official foodie. I grew up in the Midwest in the '60s, raised on Shake 'n' Bake and Chicken in a Biscuit.

Having been in the book business many years and having witnessed memoirs by Joe the Plumber; the nine-year-old *Slumdog Millionaire* star, Rubina Ali, writing about the trials and tribulations of her first eight years; and George W. Bush writing about decision making, I am less concerned about having the credentials to write a book. But a book about my beloved New Orleans and its iconic food culture was another matter.

However, in the writing of this book I have learned that most of top food critics brought little more to the job at the beginning than a passion for New Orleans and a love of our food. Those I have in spades.

My goal is to provide more than a bucket list as executed in most guidebooks, which catalog restaurants like Commander's Palace and Galatoire's or famous joints like Mother's and Café Du Monde. I admit up front that I have a knee-jerk reaction against tourist spots. Unlike most cities, generally where you see a line of waiting customers in New Orleans, don't go. It's not that there's anything wrong with Café Du Monde, Central Grocery, or Mother's. It's just that we can do so much better.

Above all else, my aim is to make *Eat Dat* story filled, as befits our city. Everyone here has a story to tell—and they're really good at telling it.

Eat Dat is built around stories. My Galatoire's profile does not focus on its hundred-year history nor provide recipes for Crab Maison or Trout Amandine. Rather, I write about John Fontenot, a Galatoire's waiter since shortly after the earth cooled, and the time Mick Jagger was sent back to the line waiting for a table. If you want the full story, Marda Burton and Kenneth Holditch have written *Galatoire's: Biography of a Bistro.*

Every story in *Eat Dat* I have heard from at least one outside source. More often the stories are well-worn chestnuts, retold a thousand times, and now a part of our restaurant lore.

I cannot guarantee 100 percent faithfulness to the original facts, as stories do tend to get embellished over time. The story of New Orleans's famously sadistic couple from the 1800s, Louis and Delphine LaLaurie, has grown over the years from torturing a few slaves to killing hundreds, using intestines as garlands and other organs and body parts as Mardi Gras throws. I doubt anyone now knows the *true* true story, but it doesn't seem to matter, as every night waves of tourists take ghost tours and gather in front of the LaLaurie mansion to hear grisly tales.

There is a phrase we here in New Orleans faithfully observe: "Never let the truth get in the way of a good story."

A NOTE ABOUT THE TITLE

Eat *Dat* is derived from the famous New Orleans Saints' chant, "Who Dat." *Dat* has become ubiquitous in New Orleans. After the Saints finally won a Super Bowl in 2009, T-shirts and bumper stickers popped up: "Repeat Dat" and "Two Dat." New Orleans anti-litter ads use the phrase "Don't Trash Dat." Dog runs and some front yards display the sign "Scoop Dat." And "Tru dat" is a commonly heard phrase, meaning "I agree" or "Yeah, you right."

There are many stories (fabrications) of where "Who Dat" originated. Copied below is a Wikipedia entry, so it must be true.

> The chant of "Who Dat?" originated in minstrel shows and vaudeville acts of the late 19th and early 20th centuries and was taken up by jazz and big band performers in the 1920s and '30s.
>
> A common tag line in the days of Negro minstrel shows was: "Who dat?" answered by, "Who dat say who dat?" Many different gags played off that opening.
>
> "Who dat?" became a familiar joke with soldiers during World War II. US fighter squadron pilots would often fly under radio silence. But after a while there'd be a crackle of static as someone keyed his mike. Then a disembodied voice would say, "Who dat?" An answer would come, "Who dat say who dat?" And another, "Who dat say who dat when ah say who dat?" After a few rounds of this, the squadron commander would grab his microphone and yell, "Cut it out, you guys!" A few moments of silence. Then . . . "Who dat?"

Many have tried to steal our "Who Dat." The Cincinnati Bengals, displaying as much creativity as Super Bowl rings (none), crafted their chant, "Who Dey."

Roger Goodell, a man much despised in New Orleans, signed off on the NFL sending cease-and-desist letters to T-shirt companies displaying the "Who Dat" phrase or the Saints' fleur-de-lis logo, claiming the NFL had intellectual property rights. After a large backlash, pointing out that use of "Who Dat" predates the NFL by thirty years and the fleur-de-lis by fifteen hundred years, the NFL backed down. My favorite protest came from *Sesame Street*. Their lawyers sent a cease-and-desist letter to the NFL, claiming they had the intellectual property rights for the letters N, F, and L.

Tru Dat.

A Note on the Restaurant Listings

👑 = The Hughie Award

I named this award after Hugh Capet, the first king of France. Where placed, the Hughie denotes a restaurant chosen as one of the top "Best of" for its category by an A-list of New Orleans restaurant critics and food historians and now judges in this book (see Appendix A).

Each restaurant profile in the book includes a $ price code, defined as follows:

$ = cheap eats with priceless flavors
$$ = drop in and pig out
$$$ = put a dent in your wallet matched by a satisfied bulge in your belly
$$$$ = expensive and worth every penny

For even more restaurant profiles and updates of newly opened ones or older ones closed, please visit www.eatdatnola.com. You may also leave your opinions and/or trash mine on the site.

CHAPTER 1

A Brief
and (Mostly) Bona Fide History of
New Orleans Food

He was a bold man that first ate an oyster. —Jonathan Swift

Writing about the history of New Orleans food should not be as difficult nor as filled with controversy as discussing the Big Bang Theory of Evolution, nor Second Amendment rights . . . except it is. We take our food *very* seriously here. You can call our streetcars "trolleys" or "trains" and it's no big deal. But, say *PRAY-leens* rather than *PRAH-leens* and we'll get all up in your face like you left dog poop in our front yard or insulted our momma.

Before you come here and ask for "local food" or "something authentic," you need to know Cajun and Creole are not interchangeable.

Creole was New Orleans's first cuisine (after you willfully ignore the Choctaw, Houmas, Attakapas, and Chitimachaw Native Americans, who predate French settlers by a few hundred years). The French migrated to New Orleans right at the time of the rise of the Restaurant Culture in Paris. For the first time, recipes were created, perfected, *written down*, and prepared for people outside the family.

When Marie Antoinette and Louis XVI visited the guillotine, the long-established traditions of French society dropped like severed heads. Chefs formerly employed in royal and aristocratic households were cut loose. Many displaced chefs opened their own restaurants in Paris, bringing with them a new "revolutionary" way of dining. Diners no longer had their meals at a common table, as was typical of taverns and roadside inns. Instead they had private tables, held by reservations, both new concepts. A whole new wave of common middle-class Frenchmen dined with fine china, cutlery, and tablecloths, all trappings of aristocracy.

These professional chefs-turned-restaurateurs catered to a new class of the less sophisticated, bordering on the unfashionable, who flocked to Paris following the end of the Revolution. Before the Revolution, there were fewer than fifty restaurants in Paris. By 1814, *Almanach des Gourmands*, the world's first food journal, launched in 1803 (or over two hundred years before Urbanspoon and Yelp), listed more than three thousand restaurants.

Most New Orleans cookbooks define Creole cuisine as the food of French settlers attempting to re-create the tastes of their homeland using what was available here in the bayous and swamps of Louisiana. Many ingredients in their written recipes simply weren't to be found here. From the Native Americans the French cooks learned about filé powder (ground sassafras leaves) and hominy (a corn kernel staple of Native American cuisine). Creole also blended flavors and ingredients introduced by other European and African immigrants. "Creole" derives from an old Spanish word meaning "mixture of color."

And here's where the controversy begins.

The first Creole cookbook was the verbosely named *La Cuisine Creole: A Collection of Culinary Recipes, From Leading Chefs and Noted Creole Housewives, Who Have Made New Orleans Famous for Its Cuisine*, written by Lafcadio Hearn in 1885. We forgive Lafcadio his title because his words in other books helped create the image of New Orleans as an exotic locale that still draws nine million tourists here every year. Beginning in 1900 and spanning sixteen editions, *The Picayune's Creole Cook Book* was called "the ultimate cook book on Creole cuisine," and the "most notable among early-twentieth-century food writings." These two books and practically every other Creole cookbook published thereafter push the often-repeated formula of Creole cooking being 75 percent French, 20 percent combined Spanish, Italian, German, and Irish, and 5 percent Indian and African.

However, Lolis Eric Elie, a locally renowned writer, editor, columnist, historian, award-winning documentary filmmaker, and founding member of the Southern Foodway Alliance (established for the preservation of Southern food traditions), takes the well-reasoned position that all these books have gotten it wrong:

> If you define Creole cuisine by its emblematic dishes—red beans and rice, gumbo, jambalaya, fish court bouillon, chicken and shrimp étouffée, shrimp Creole, shrimp rémoulade, smothered okra and crawfish bisque, to name the most prominent—well, most of these have no direct parallels in Europe, though they have plenty of siblings and cousins in the integrated cuisines of the Americas, not only Francophone portions but Hispanophone ones as well. Whether you're in Haiti, Puerto Rico, or Louisiana, shrimp Creole contains shrimp, tomato sauce, and rice. Beans and rice is standard in the Creole world but not the French one. And although jambalaya is often compared with paella, the method of preparation has more in common with jollof rice, thiebudjen, and other composed rice dishes of West Africa.

Where the original *Picayune's Creole Cook Book* **claims,** "Some sources say it [gumbo] derives from the Choctaw word 'kombo,' which means sassafras. Whatever the source, gumbo is based on the French soup Bouillabaisse," Elie responds:

> That dish lacks any connection at all to the seafood soup of Marseilles. Gumbo does, however, have much in common with the okra soups and stews that are commonly found in Western Africa.
>
> The word gumbo is derived from the word for okra in many Bantu languages. It seems highly unlikely that French Creoles would apply a Bantu term to a French dish. In fact, if you are shopping for okra in France, you must use the African word gombo, as the French language hasn't its own term.

Rudy Lombard in his 1978 book *Creole Feast* writes:

> It is difficult to arrive at a universally satisfying definition of Creole cuisine. All such attempts in the past have failed to achieve a consensus, and have seldom been used twice; several key influences or individuals are always left out or changed.

So . . . in starting out my book with the intent to clarify Creole and Cajun cuisines, I guess I have failed miserably. Where it is difficult to isolate where Creole cooking came from, we do know what it is. We do know its importance as America's finest homegrown cuisine. In his 1930 book *America Set Free*, Count Hermann Alexander Graf von Keyserling writes:

> Nowhere did the absolute superiority of real culture strike me so forcibly as there. . . . New Orleans is the one place in America where cooking is considered an art.

Now, Cajun food is not really a New Orleans cuisine at all. It developed in rural southwest Louisiana, today about two-hour drive from the city. The Acadians were French settlers in Canada, forced to leave their homes during Le Grand Dérangement, or the Great Upheaval (1755–1763), because they refused to sign an unconditional oath of allegiance to the conquering British. By the time the displaced Acadians had made it all the way down to Louisiana, they had become identified by the shortened form "Cajuns."

The Cajuns were trappers, farmers, and fur traders. They ate pretty much whatever they trapped, shot, or hooked outside their front doors. To make it edible, the food was often heavily seasoned (i.e., spicy). Because Cajuns were not especially wealthy, they tried not to waste any part of a butchered animal. Cracklins are a popular snack made by frying pork skins. Boudin, a signature Cajun food, is created

The Katrina Culinary Tale

August 29, 2005. The story of Hurricane Katrina is filled with heartbreak, heroism, and ultimately hope. So too is the food and restaurant chapter of the Katrina story.

With over 80 percent of the city underwater, some places by as much as twenty feet, most of our restaurants were impacted. Even those without flood damage had to deal with the cleanup (and a whole lot of maggots and flies) after storage and food lockers had gone months without electricity.

New Orleans lost many top restaurants that day. Mandich had been tagged by restaurant critic Gene Bourg as "the Galatoire's of the Ninth Ward." Around since 1922, Mandich had become a hallowed spot for locals and a *must* venture for many visitors. Mandich was known for its bright pink exterior and the lively crowd of regulars who'd welcome first-timers by yelling out, "Get the trout!" The menu was loaded with longtime and signature selections like Oysters Bordelaise, roast duck with sweet-potato sauce, Trout Mandich, and a spicy red bean gravy made into soup. Joel and Lloyd English, owners and chef since 1939, looked at the flood as the sign to retire. They sold the building, and it's now a small grocery store.

Another victim was Barrow's Shady Inn (what a great name), open since 1943. Owner Billy Barrow forever tinkered with the look of his restaurant, once buying all the neon signs from a nearby nightclub and casino about to close in order to "class up" his place. The Shady Inn was decorated with lava lamps (before they were retro-cool), odd photographs of shoes, and a watercolor painting of Brennan's restaurant. Barrow never tinkered with his famous wild-caught,

pan-fried, cayenne-pricked catfish. Loyal patrons insisted Barrow's was the All-Time Best Fried Catfish in New Orleans. Billy Barrow was hit by a car and killed in the late '90s. His daughter took over the restaurant without missing a beat. After Katrina, she tried to open another Shady Inn on the West Bank, but it never caught on.

Other restaurants lost to the storm and whose names should be carved into the stone of a culinary memorial include Bruning's, dating to 1859; La Cuisine; Christian's, a Mid-City staple; Marisol; Gabrielle; Mango House; Indigo on Bayou Road; Nick's; a steak house, Chateaubriand; Rene Bistrot; the romantic Bella Luna; the decidedly unromantic Charlie's Delicatessen; Michael's Mid-City Grill; and Cobalt & Lulu's.

While the loss of these individual restaurants is a sad chapter in New Orleans culinary history, the overall Katrina tale is not. The week before Katrina, there were 809 restaurants in the city. Today, New Orleans has more than thirteen hundred. No other American city has experienced such explosive restaurant growth.

The return of certain restaurants is also a huge part of the Re-New New Orleans, none more so than Willie Mae's Scotch House. Earlier in 2005, Willie Mae's had won an "America's Classic" award from the James Beard Foundation. Three months after receiving the Beard Award, the restaurant was destroyed by Katrina. Willie Mae Seaton, in her late eighties, packed up her medal and evacuated. Then, anxious about her restaurant, she boarded a plane in Houston and, without telling her family, made her way back to New Orleans. Police found her

huddled in front of the Scotch House. She told them about the James Beard Award, and they called the James Beard Foundation and the James Beard Foundation called Lolis Eric Elie, a friend of Willie Mae's and a founding director of the Southern Foodways Alliance. The SFA recruited foodies from all over the country to volunteer to rebuild Willie Mae's.

"It was a hell of a deal we offered them," Elie says. "We said, 'You pay your own transportation, you pay your own hotel, we give you one meal a day, and you work ten hours a day.' And folks did it." It took three years and more than $200,000 in private donations to get Willie Mae's Scotch House back in business. On re-opening night in April 2007, Willie Mae Seaton was helped out in the kitchen by two James Beard Award–winning chefs, Ann Cashion and John Fleer. James Beard nominee James Currence waited tables. "Based on that kind of firepower," said Elie, "this was the best restaurant in America that day."

Like any good story, the culinary Katrina tale has heroes and villains. For a short while, even Emeril Lagasse was vilified. *Times-Picayune* restaurant writer Brett Anderson wrote a blistering commentary titled "Where's Emeril?" for his failure to come quickly back to the city where he owns three restaurants. Emeril was on a book tour at the time of the flood. When he did return, Emeril tells how he was harassed at a supermarket near his West Bank home, and then got "cut off on the road by a family throwing me the bird." Emeril's ongoing contributions to the community (he established the Emeril Lagasse Foundation, which has granted over $5.3 million to children's education and culinary arts programs in New Orleans) plus time served have largely returned him to the city's good graces. He won the 2013 James Beard Humanitarian Award.

New Orleans is less forgiving of Ruth's Chris Steakhouse. They moved headquarters to Florida within a week of the storm. Dixie Beer's label may still say "New Orleans Slow Brewed," as it had been since 1907, but since Katrina the beer is made in Wisconsin.

Probably the #1 and ongoing villain is *GQ* food critic Alan Richman. He came to New Orleans in 2006, just as the city and her restaurants were beginning to recover, and did his best to hock a loogie in the sauce. He compared the French Quarter to Tijuana, questioned what exactly was worth rebuilding or restoring, said roux was pretty much like cornstarch, added that most of the population was too drunk to care what they were eating, and, most infamously, opined, "Supposedly Creoles can be found in and around New Orleans. I have never met one and suspect they are a fairie folk, like leprechauns, rather than an indigenous race." Not surprisingly, when his venom-filled but void-of-facts article appeared, New Orleans unleashed a backlash. Poppy Tooker wanted to throw him in a back room with the Neville Brothers. *Times-Picayune* food critic Brett Anderson wrote, "Richman's story is a weakling's idea of what it means to be tough." When the *New York Times* ran a piece about the resulting furor, Richman was boorishly unrepentant: "If people want to call themselves Creoles, fine," he said. "I am now calling myself a tight end for the New York Giants."

New Yorker Anthony Bourdain became New Orleans's top defender. Not content to nominate Richman for a "Douchebag of the Year" award, he's dedicated an entire chapter in his book *Medium Raw* to the *GQ* critic. It's titled "Alan Richman Is a Douchebag." Bourdain was also a co-writer for HBO's *Treme* and created a scene in which Janette, the New Orleans chef played by Kim Dickens, now working in New York, discovers that Richman is in her restaurant and takes the opportunity to throw a Sazerac in his face.

Where Richman has joined Roger Goodell and Dennis "bulldoze New Orleans" Hastert on the Most Hated List, Katrina made beloved stars out of John Besh, Scott Boswell, Bob Iacovonne, Paul Prudhomme, Donald Link, and a number of other noted chefs who rushed back as soon as possible to dish out food. Perhaps because of his boyish good looks, deep local roots, and can-do Marine background, John Besh became the poster boy for New Orleans recovery. After Katrina, he became nationally known as the ex-Marine who rode into the flooded city with a gun, a boat, and a bag of beans to feed New Orleans. In truth, Besh was initially as freaked out by Katrina as the rest of the city. "We came back fast and furious, but we were here with a refrigerator full of food and no one to cook it for." He had just taken out a large loan to pay off his partners when the storm shut down his restaurant and took away all his paying customers. At the suggestion of an old Marine Corps buddy, he decided to cook food for stranded residents and first responders. It turned out to be a smart (lucrative) move. Quickly arranging a series of emergency catering contracts to feed law enforcement, government, and oil rig workers, he made enough money to bankroll the expansion of his businesses. He's now involved in six New Orleans restaurants—August, Besh Steak, Borgne, Domenica, Lüke, and American Sector, with a seventh, La Provence, outside the city in Lacombe. Besh now employs more than three hundred people; the number was half that before the storm.

Katrina can also be held responsible for taking the lives of two of the city's food icons.

from the ground-up leftover parts of a hog after the best meat is taken. Most often boudin is served as a type of sausage made from pork, pork liver, rice, garlic, green onions, and other spices. Boudin balls are commonly served in southern Louisiana restaurants and are made by taking the boudin out of the natural casing, rolling the ground meat into a ball, and then deep-frying it.

As much as what they eat, rural Cajuns are known for how they eat. Cajuns view food as the chance for a community event.

A *boucherie* is a pig-slaughtering party where Cajuns gather to socialize, play music, dance, and eat meat with side dishes of meat. They use of every last bit of the animal, including organs and variety cuts in sausages and the inaccessible bits in the head as head cheese.

The crawfish boil is a celebratory event where Cajuns boil crawfish, potatoes, onions, and corn in large pots over propane cookers. Lemons and small muslin bags containing a mixture of bay leaves, mustard seeds, cayenne pepper, and other spices, commonly known as "crab boil" or "crawfish boil," are added to the water for seasoning. The results are then dumped onto large, newspaper-draped tables and eaten by hand. If crawfish are not around, shrimp and crabs are served in the same way. Attendees are encouraged to "suck the head" of a crawfish by separating the abdomen and sucking out the fat and juices.

How Cajun cuisine became a part of the New Orleans food scene is largely attributable to one man—Paul Prudhomme. Prudhomme was a "real" Cajun, raised on a farm near Opelousas. Without electricity, when he was a young boy Paul's momma used to hoist him up to the rafters, the hottest part of the house, to test when the bread yeast had risen. He opened his first restaurant in his hometown in 1957, a hamburger joint called Big Daddy O's Patio. In 1970 he moved to New Orleans to work as a sous-chef at Le Pavillon Hotel, then left a short while later to be the chef at the new Maison du Puy restaurant. After only five years on the New Orleans restaurant landscape, Prudhomme was hired as executive chef at the cornerstone restaurant Commander's Palace. Then in 1979 Paul and his wife Kay opened the restaurant that would change everything. K-Paul's Louisiana Kitchen almost immediately created continual lines around the block of locals and tourists waiting to eat his "authentic" Cajun food and signature dishes like turducken (a turkey stuffed with duck, stuffed with chicken) and blackened redfish. His redfish was so popular the commercial fishing industry had to shorten the season and impose restrictions or the fish would have become extinct.

In 1980, Paul Prudhomme was made a Chevalier (Knight) of the French Ordre National du Merite Agricole in honor of his work. His first cookbook, *Paul Prudhomme's Louisiana Kitchen*, was given a Culinary Classic Book Award in 1989 by the International Association of Culinary Professionals.

The country boy, born 155 miles from New Orleans, has permanently changed New Orleans food culture.

Seafood is at the heart of both Creole and Cajun cuisine. The Gulf Area is blessed with an abundance of sustainable shrimp, oysters, crawfish, blue crab, soft-shell crab, redfish, drum, and catfish. Oh, and gator if you want to group it as seafood. I have heard that New Orleans produces one third of all seafood consumed in America. But when I said that to people in Seattle or Boston, they replied, "Yeah. We say the same thing." I can write, without question, that 90 percent of the crawfish eaten each year comes from Louisiana, that we catch between 100 and 120 million pounds of shrimp per year, and that in a blind taste test consumers chose Louisiana oysters over all others 85 percent of the time.

New Orleans has a wealth of seafood restaurants and oyster houses: G. W. Fins, Drago's, Deanie's, Red Fish Grill, Oceana, Ralph & Kacoo's, Donald Link's new Pêche, Acme, Felix's, and the incomparable Casamento's. But you can get decent seafood in every restaurant in New Orleans. Even our steak houses like Chophouse and Dickie Brennan's have at least three seafood entrees.

With the focus on seafood, Cajun, and Creole, the one overlooked pillar of New Orleans cuisine is Vietnamese. Toronto has great Thai restaurants. With Beijing Pie House, Chef Chu's, Dintaifung, Newport Tan Cang, and R&G Lounge, California seems to wear the mantle for best Chinese restaurants. But it's New Orleans that has the best Vietnamese food in North America.

Vietnamese chefs, restaurants, and groceries have operated here since 1976, after the arrival of the Vietnamese immigrant-exile population following the fall of Saigon. Prior to April 1975, Vietnamese numbered just fifteen thousand in all of America, but by the '80s fifteen thousand lived in Louisiana alone, most in the New Orleans area. When immigrants arrived, carrying family recipes, they set up shop in communities on the edges of New Orleans East and on the West Bank.

In 1976 To Hong Duc opened the first Vietnamese restaurant in the area, Hong-Lan. The same year, Duc also participated in New Orleans's France-Louisiana Bicentennial Festival, where his Vietnamese dishes were served alongside legendary restaurants like Antoine's. Hai Nguyen came from Saigon to open the Asian Restaurant in 1978 in a suburban strip mall. He closed it two years later, not because the Asian Restaurant didn't have enough customers, but because it had too many. The *Times-Picayune* reported his experience: "The American Dream began to turn into a nightmare." Nguyen grew weary of working eighteen-hour days to serve the long lines outside his front door.

Crossing the bridge out of New Orleans to the West Bank, a bridge commonly called the Crescent City Connection, we find Gretna, where many Vietnamese settled. There are a number of outstanding Vietnamese restaurants in the area— Pho Bang, Kim Son, Hoa Hong 9 (or Nine Roses), and perhaps the best food, Tan Dinh. The best story is Pho Tau Bay, where American-born GI Karl Tackas fell in love first with Vietnamese food during the war and then with Tuyet, the daughter of the owner of his favorite Saigon restaurant. He married Tuyet, learned cooking from her family, and now mans the kitchen at Pho Tau Bay. A little farther out in Slidell are Pho Bistro, Saigon Pho, and Saigon Restaurant. Dong Phuong Oriental Bakery, in New Orleans East, is a restaurant, retail store, wholesaler, and caterer

Joseph Casamento

Joseph Casamento was born on the second floor of 4330 Magazine Street in 1925. He lived at that address his entire life. He worked downstairs on the first floor at the restaurant his dad opened in 1919. As a young teen, he delivered food from the restaurant on his bicycle. Then, for more than fifty years, he was one of the best oyster shuckers in New Orleans.

Joe was a creature of habit. He had the same dinner every night, a ham sandwich, some cookies, and Häagen-Dazs ice cream. It had to be Häagen-Dazs.

When his parents passed, Casamento took on every task at the restaurant, with the exception of cooking. He was allergic to the corn batter used for the fried seafood and so stayed out of the kitchen. Reflecting Joe's nature as a creature of habit, the menu never changed. He wasn't keen on spicy food nor experimental dishes. Casamento's in the 1920s and Casamento's of today were built around oysters, shrimp, and catfish.

With the exception of going to the Philippines as a soldier in World War II, Casamento never left New Orleans. "He didn't travel at all," says Linda Gerdes, his daughter-in-law who now owns the restaurant with her husband C. J. "There was a rumor around that we closed every summer so Joe could go back to Italy. He'd never been to Italy, never intended to go to Italy. He'd say, 'My dad left Italy. Why would I go back?'"

Casamento turned eighty two months before Katrina, then evacuated with family friends to Mississippi. He talked with C. J. from his hotel room the evening the storm hit New Orleans. "I could hear it in his voice, he was panicking," C. J. said. "I told him he had to calm down. He had emphysema real bad." Joe went to sleep, and about six hours later the people he was with called C. J. to say they'd found him dead on the floor. "He never lived anywhere else," Linda said. "He was born there [the restaurant], literally, and he probably would have died there if it wasn't for Katrina."

and considered makers of the best *banh mi* (called Vietnamese po' boys). Dong Phuong's bakery supplies the baguette-style bread for nearly every restaurant in the area that offers *banh mi*.

The reason I devote so many words to our Vietnamese restaurants is because I will give them short shrift elsewhere. *Eat Dat* is primarily intended for visitors to New Orleans. As such, most readers will be less interested in our Vietnamese restaurants, or Chinese, Thai, Indian, Middle Eastern, or pizza parlors. The book will mostly focus on what visitors might call "authentic" or "local," but know that in so doing, I will be leaving out a number of good restaurants that don't seem to

IN MEMORIAM:
Austin Leslie

Austin Leslie was one of the great, real Creole chefs in the country. He was called by many "The Godfather of Fried Chicken," but he was a master of the full range of Creole cooking, like gumbo, stuffed peppers, and virtually every other dish.

He was born in New Orleans on July 2, 1934, and he began his food career as a boy, delivering herbs, peppers, and celery to his neighbors in the projects. As a teenager he delivered fried chicken by bicycle for Portia's Fountain restaurant on Rampart Street. He exploded onto the New Orleans culinary scene in 1975 when his aunt Helen retired and sold him her Chez Helene restaurant. Despite the modest surroundings of the original location in Treme, it became the classic "underground" restaurant, with good food, reasonable prices, and an off-the-beaten-path (non-touristy) location. He then built a steady clientele of locals and more and more tourists. Local food critics gave him rave reviews, and national ones, such as R. W. "Johnny" Apple of the *New York Times* and Calvin Trillin of the *New Yorker* joined the chorus. Chez Helene was compared to the signature New Orleans restaurants Antoine's, Brennan's, and Commander's Palace. The restaurant served haute Creole dishes like Oysters Rockefeller, but served them on bent tin pie plates. Leslie's menu was mostly filled with down-home dishes like mustard greens, fried chicken livers, buttery cornbread, and what was considered the best fried chicken around.

With his big smile, muttonchop sideburns, diamond-and-gold crab pendant, trademark yachting cap, and the gift of gab, Chef Austin was a local celebrity. Business deals came flying at him, including French Quarter and Chicago versions of Chez Helene, a chain of fried

---

fit. Milkfish, New Orleans's first Filipino restaurant, doesn't fit *Eat Dat* for two reasons. Not only is the food a far cry from "local," but Milkfish is a popular pop-up that keeps popping up in different locations around the city, making it impossible to place the entry in any of *Eat Dat*'s geographically arranged chapters. For the growing number of enthusiastic fans, the restaurant is a culinary version of *Where's Waldo*. Milkfish started as one night only in Rio Mar in the Warehouse District, then Sundays only in Maria's Bar in the Marigny, then seven nights a week at the Who Dat Café. Most recently, Milkfish was located in A Mano, just on Sunday, and in Cibugnu, just on Monday and Tuesday. A Mano is about to close.

In addition to Vietnamese food now being exceptionally well represented throughout the city, every dive bar now seems to come with an ethnic or BBQ pop-up restaurant buried in the back or a food truck resting just outside. Falafels, Filipino, and Slavic soul food are all part of the *New* New Orleans food scene. While

chicken restaurants, and a cookbook deal. His distinctive style became the inspiration for the TV series *Frank's Place* with actor Tim Reid playing the chef. Leslie said, "Seems like everyone wanted to use my name to sell this, my face to sell that. I made the mistake of listening."

Despite Chez Helene's success, the neighborhood became unsafe. Cabdrivers would not bring guests to the area. Hotel concierges stopped recommending the restaurant. As Leslie himself said, "The real problem was that I was sitting on dynamite. The dope fiends and pushers were moving into the neighborhood. Now don't get me wrong, I know the streets. I've lived my whole life around pimps and whores. They've got a job to do same as me. But this was something different." Leslie moved his business to the French Quarter and opened a branch in Chicago. But the new location did not have the same charm as the original. Leslie declared bankruptcy in 1989 and, after thirty years, the last Chez Helene closed its doors for good in '94. The building that housed the original restaurant burned down shortly after. Leslie was a legendary but nomadic chef around New Orleans his latter years, perhaps best known for teaming up with Jacques Leonardi to create Jacques-Imo's.

During the flooding after Katrina, the seventy-one-year-old Austin Leslie, like many, was trapped in his attic for two days in stifling humidity and near one-hundred-degree heat. He was later rescued and relocated to the New Orleans Convention Center until being taken to Atlanta. On September 28 he was admitted to an Atlanta hospital for a high fever and died the next day. Hearing of his death, Leah Chase said, "You think you lose big when you lose your house, but here we lose a person, a person that could help us uplift everything." On October 9, Austin Leslie was honored with the first post-Katrina New Orleans Jazz Funeral.

many tourists lust to sample our old standards like beignets, boiled crawfish, and gumbo, more attentive travelers will discover New Orleans's unique take on all the current farm-to-table, artisan-butcher, salted-caramel, butter-cookie food trends.

New Orleans maintains the difficult balancing act of continuing to support the Cajun and Creole food traditions, which are major draws for most tourists and, like jazz music, an essential part of New Orleans history and culture, while expanding into current food movements, or what the *New York Times* called a "gastronomic youthquake," so that New Orleans will remain as relevant, food-wise, as cities like New York or San Francisco.

John Fontenot, Galatoire's superstar waiter

CHAPTER 2

The French Quarter

I came to New Orleans back in 1994 doing the Interview with the Vampire *movie and fell in love with the city. It got under my skin. Everything was sexy and sultry. I'd ride my bike all over the place, amazed by the architecture. I'd return to New Orleans every chance I could. What can I say; it's got the best people, the best everything. It's the most interesting city in America.*

—Brad Pitt, French Quarter resident

It ain't burnt, Rosemary, it's blackened. ♔

—Bunny Matthews, Yat chronicler

The French Quarter was the whole of New Orleans for more than one hundred years. Founded in 1718 by French Canadian Jean-Baptiste Le Moyne de Bienville, or JB for short (though there is no evidence of him ever being called that), it was designed as a perfect six-street-by-twelve-street grid. The streets were named after Catholic saints and French nobility, with the occasional war hero sprinkled in later. Governor Nicholls Street is named after two-time Louisiana governor and Civil War hero Francis Nicholls. He lost both his left arm and left leg in the war. His political campaign used the slogan "What's left of me is all right." The great fire of 1788, followed by the pretty big but not so great fire of 1794, destroyed practically the entire city. The beautiful buildings you see today were predominantly rebuilt during Spanish rule and are Spanish in design. Drawn in by the historic architecture and the ability to walk the streets with open alcohol containers, tourists flock here to make the French Quarter overwhelmingly the most visited section of the city. Many spend most of their time on Bourbon Street, beckoned by the smell of urine and vomit wafting through the air like an undeniable siren's call. Others (hopefully more) are drawn to the classic

---

♔ A Yat is a native of New Orleans who speaks the Yat dialect, a term derived from the common expression "Where y'at?"

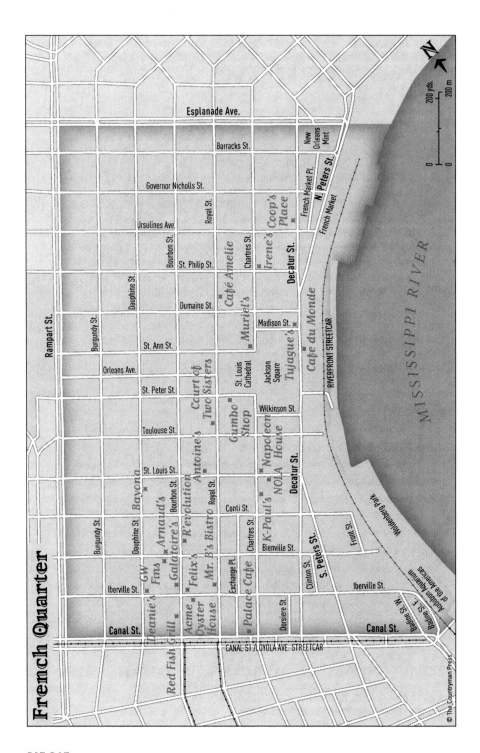

French Quarter

Esplanade Ave.

Barracks St.

New Orleans Mint

Governor Nicholls St.

French Market Pl.

Royal St.

Coop's Place

Ursulines Ave.

N. Peters St.

Bourbon St.

Chartres St.

Irene's

French Market

St. Philip St.

Café Amelie

Decatur St.

Dauphine St.

MISSISSIPPI RIVER

Dumaine St.

Muriel's

Burgundy St.

St. Ann St.

Madison St.

Café du Monde

Rampart St.

Orleans Ave.

Jackson Square

Tujague's

RIVERFRONT STREETCAR

St. Peter St.

St. Louis Cathedral

Court of Two Sisters

Toulouse St.

Gumbo Shop

Wilkinson St.

Antoine's

Napoleon House

Decatur St.

St. Louis St.

Revolution

NOLA House

Bayona

Bourbon St.

Royal St.

Conti St.

Woldenberg Park

Burgundy St.

Arnaud's

Mr. B's Bistro

Chartres St.

K-Paul's

Bienville St.

Dauphine St.

Galatoire's

Felix's

Bienville St.

Front St.

GW Fins

Palace Cafe

Exchange Pl.

S. Peters St.

Iberville St.

Deanie's

Acme Oyster House

Dorsiere St.

Clinton St.

Iberville St.

Audubon Aquarium of the Americas

Canal St.

Red Fish Grill

Canal St.

Bienville St. W.

Bienville St. E.

CANAL ST./LOYOLA AVE. STREETCAR

200 yds.

200 m

© The Countryman Press

restaurants: Antoine's (1840), Tujagues (1856), Galatoire's (1905), Arnaud's (1918), and (depending on when you read this) Brennan's (see page 46 for the story). With the constantly renewable resource of tourists, the neighborhood is also home to the highest-volume oyster house, Acme, most active po' boy stand, Johnny's, and #1 volume seafood restaurant, Deanie's.

ACME OYSTER HOUSE

724 Iberville St. • (504) 522-5973 • $$
HOURS: 11:00 a.m.–10:00 p.m. Sun–Thurs; 11:00 a.m.–11:00 p.m. Fri and Sat

If this is your second visit to New Orleans, you've already eaten at Acme. Everyone eats at Acme their first visit. There's always a line. If it's too long, catty-cornered across the street is Felix's Restaurant & Oyster Bar, two doors down is Bourbon House, and just around the corner is Red Fish Grill. All three have raw oyster bars and are probably better than Acme. They need a better neon sign to compete with Acme's "Waitress Available Sometimes."

Acme opened its doors on Royal Street in 1910. After a fire, not *the* fire, they

A Sometimes Available waitress caught on film

moved to their present location in 1924. They shuck and serve ten thousand raw oysters a day, every day. They encourage oyster gluttony with their fifteen dozen challenge. If you eat fifteen dozen in an hour, you don't get them free, but you do get your name placed up on the wall. Don't even think about setting the record. Sonya Thomas, aka the Black Widow, a professional eater, holds that by having eaten forty-seven dozen . . . in eight minutes. If I hadn't seen her do it in person at the Oyster Festival, there's no way I'd believe what I just wrote. Michael Jordan with a basketball had nothing on Sonya Thomas in front of oyster trays.

There's nothing terribly wrong with Acme. It's simply that with their checkered tablecloths and the canned chipperness of the servers, that most everything is fried, fried, and fried, that they'll serve you crawfish out of season (shipped in frozen from California), and that the tourists dining at the next table will be wearing just-bought "I got Bourbon Faced on Shit Street" T-shirts, the place feels like a New Orleans version of Applebee's or T.G.I. Friday's.

REASON TO GO: To say you did.
WHAT TO GET: A mere dozen or two will do.

ANTOINE'S

713 St. Louis St. • (504) 581-4422 • $$$$
HOURS: 11:30 a.m.–2:00 p.m., 5:30 p.m.–9:00 p.m. 7 days a week

Antoine's is the oldest restaurant in America (*owned by one family*). Many of our oldest, biggest, longest claims come with a qualifying phrase. We claim Canal Street is the widest street in America, for instance. As you're about to argue, "But what about . . ." we'll chip in, "The widest *street* in America. Of course there are wider avenues and boulevards." Union Oyster House in Boston (1826) is the oldest restaurant—but it's had several owners.

A city block in size, Antoine's is a labyrinth of fourteen dining rooms, each with its own unique history. The Mystery Room got its name during Prohibition. Patrons would go through a door in the ladies' restroom to a secret place and return with a coffee cup filled with illegal booze. When asked where they'd gotten alcohol, the response was, "It's a mystery to me." The Japanese Room was designed with Oriental motifs. The red walls of the Rex Room are lined with memorabilia from notable past diners like General Patton, the Duke and Duchess of Windsor, President Roosevelt, Judy Garland, Carol Burnett, Whoopi Goldberg, Pope John Paul II, and, let's not forget, Don Knotts.

It was actually founder Antoine Alciatore's son, Jules, who made the restaurant an institution. Jules served as apprentice under his mother for six years before she sent him to France, where he learned in the great kitchens of Paris. He had a talent for creating new dishes, such as his invented Oysters Rockefeller, named for the richness of the sauce and the money-green color of the herbs and vegetables. He also created Oysters Bienville and Trout Marguery.

REASON TO GO: The history.

WHAT TO GET: Oysters Rockefeller and a loan from the Rockefellers—it ain't cheap. Pompano fish is $40, lamb chops are $45, and chateaubriand is more than your hotel room for the night.

ARNAUD'S

813 Bienville Ave. • (504) 523-5433 • $$$

HOURS: 6:00–10:30 p.m. Mon–Sat; 10:00 a.m.–2:30 p.m., 6:00–10:00 p.m. Sun

French wine salesman Arnaud Cazenave opened his restaurant in 1918. Like Antoine's, Arnaud's also has fourteen different dining rooms, but it trumps Antoine's with six different menus: A La Carte Dinner Menu, Sunday Brunch and Jazz Menu, French 75 Menu, Table d'Hote Menu, Dessert Menu, and Speakeasy Menu. Arnaud's also has live jazz music and a Mardi Gras Museum that closely resembles Liberace's closet.

In 1978, sixty years after opening, Arnaud's was acquired by Archie and Jane Casbarian. Casbarian sought to return Arnaud's to the roots from which it had strayed by both restoring the property and reinvigorating the cuisine. The restaurant is currently best known for its crab cakes, veal tournedos in mushroom sauce, and crawfish tails in brandy/lobster sauce.

As an added treat, you can buy a plaque placed above a table, marking it as your own, for only $10,000.

REASON TO GO: The history is a bit less than Antoine's, but the food is a bit better.

WHAT TO GET: Heck, you're on vacation. Why not splurge and buy a table?

AUNT SALLY'S PRALINE SHOP

810 Decatur St. • (504) 524-3373 • $

Aunt Sally's is perfectly located a few doors from Café Du Monde. Through the large viewing window, you can watch employees pouring out liquid praline batter onto a hot stove. This sideshow gives your digestive system just a moment to process the beignets and chicory coffee you consumed next door before you barge inside to buy one or more of Aunt Sally's three flavors of praline: original, chocolate, and—for the "I put ketchup on my ketchup" type of eater—triple chocolate.

♛ BAYONA

430 Dauphine St. • (504) 525-4455 • $$$
HOURS: 6:00 p.m.–9:00 p.m. Mon–Sat; 11:30 a.m.–2:00 p.m. Wed–Sat

Bayona is, without question, my favorite restaurant in the Quarter. Owner and chef Susan Spicer is pure genius. She and her restaurant have won about every award available. She's received the James Beard Award, the Mondavi Culinary Excellence Award, the Ivy Award, and was inducted into the Fine Dining Hall of Fame. In 2010, Spicer was inducted into the James Beard Foundation's Who's Who of Food & Beverage in America, followed up by her 2012 induction into the Culinary Hall of Fame.

Chicken à la Spicer

Bayona's cuisine is Northern African, Mediterranean, French, and sometimes Asian. Spicer likes to experiment. She may change the menu as often as twice a year because she wants to keep growing as a chef.

Even dishes that sound terrible are delicious. My wife ordered and then tried to foist on me a nasty-sounding peanut butter and duck sandwich. After my lengthy protestation, I finally tried it and it was—fantastic. I then thought to myself, "Idiot! What's Thai food but chicken or duck with peanut sauce?"

REASON TO GO: If you're really shallow, because Susan Spicer was the basis for the character Janette Desautel in HBO's *Treme*. For all others, because Bayona is the best restaurant in the Quarter.

WHAT TO GET: Grilled shrimp with black bean cake and coriander sauce, or Covey Rise Farm duck breast and confit crepe with date molasses and pistachios. If neither is offered when you dine—anything else.

BENNACHIN

1212 Royal St. • (504) 522-1230 • $$

HOURS: 11:00 a.m.–9:00 p.m. Sun–Thurs; 11:00 a.m.–10:00 p.m. Fri and Sat

Bennachin is an African restaurant with dishes from Gambia and Cameroon (so none of that spongy, gag-inducing bread from Ethiopia that I alone seem to hate). Their best menu items are Akara, Egusi, Sisay Singho, and their signature Jama Jama, which is also served from a tent each year at Jazz Fest. I'll assume you don't know any of these dishes. I'll leave it at that and hope your curiosity leads you to the door of owner and chef Fanta Tambajang.

> REASON TO GO: African restaurant with plenty of vegetarian options.
> WHAT TO GET: Something you've never heard of nor tasted.

BOMBAY CLUB

830 Conti St. • (504) 586-0972 • $$

HOURS: 5:00 p.m.–10:00 p.m. Sun–Thurs; 5:00 p.m.–12:00 a.m. Fri and Sat

The key word in Bombay Club is "Club." To enter, you weave your way through the enclosed, tunnel-like private driveway of the Prince Conti Hotel. Once inside you'll feel miles (and decades) away from the nearby Bourbon Street in what masquerades as an opulent Gentleman's Club from an era before you were born. The windowless room is decorated with overstuffed leather wingback chairs, rich wood, oil portraits, and, in the far corner, a piano that accompanies retro-sounding crooners each evening.

The kitchen serves contemporary Creole, including house-cut steaks, grilled to order, and a very un-Creole-sounding English stout pie. The Bombay Club is best known for its velvet-lined cocktail menu with 120 specialty martinis. The bar also serves Diet Sierra Mist from a soda gun.

> REASON TO GO: If you packed an ascot and a silk smoker's jacket, this is a *must*.
> WHAT TO GET: I suggest the steaks. I encourage Diet Sierra Mist, from a soda gun.

BOURBON HOUSE

144 Bourbon St. • (504) 522-0111 • $$

HOURS: 6:30 a.m.–10:00 p.m. 7 days a week

At Bourbon House—located close to Canal, at the end of the first block of Bourbon Street—the huge floor-to-ceiling plate-glass windows look out on tourists dressed in questionable fashion with feather boas and Mardi Gras beads out of season. But you'll be dining a few blocks before the serious riffraff and perpetual smell of vomit on New Orleans's most infamous street.

Dickie Brennan opened his restaurant in 2002 and serves respectable versions of many Creole standards like seafood gumbo or barbecue shrimp, plus a few signature spins like the Plateaux de Fruits de Mer, a selection of shucked oysters, Gulf shrimp, assorted seasonal seafood salads, and marinated crab fingers. There's a large oyster bar, unfortunately framed by a huge plasma TV.

The restaurant is as much known for its extensive and impressive selection of small-batch and single-barrel bourbons as its food. The Frozen Bourbon Milk Punch should be as famous as the more popular Hurricanes, Grenades, and Huge Ass Beers found farther down the street.

REASON TO GO: Gear up with some solid food before venturing down Bourbon Street.

WHAT TO GET: Bourbon Milk Punch to get a jump start.

BROUSSARD'S

819 Conti St. • (504) 581-3866 • $$$
HOURS: 5:30 p.m.–9:00 p.m. Tues–Thurs; 5:30 p.m.–10:30 p.m. Fri and Sat

Joe Broussard, the founder of the restaurant, was a small, intense man, much like his hero Napoleon Bonaparte. Joe chose to base the theme of his restaurant on the "Little Corporal." Until Joe's death in 1968, Napoleon was everywhere you looked—Napoleonic statues and paintings along with many other references on the menu and as names of specialty drinks. After Broussard died, the restaurant closed for a short time. In the early 1970s Joe Segreto took over as only the second owner and did an extensive remodeling prior to reopening. Segreto placed his stamp on many of the design features with the creation of the Broussard's Crest.

Broussard's serves a blend of French, Spanish, Indian, Caribbean, Cajun, and Creole influences. The dining rooms, the bar, a lobby with hand-painted tiles, and a lush and leafy courtyard remain a beautiful and distinctly New Orleans place to dine. You do need to prepare yourself for service at a New Orleans pace (slow).

REASON TO GO: It's one of the more romantic settings in the Quarter.

WHAT TO GET: Hidden among traditional dishes served at many restaurants are a few gems rarely seen on other menus, like pompano and veal sirloin.

CAFÉ AMELIE

912 Royal St. • (504) 412-8965 • $$
HOURS: 11:00 a.m.–4:00 p.m., 6:00–9:00 p.m. Wed–Sun

Café Amelie had the misfortune to open months before Hurricane Katrina, but the great fortune to have secured perhaps the most romantic location in the French Quarter. The restaurant's 150-year-old Princess of Monaco courtyard offers picturesque outdoor dining in a garden setting. If rain or heat is a factor, dine inside the historic Carriage House. Chef Jerry Mixon worked with Paul Prudhomme and Kevin Vizard, among other chefs, before taking over at Café Amelie. Beyond standard Creole dishes, Chef Mixon gives the restaurant a unique spin by serving fresh salads, small plates, and creative dishes like local satsuma-pepper-glazed jumbo shrimp. *Where* magazine chose it as its "Favorite Outdoor Dining Spot" and *Where Yat*, a different magazine, has voted it "Best Brunch" five years in a row.

> REASON TO GO: The Princess of Monaco courtyard almost as much as the food.
> WHAT TO GET: I have never had their satsuma-pepper-glazed jumbo shrimp, but it sounds like a good start to me.

CAFÉ DU MONDE

800 Decatur St. • (504) 525-4544 • $
HOURS: Always open

In a city loaded with *must do* restaurants, bars, music clubs, historical buildings, and horse-drawn or airboat-propelled tourist rides, somehow sitting under a green-and-white awning at a too-small, unclean table, served by waiters who seem more suited to wordlessly taking your ticket at the Superdome, eating a small square hunk of deep-fried dough smothered with powdered sugar has become the #1 *must do* experience in New Orleans. If only the Pennsylvania Dutch settlers had given a cute name to funnel cakes like "hoofdkussens" and put a stand in Times Square, they'd all be millionaires today.

Café Du Monde began serving beignets and chicory coffee in 1862. Some say the extra-strong chicory coffee was to shoo away the startled taste buds of the occupying and unwelcome Union soldiers. Beignets were declared the official state donut of Louisiana in 1986, much to the chagrin of jelly-filled and French crullers.

A word of warning: Beignets were meant to be eaten hot and fresh from the fryer. Do not take a bag back to the hotel room. Do not bring them on a plane for family and friends. Beignets turn into crusty, stale goo once your feet hit Decatur Street.

Child expertly eating at Café Du Monde

A second word of warning: Do not wear black or dark blue. The visible powdered sugar smears will betray where you've eaten.

REASON TO GO: Get a fix of New Orleans–style heroin.

WHAT TO GET: As if you have a choice. They serve only beignets.

CAFÉ GIOVANNI

117 Decatur St. • (504) 529-2154 • $$$

HOURS: 5:30–10:00 p.m. Sun–Thur; 5:30–11:00 p.m. Fri and Sat

Chef-owner Duke Locicero has crafted a menu that mixes Italian, Creole, French, and American in what is termed "New World Italian." To others it may seem schizophrenic, Southern Italian and Louisiana styles sharing a menu as comfortably as Michael Jackson and Lisa Marie Presley shared the bridal suite in the Dominican Republic. The dining room is single-mindedly old New Orleans, with tall ceilings, mirrors, and a faux courtyard. Chef Duke has won with numerous awards, including USA Chef of the Year Award from the American Tasting Institute. One of the most entertaining meals to be had in New Orleans is at Café Giovanni on a Wednesday, Thursday, or Friday night when live opera performers slide among the tables, accompanied by a superb, but stationary, pianist.

REASON TO GO: Puccini with pasta. What's better than that?

WHAT TO GET: A reservation for dinner, Wednesday through Friday.

SOUTHERN DISCOMFORT:
The Shakespearean Drama
OF THE *Brennan Family*

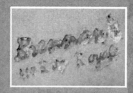

Right here I should be writing about the distinguished Brennan's Restaurant, a world-famous fixture on Royal Street in the French Quarter for sixty-five years, inventor of the flaming Bananas Foster dessert, inventor of the Bloody Bull, a Bloody Mary–like concoction with beef bouillon, and inventor of Eggs Husard, an effulgent egg dish with sauce on top of sauce, Marchand de Vin and Hollandaise. You'd pay over $20 . . . for eggs . . . but, once tried, you'd think it's worth it. I *should*, but I can't because the restaurant has been padlocked since June 27, 2013, after Ralph Brennan purchased the building at auction and evicted family member and the up-to-then owner, Pip Brennan. We await a judge to sort out the mess.

The story of the Brennan family and their restaurant empire has always read like a Shakespearean drama. This one too begins with a larger-than-life patriarch, Owen Brennan. Owen was born in the Irish Channel section of the city. He felt a strong sense of family obligation to take care of not just his wife and kids, but parents, siblings, and their kids as well. He was a tireless worker, buying interest in a gas station, then drugstore, and becoming the bookkeeper for a candy company. He worked as a liquor salesman and district manager for Schenley Company and temporary manager of the Court of Two Sisters Restaurant. In 1943, Owen bought an historic Bourbon Street bar, the Old Absinthe House. He made a huge success out of the formerly dilapidated establishment through his mixture of

P. T. Barnum showmanship and brimming gregariousness.

Owen added staged mannequins of the pirate Jean Lafitte and Andrew Jackson in what he called the "Secret Room." He invited visitors to attach their business cards to the walls. Thousands upon thousands of cards and autographed papers still hang from the walls and ceiling. He created specialty drinks like the Pirate's Dream, which he called "the high brow of all low brow drinks," and the Absinthe Frappe.

But it was Owen himself who drew customers and created loyal patrons. It was once written that Owen would hit his customers over the head with his personality—"a blow from which few tourists, writers, movie celebrities or presidents ever completely recovered." His bar became a destination for visitors and included as its "regulars" movie stars Vivian Leigh, John Wayne, Robert Mitchum, Barbara Stanwyck, Robert Taylor, Gary Cooper, and Jane Russell, as well as national magazine writers and syndicated columnists Earl Wilson, Walter Winchell, Hedda Hopper, Dorothy Kilgallen, Robert Ruark, and Lucius Beebe, resulting in many stories written about Owen and his bar in national publications. The Old Absinthe became a regular stop for visiting presidents Franklin Roosevelt and Dwight Eisenhower.

Often hearing complaints from his inebriated patrons about various local restaurants, Owen would sometimes relay their comments directly to the restaurant owners. One, Count Arnaud, ungraciously replied, "You're forever telling me about the complaints you hear. If you think you can do better, why don't you open a restaurant?" Arnaud then taunted Brennan that no Irishman could run a restaurant that was more than a hamburger joint. Owen responded, "I'll show you and everybody else that an Irishman can run the finest French restaurant in this town!"

In 1946, Owen Brennan leased the Vieux Carré Restaurant directly across the street from the Old Absinthe House. His stubbornness pushed him to work extremely long and hard hours to put his restaurant on the culinary map. Add in his "Irish smile" and the restaurant quickly became a famous institution, as popular and praised as New Orleans's oldest and best French and Creole establishments. He was called the "wonder man" of the New Orleans restaurant industry. As a family-first Irishman, he employed two of his younger sisters, Adelaide (bookkeeper) and Ella (kitchen supervisor), as well as a younger brother, John.

In 1954, when it became time for Brennan to renew his lease on Bourbon Street, his landlord demanded 50 percent of the profit from the restaurant. Unwilling to meet these demands, Owen found its present location on Royal Street. He was under a tremendous amount of stress as a result of his decision to move. At that time, Royal Street was not the busy boutique- and restaurant-lined street it is today. On November 4, 1955, Owen attended a dinner at Antoine's Restaurant, enjoying exquisite wines, superb food, and the company of good friends. The next morning, his wife was unable to wake him. At the age of forty-five, Owen Brennan had died of a massive coronary in his sleep, just prior to the restaurant's relaunch. His photograph and the news of his passing were front-page headlines for New Orleans's *Times-Picayune*. *Time* magazine included the report in its "Milestones."

This was when the trouble started. Although grief overwhelmed his family, Brennan's Restaurant still opened in its new Royal Street location on schedule. The restaurant was left to Owen's wife Maude and their three sons, Pip, Jimmy, and Ted (on paper). His sister, Ella, was still the kitchen supervisor. Her strong will and leadership ability enabled her to assume the role of manager of Brennan's Restaurant. Maude had not been involved at Brennan's in a managerial capacity and none of their three sons was old enough to take control.

As time passed, Ella sought to enlarge her legacy. In 1963, under Ella's direction, Brennan's purchased a second restaurant in Biloxi, Mississippi. In 1969, the Brennan family purchased a New Orleans restaurant from the 1800s, Commander's Palace, as well as a family-style restaurant in Metairie. Then came the opening of Brennan's of Dallas, Houston, and Atlanta and an intended chain of two hundred steak houses. Ella informed the family that she intended to assume the ownership of substantially more stock than her usual percentage. The family did not receive this news graciously.

Maude had sold stock to her father-in-law. When he and his wife died, their stake was left to *their* five children and three grandchildren. So now there was a bushel of Brennans involved in the business. The stock of each expansion was divided equally among the now multiple family stockholders. Ella and her siblings assumed control of the stock while Maude and her three sons became the minority stockholders.

Accountants and attorneys were called in. No proposal splitting the restaurants was acceptable to Ella as long as she was not awarded the original Brennan's Restaurant. After months of negotiations, Maude, Pip, Jimmy, and Ted assumed complete control of Brennan's Restaurant on Royal Street. Ella, with her brothers and sisters, took over the then six expansion restaurants. The result created a family schism.

Another accountant and attorney agreement was made in 1979 by members of the clan that restricted the signers from opening any restaurant with the name "Brennan" or "Brennan's." But the contract did not prevent the younger generation of non-signers from doing just that. Ralph and Dickie, sons of John and Richard Sr., opened Dickie Brennan's Steakhouse in 1998 and caused confusion for diners who thought they were eating at the original Brennan's Restaurant. This led to a very complicated lawsuit.

The most recent spat could be viewed as another Katrina victim. Blake and Clark Brennan, sons of Pip, grandsons of Owen, started managing the original Royal Street restaurant in 1995 and were making plans to expand when Hurricane Katrina struck. Ted, Pip's brother, and Bridget, Ted's daughter, accused the brothers of abandoning their positions without notice before repairs could be completed. Blake and Clark, however, claim Ted had informed them just before Katrina that they would never be anything but employees of the restaurant and should leave if they weren't satisfied. Ted and Bridget claim they have been solely in control of Brennan's since Pip

sold his shares more than two years prior. Pip, however, claims he is entitled to keep control over his shares because Brennan's Inc. hasn't fully compensated him for the stock sale. Need a flow chart or slide rule yet?

Ralph Brennan, a cousin of Ted and Pip who owns Ralph's on the Park, Mr. B's Bistro, and Red Fish Grill, inserted himself into the squabble when his corporation, LEGGO 4, LLC, acquired the restaurant at a sheriff's auction and promptly evicted Pip, Clarke, and Blake, temporarily closing Brennan's. Pip called an emergency shareholders' meeting to try to remove Ted and Bridget as directors. After the meeting adjourned, Pip and his sons allegedly entered the closed restaurant without permission and tried to call a staff meeting, prompting Bridget to call the police.

In a lawsuit filed in federal court, Pip Brennan claims he is owed $2 million since selling his shares in 2010 and accuses Ted Brennan of not doing enough to stop the foreclosure and auction, and he's filed an injunction to overrule the sale to Ralph Brennan and LEGGO 4. He has also filed a motion to dismiss cousin Ralph's motion to dismiss Pip's lawsuit against Ralph. Meanwhile, Bridget and Ted have both denied Pip's accusations. Ralph Brennan claims he has tried to inject capital into the sinking restaurant for the past two years but has been denied. Pip claims to "have emails, phone records and witness testimony" against them all and that Ted "would reap an enormous personal benefit from the uncontested foreclosure." So much for Owen Brennan's vision of family bonds.

All we want is our Eggs Husard back . . . and you can now get them at Dickie Brennan's new restaurant, Tableau, at least until Pip sues Dickie over the rights to the recipe.

CENTRAL GROCERY

923 Decatur St. • (504) 523-1620 • $
HOURS: 9:00 a.m.–5:00 p.m. Tues–Sat

Salvatore Lupo, a Sicilian immigrant, opened the grocery store in 1906 and famously invented the muffuletta to feed the Sicilian and Italian truck drivers driving produce to the French Market. The muffuletta is layers of Genoa salami, ham, mortadella (similar to baloney), provolone cheese, and olive salad with garlic and chunks of vegetables served on a large round bread with sesame seeds. Here and in other places serving muffulettas, you generally will be more than filled up by just half a sandwich.

Now, just because they were invented here doesn't mean Central Grocery's are the best muffulettas. Many prefer them two doors down at Frank's. I like them best at Napoleon House. The latter two serve them heated whereas Central Grocery, in order to handle the line-out-the-door demand, makes them each morning before opening and has whole and half sandwiches plastic wrapped and waiting. The staff at Central Grocery is often less than welcoming. For God's sake, don't snap a photograph inside their hallowed store or you'll be snapped at as though their sandwiches were in the Witness Protection Program.

For me, the real reason to go is to step back in time and experience an old-school Italian grocery. The shelves are stocked with two-quart cans of clam juice, packages of marinated baby octopus, industrial-sized olive oil tins, and boxes of imported pasta. But, if you want to buy any of these items, you'll have to wait in a long line of muffuletta shoppers.

REASON TO GO: Old-world grocery and birthplace of the muffuletta.
WHAT TO GET: A quick photograph and then run like hell.

CLOVER GRILL

900 Bourbon St. • (504) 598-1010 • $
HOURS: 24 hours 7 days a week

Company Burger on Freret Street has the best burgers in New Orleans. Camellia Grill has the longer history and the more stylin' waiters. But Clover Grill, open twenty-four hours, is my favorite burger joint. Located on the other side of the Velvet Rope (that marks where the girls-gone-wild, frat-boy party section of Bourbon crosses over—literally—into the GLBT section), Clover Grill is as eccentric as the people who dine there. The late-late night is the best time to go for food and people-watching. You can sit at one of their eleven (not ten or twelve) counter stools or try to slide into a jammed-in table with wobbly legs. You'll be greeted by a conversational, only slightly intrusive, and sometimes questionable-gender waiter/

Clover Grill at peak hours (3:00 a.m.)

waitress wearing a "We love to fry and it shows" T-shirt. Your burgers will be fried under a hubcap to keep the grease in. There are a variety of clocks on the wall displaying the current time in distant lands like Baton Rouge and Chalmette (i.e., same as New Orleans). If you can pull it off (and they'll be watching you to see that you don't), try to steal the menu on the way out. Clover Grill's menu is embedded with quips like, "We're here to serve you and make you feel better-looking than you really are," and "Have character, don't be one." They also serve a very good omelet first concocted "in a trailer park in Chalmette, Louisiana," the menu claims.

REASON TO GO: A lively, if downtrodden, twenty-four-hour burger joint.
WHAT TO GET: The menu, if you can.

COOP'S PLACE

1109 Decatur St. • (504) 525-9053 • $$
HOURS: 11:00 a.m.–3:00 a.m. Sun–Thurs; 11:00 a.m.–4:00 a.m. Fri and Sat

Depending on your sensibility, Coop's Place is either cozy or cramped, hole-in-the-wall chic or *Kitchen Nightmares* shabby. It *is* an experience no matter what, as drunks sing along (poorly) to the jukebox with a chorus coming from the noisy video poker machines and balls banging away on the pool table. While it feels like a place serving day-old grilled cheese sandwiches, Coop's menu is surprisingly broad and even more surprisingly quite good. Many feel their jambalaya is the best in New Orleans. They also serve fried alligator bits that have actual flavor and are not merely something you'd eat on a dare. They do a decent redfish, a much more than decent duck quesadilla, and the tasso they smoke in house.

Open till 3:00 a.m. (4:00 a.m. on weekends), Coop's offers a less touristy (well, a little less touristy) spot than Café Du Monde to ingest hangover blockers.

REASON TO GO: Quarter Rat Regulars and First Time Tourists mixed together in a darkened, noisy, sticky canteen.
WHAT TO GET: Jambalaya.

COURT OF TWO SISTERS

613 Royal St. • (504) 522-7621 • $$$
HOURS: 9:00 a.m.–3:00 p.m., 5:30–10:00 p.m. 7 days a week

The restaurant was once the governor's mansion in 1732 and later the residence of Emma and Bertha Camors, for whom the restaurant is named. The two sisters never spent a day in the restaurant business. They owned a notions shop on this very spot and died there within two months of each other in 1944. They lie next to each other at St. Louis Cemetery No. 3. Their pictures are posted together on the walls of the restaurant. Joe Fein bought the historic location in the '60s and converted the space into a restaurant. His sons, Joe III and Jerome, run it today.

Court of Two Sisters offers respectable versions of Creole standards like Oysters Rockefeller, roast duck, and a bowl of gumbo. Their famous buffet has eighty items. But the draw is primarily the intensely photogenic old-

world courtyard with original gaslights, flowing fountains, and the largest wisteria plant I have ever seen. It blooms in April if you're planning your trip around the Court of Two Sisters courtyard. There's also a strolling jazz trio seven days a week.

REASON TO GO: The courtyard is extremely beautiful.
WHAT TO GET: Pictures of the courtyard. The food is good too.

CRESCENT CITY BREWHOUSE

527 Decatur St. • (504) 522-0571 • $$
HOURS: 12:00 p.m.–10:00 p.m. Mon–Thurs; 11:30 a.m.–11:00 p.m. Fri–Sun

Wolfram Koehler, an expat Yat from Germany descended from several generations of brewmasters, opened the Brewhouse in 1991. It feels designed to give tourists exactly what they want in a French Quarter establishment. Old brick building; front doors flung open where a jazz band serves as the "check it out" hawker; neon signs in the window; New Orleans art lining the walls; an oyster-shucking bar—check, check, check, check, and check. The Brewhouse adds its signature note, house-brewed beers, in beautiful copper tanks behind the bar.

REASON TO GO: To dine (and drink) in what feels like a classic old New Orleans spot (opened in 1991).
WHAT TO GET: Raw oysters in season. German sausage platter (always in season).

DEANIE'S

841 Iberville St. • (504) 581-1316 • $$
HOURS: 11:00 a.m.–10:00 p.m. Sun–Thurs; 11:00 a.m.–11:00 p.m. Fri and Sat

Deanie's is the ≠1 seafood restaurant in New Orleans. In volume, that is. Located in the French Quarter and able to seat 350 diners, they serve one (1) sirloin steak option. Everything else is seafood. Portions are spilling off the plate. The original Deanie's, opened in Bucktown (near Lake Pontchartrain) in 1961, is supposed to be better. I've only been to the one in the Quarter. It is a top choice if you're traveling with young kids. The atmosphere is lively so no one will notice any kind of temper tantrum and there are decorative aquariums and plenty else for easily bored eyes to see while fidgeting and letting their dinner get cold.

REASON TO GO: If you have kids or like a lively atmosphere that could include lively kids.
WHAT TO GET: Seafood, lots and lots of seafood.

DICKIE BRENNAN'S STEAK HOUSE

716 Iberville St. • (504) 522-2467 • $$$

HOURS: 5:30–10:00 p.m. 7 days a week; 11:30 a.m.–2:30 p.m. Fri

Dickie Brennan's is a traditional steak house but with a New Orleans spin and a Brennan's flare. All steaks get sprinkled with a house seasoning blend before broiling and are slathered with a special Creole compound butter. The chef also feels the New Orleans itch to scatter fried P&J oysters over the house filet. Along with P&J oysters, all other local seafood is sourced from New Orleans Fish House, the meats mostly from the revered Covey Rise Farms. More recently, Dickie Brennan's began working with Chappapeela Farm to provide duck. The ducks show up in the DBLT (duck, bacon, lettuce, and tomato sandwich). Everything served receives the Brennan's attention to detail. Not just the béarnaise sauce, but the Worcestershire also is made in house. The sides get a little lagniappe. The sweet-potato mash is swirled with compound butter made with pecans and molasses.

> REASON TO GO: It's a Brennan's. They serve steak. No third reason should be needed.
> WHAT TO GET: Even at a renowned steak house, I'd be tempted by a DBLT.

FELIX'S

739 Iberville St. • (504) 522-4440 • $$

HOURS: 11:00 a.m.–10:00 p.m. Sun–Thurs; 11:00 a.m.–11:00 p.m. Fri and Sat

Felix's needs to hire a publicist. It is located almost right across the street from Acme Oyster House. It's nearly as venerable, having been around since 1935. It has its own neon sign, stating, "Oysters 'R' In Season" rather than "Waitress Sometimes Available." And the food is just as good, many feel better. Felix's does all the alligator bits, jambalaya, red beans and rice, boiled or fried seafood, including oysters done multiple ways (Rockefeller, char-grilled, and raw) to draw in any tourist. Yet while there's always a line in front of Acme, there is rarely, if ever, one trying to get into Felix's. Maybe it's the service staff, who are notoriously inattentive.

> REASON TO GO: It's Acme without the wait . . . until you get to your table.
> WHAT TO GET: That dozen or two you intended to get at Acme are just as good here.

FIORELLA'S

1136 Decatur St. • (504) 553-2155 • $$

HOURS: 11:00 a.m.–10:00 p.m. Sun–Thurs; 11:00 a.m.–2:00 a.m. Fri and Sat

Fiorella's has entrances on two streets. The French Market side opens to a former grocery store now turned into a dilapidated diner. The Decatur Street side was a former seafood house and has retained an assortment of faux portholes and seafaring decorations. While the decor may be off-putting to some and bizarre to all, they serve hearty comfort food like liver and onions cooked in Abita beer gravy and served with mashed potatoes, hefty hamburger steak with grilled onions, and their signature fried-to-order chicken. *Southern Living* magazine has praised Fiorella's fried chicken. One thing to note: They don't start frying your chicken until you order it. So, while fresh, it may take a half hour or more to be served. If you find waiting for your food to be odious, forcing you to do something disturbing, like have a conversation, you should pick another restaurant (in another city).

Fiorella's will also deliver, so rather than waiting at your table you can be in your hotel bed, watching TV. There's a YouTube video of a Fiorella delivery (by the brilliant local performer Clint Maedgen, who really was a Fiorella delivery boy, singing "A Complicated Life") that I think perfectly captures the spirit of New Orleans in five minutes and seven seconds (www.youtube.com/watch?v=dzVCHv6FSbg).

REASON TO GO: Comfort food in a visually uncomfortable setting.
WHAT TO GET: Order the fried chicken . . . then wait.

FRANK'S

933 Decatur St • (504) 525-1602 • $$

HOURS: 10:00 a.m.–11:30 Tues–Sun

Frank Gagliano opened his muffuletta shop in 1965 and boldly placed it only a few doors down from the iconic Central Grocery. That'd be like opening a hot dog stand in Coney Island next to Nathan's. *Frankly* I think Frank's muffulettas are superior to Central Grocery's. When Frank's sons took over, it expanded into a neighborhood-style, full-menu restaurant. You now have the tough choice to eat downstairs, crammed in among a counter, too many tables for the space, wine racks, and service bar (but with the oldest and most colorful waiters), or upstairs in a much nicer (quieter) room with a balcony overlooking the river and looking down on tourists heading in and out of the French Market.

♕ GALATOIRE'S

209 Bourbon St. • (504) 525-2021 • $$$$

HOURS: 11:30 a.m.–10:00 p.m. Tues–Sat; 12:00–10:00 p.m. Sun

Galatoire's was founded in 1897 by French immigrant Jean Galatoire and moved to its current location on Bourbon Street in 1905. Five generations of descendants of Jean Galatoire owned the Creole restaurant until 2009, when they sold controlling interest to Todd Trosclair, who, in turn, sold his interest to New Orleans businessman and political candidate John Georges.

There have been some other changes over the years that regulars have found quite disturbing. The restaurant proudly took no reservations until Galatoire's created an upstairs dining room in 1999. For the street-level main dining room, patrons continue to stand in long lines on the sidewalk, often sweltering in their suits. Men must wear jackets. If you don't have one, there's a rack of ugly, high-polyester-content ones by the front door. There are many tales of the famous and well-heeled from Mick Jagger to U.S. senators trying to jump the line and being turned back. When Charles de Gaulle visited New Orleans, he tried to call for reservations. After being told Galatoire's did not accept reservations, the French president invoked, "Do you know *who* I am?" They replied, "Why, yes, Mr. President. But, do you know *where* you're calling?"

Sadly, Galatoire's has removed the double set of French doors at the entrance, which served as a sort of decompression chamber between the riffraff on Bourbon Street and the old-world grace once inside. The loss of the double doors caused the most uproar with patrons since Galatoire's fired Gilberto Eyzaguirr, a waiter of twenty-two years, or since they switched from shaved ice to cubed. Don't think for a minute there aren't regular patrons still upset about that.

The feeling of tradition is created by the mirrored walls, tiled floor, slow-moving paddle fans, white linens; each table is set with its own glass water bottle plus bottles of Tabasco and Worcestershire sauce, bowls full of lemon wedges—specifically designed for fine-tuning a Bloody Mary. You'll be served by waiters in tuxedos, all male until recently. But the classic New Orleans experience is most enhanced by the regular cast of characters who dine there. This is particularly true on Fridays, when some of New Orleans's upstanding citizens come for lunch every week. Both Tennessee Williams and Truman Capote had their special tables where they sat for Friday lunch and drank their way into Friday dinner. Marian Patton Atkinson was a Friday lunch regular, usually joined by Mrs. Henri Viellere, known to her friends as Peachy. They would hold court at their table the rest of the afternoon, dressed in their churchgoin' finest, including hats. Since Ms. Atkinson's passing, there is a commemorative brass plaque bolted to wall by "her" table.

Many of the waiters have worked the tables since shortly after the earth cooled and are as much a reason to dine at Galatoire's as the Trout Amandine. Veteran waiters are not a luxury but a necessity here in order to decipher, interpret, and advise you on the five-page menu with well over one hundred options. While the regulars know the difference between creamy Shrimp Maison and spicy Shrimp Rémoulade, they may need a reminder choosing between Trout Marguery and Trout Meuniere. You may request your waiter by name prior to being seated. Several, like Lee McDaniel, Robert Wong, and John Fontenot (pictured above) are virtual rock stars. The five-foot, four-inch John Fontenot has been serving customers with food, drink, and a steady diet of cornball Cajun jokes, told in his rural Ville Platte accent, since the mid-'60s. John lets his customers choose the level of bawdiness (from 1 to 10) for the jokes they wish to hear as he serves their meal.

If I may photobomb your waiter's suggestions, get the Grand Gouté appetizer. Gouté roughly translates as "big taste." Tomato slices separate dollops of Shrimp Rémoulade, Crabmeat Maison, and Shrimp Maison, and can, for a price, be joined on the plate by a skewer of oysters en brochette.

Galatoire's classic dishes of Trout Amandine, stuffed eggplant, Shrimp Rémoulade, Crab Maison, and Oysters Rockefeller are prepared, served, and taste exactly as they did when the then double French doors opened in 1905.

REASON TO GO: To experience the part of New Orleans that hasn't changed since the turn of the (twentieth) century.

WHAT TO GET: A couple of Sazeracs and then settle in for the next few hours.

GALVEZ

914 N. Peters St. • (504) 595-3400 • $$$
HOURS: 4:00–10:00 p.m. Tues–Sat; 10:00 a.m.–3:00 pm, 4:00–10:00 p.m. Sun

Galvez is the one and only New Orleans restaurant offering a good view of the Mississippi River. Unlike other river towns such as Savannah, San Antonio, and Cleveland (hey, don't knock John's Steakhouse on the Cuyahoga until you've tried it), New Orleans is below sea level. A romantic walk along the Riverwalk could easily lead to a breakup. On one side is an ugly retaining wall so we don't drown. On the other is the mighty Mississippi, nicknamed the Big Muddy for a reason. It's a big brown river. Our riverfront is not lined with cute boutiques, populated by street performers (the meth dealers are a little bit entertaining), nor dotted with restaurants.

Galvez's main dining room on the second floor has large windows that give a sweeping view of the Mississippi River and are opened in pleasant weather to offer the breeze and the sounds coming off the river. Chef Laura Cedillo and her brother Cesar Cedillo opened Galvez in Bella Luna's old location. Laura ran a pan–South American restaurant in New York, but at Galvez, her menu is a litany of old-world

View of the Mississippi River from the Galvez dining room

Spanish dishes (the shrimp ceviche is pretty great) with a little French and some classic Creole.

REASON TO GO: The view.

WHAT TO GET: They do tapas best of all.

GREEN GODDESS

307 Exchange Place • (504) 301-3347 • $$

HOURS: 11:00 a.m.–9:00 p.m. Wed–Sun

When eating at the Green Goddess, patrons can choose to sit in their tiny and uncomfortably cramped interior or outside under an umbrella on Exchange Alley, a cobblestone street free of traffic. There's something very Barcelona and beautiful about the outdoor setting (I write, having never been to Barcelona).

Until recently, there were two brilliant chefs, Paul Artigues doing breakfast and lunch and the highly creative, capricious Chris DeBarr cooking dinners. Like a lot of really creative people, Chris grew impatient and moved frequently, from Commander's Palace to Delachaise to Green Goddess; then Serendipity, which he opened six months before quitting his own restaurant and moving to Houston. At Delachaise he concocted a chestnut flour tagliatelle and Irish cheddar grilled cheese sandwich. At Green Goddess he made up dishes like ravioli made not with pasta but with ultra-thin slices of golden beets bursting with chevre and drizzled with flavored oils and saba, a honey-like grape syrup. Now Paul Artigues is the whole show. I've had his watermelon-ginger soup, garnished with avocado and crabmeat. On a really hot day, there is nothing more perfect than a cold watermelon-ginger soup. I've had an off-the-menu appetizer of shrimp, eggplant casserole, and fried green tomato. For my son, the chef made a dessert of praline ice cream, caramel, whipped cream, and bacon. The bacon made it. Now, having just written about bacon, I will note that Green Goddess is also my ≠1 choice for vegetarians. About a third of the menu is vegetarian at any given time.

REASON TO GO: A perfect cobblestone street bistro setting.
WHAT TO GET: Let the chef be your guide to off-the-menu territories.

GUMBO SHOP

630 St. Peter St. • (504) 525-1486 • $$
HOURS: 11:00 a.m.–10:30 p.m. Sun–Thurs; 11:00 a.m.–11:00 p.m. Fri and Sat

The Gumbo Shop serves seafood okra gumbo and chicken andouille gumbo every day of every year and, if you're lucky, some days duck and oyster gumbo and has been doing so for more than a hundred years. That's over 36,500 days of serving gumbo. Practice makes perfect. *New Orleans* magazine chose the Gumbo Shop as best gumbo multiple times, and the *Best of New Orleans* gives them the status of Red Auerbach's Boston Celtics, picking them as the best gumbo in 1999, 2000, 2001, 2002, 2003, 2004, 2005, 2006, 2007, 2008, and 2009. They serve much more than gumbo, offering covers of all the Top 40 hits: jambalaya, red beans and rice, shrimp Creole, crawfish étouffée, blackened fish. *Where* magazine chose Gumbo Shop for its Best (overall, not just gumbo) New Orleans Cuisine award.

REASON TO GO: Gumbo.
WHAT TO GET: Gumbo.

G. W. FINS

808 Bienville St. • (504) 581-3467 • $$$
HOURS: 5:00–10:00 p.m. Sun–Thurs; 5:00–10:30 p.m. Fri and Sat

Zagat rated G. W. Fins as Best Seafood Restaurant in New Orleans. *Forbes* tagged G. W. Fins as one of the Top 10 Seafood Restaurants in all of America. *Esquire* magazine designated G. W. Fins one of America's Top 20 Best New Restaurants, seafood or otherwise. But the real honor, Appendix A in this book, places them at ≠1 seafood restaurant.

G. W. Fins prints a new menu every day to take advantage the freshest fish they can find, both local standards like oysters or redfish as well as the best, sometimes exotic, catch from around the world: lobster dumplings with fennel and tomato, Chilean sea bass braised in a hot and sour shrimp stock and served with sesame spinach, cashew- and peppercorn-crusted swordfish, king crab from Alaska, blue nose bass from New Zealand, New Bedford sea scallops served with mushroom risotto and mushroom butter.

> REASON TO GO: Pretty much *everyone's* choice as Best Seafood Restaurant in New Orleans.
> WHAT TO GET: The freshest fish they've got, which you'll only know when you get there.

IRENE'S

539 St. Philip St. • (504) 529-8811 • $$$
HOURS: 5:30–10:00 p.m. Mon–Sat

Veteran of several Italian restaurants around town, Irene DiPietro opened Irene's with her former partner Tommy Andrade (see Tommy's in chapter 6) in the early 1990s. While the restaurant does a decent red sauce, they are better with dishes that rely on olive oil or garlic. Top choices would be Oysters Irene (with pancetta and Romano), Chicken Rosemarino (roasted half, with garlic and rosemary), Duck St. Philip (raspberry and pancetta demi-glace), and cioppino (Italian fish stew with pasta). The restaurant is housed in an old pasta factory, from back when this neighborhood was known as Little Palermo because of the number of Sicilians living on these blocks. The interior might have been the inspiration for the Buca di Beppo chain. The walls are chaotically littered with photographs of Italian American icons, a shelf with a porcelain chicken, and a mystery nun. The problem is the interior is not large enough to accommodate everyone who wants to eat there. The wait can be l-o-n-g.

> REASON TO GO: To dine on Italian food inside an old pasta factory.
> WHAT TO GET: Something other than standard red sauce Italian.

IRIS

321 N. Peters St. • (504) 299-3944 • $$$
HOURS: 6:00–10:00 p.m. Mon, Wed–Sat; Fri lunch 11:30 a.m.–2:00 p.m.

After working together at Lilette, chef Ian Schnoebelen and partner Laurie Casebonne, dining room and wine boss, opened their restaurant in January 2006 and were named Best New Restaurant at the end of 2006 by *New Orleans* magazine. They then changed locations from the original Uptown neighborhood bistro to a more spacious fine dining establishment at the Bienville House Hotel in the French Quarter.

Their menu focuses on fresh, seasonal ingredients presented in inventive ways you'll find at no other restaurant in New Orleans. A very partial list from their constantly changing menu would include seared sushi-grade yellowfin tuna with green papaya salad, king oyster mushrooms, and blood orange–ginger vinaigrette; Merguez (lamb sausage), shimeji mushrooms, and sauerkraut; and Kurobuta pork cheeks, raw vegetables, Italian herb vinaigrette, and fried shallots. Or why not try the Gulf shrimp, coconut broth, baby bok choy, shiitake mushrooms, Thai basil coulis, and fried ginger? And lest you forget, try the snapper, baby beets, baby turnips, lacinato kale, roasted tomato "chips," and fennel and olive vinaigrettes—or for the more adventurous (as if the last dishes listed were not adventurous enough), the veal sweetbreads, risotto, shiitake mushrooms, and sage.

REASON TO GO: A wildly creative menu.
WHAT TO GET: Something wild and creative. Can't go wrong with blood orange–ginger vinaigrette.

JOHNNY'S
511 St. Louis St. • (504) 524-8129 • $
HOURS: 8:00 a.m.–4:30 p.m. 7 days a week

Mr. Johnny and Ms. Betty de Grusha opened a grocery store and sandwich shop at 506 Chartres. In 1950, to keep up with expanding business, Johnny and Betty moved to their current location at 511 St. Louis Street. The business continues to thrive today under the third generation of the de Grusha family. Everything here is big. Big crowd, big menu, big big selection of po' boys in every manner of seafood and meat varieties, including the Judge Bossetta Special, their version of a "meat lover's" po' boy with two types of sausage and ground beef.

By sales alone, Johnny's po' boys would be New Orleans po' boy champion. By sales alone, McDonald's would be the finest restaurant in America. Few would champion Johnny's as our best po' boys, but they're perfectly good, the atmosphere is lively, and you're likely to be called *Sweetie, Baby,* or *Honey* at least three times before you leave.

REASON TO GO: Sweetie, you don' need no reason to eadda po' boy.
WHAT TO GET: Honey, any of 'em, from a long, long, list of po' boys.

♔ K-PAUL'S LOUISIANA KITCHEN

416 Chartres St. • (504) 596-2530 • $$$
HOURS: 5:30–10:00 p.m. Mon–Sat; 11:00 a.m.–2:00 p.m. Thurs–Sat

Chef Paul Prudhomme by artist George Rodrigue

Paul Prudhomme, the Dom DeLuise look-alike, is a real-deal Cajun who, more than anyone, put Cajun food on the culinary map. There are those that consider him right up there with Julia Child or Alice Waters as one of this country's most important chefs. His original idea was to do lunch only Monday through Friday, have fun, serve good food, and take a lot of vacations. Eleven best-selling books, three videos, 130 TV episodes, and a line of Magic Seasoning Blends sold in more than thirty countries later, it hasn't turned out that way. Sitting one day in his test kitchen, Chef Paul revealed that he regrets nothing. He is, after all, a millionaire. But, when he looks back, the perfect moment in time was back when he was "nobody" in a modestly sized restaurant, his wife Kay was still alive and blithely working the small front room, and Paul was in back cooking, tasting, and knowing every dish sent out was "perfect."

K-Paul's now seats over two hundred. It is best known for blackened fish—drum, yellowfin tuna, or redfish (the latter he made so popular, redfish was nearly made extinct)—and also for other signature dishes like the blackened beef tenders with debris sauce (debris is meat that's left after the more choice cuts have been cut away for other uses), bronzed fish with hot fanny sauce, and sweet-potato pecan pie. A special treat offered at K-Paul's is their open-air kitchen where you can watch as your dinner is prepared.

REASON TO GO: Great Cajun food by the greatest of Cajun chefs.
WHAT TO GET: Blackened [fill in the blank].

KILLER POBOYS

811 Conti St. (inside Erin Rose Bar) • (504) 252-6745 • $
HOURS: 12:00 p.m.–12:00 a.m. Wed–Sun

I used to feel the difference between the best po' boys and the also-rans was paper-thin. Parkway Bakery usually won "Best of" competitions, many swear by Domilise, I myself preferred Guy's. Cam Boudreaux has changed all that. A former chef in Arnaud's, Cam ventured out on his own to take po' boys to a higher level. He has succeeded. Killer PoBoys is a pop-up restaurant, where you place your order and pick up through a small window cut through the back of the decidedly seedy, bright Pepto-abysmal pink Erin Rose Bar. There are a few high tables in back if you choose to eat inside. Cam's detailed description of how they make just one of their po' boys underlines what his talent and passion bring to the table: "We marinate the pork bellies in the flavors of the Dark and Stormy rum cocktail, because rum, ginger and pork sing so well together. Although, traditionally the cocktail is made with very dark rum, we use Old New Orleans cajun spiced rum mixed with Steen's Cane Syrup (another great product) and copious amounts of fresh ginger. The addition of the cane syrup gives that molasses aroma and body that is present in the cock-

Cam Boudreaux with his business, creative, and life partner, April Bellow

tail, while the ginger creeps with a pleasant bite, balanced with the heady aroma of rum. After a rub of kosher salt and a massage of marinade we let the belly ride for at least 12 hours in the cooler, and then gently roast them, cool them and eventually slice and glaze them with more of that killer sauce for each Poboy. Glazed, hot and sticky we dress the belly up with a squeeze of fresh lime, our mellow house aioli, and a crunchy and pleasantly sour lime cabbage slaw."

The same attention goes into their shrimp with Asian slaw po' boy, and the Guinness- and garlic-braised beef po' boy, and the roasted seasonal vegetable po' boy, and all their sides. But beware the potato salad. Cam loves his horseradish. The first bite will hit your sinuses like a haymaker.

REASON TO GO: For the first and only time, don't listen to the expert judges in Appendix A. I think this is the ≠1 Best Po' Boy place.
WHAT TO GET: All of them.

KINGFISH

337 Chartres St. • (504) 598-5005 • $$$

HOURS: 11:00 a.m.–2:30 p.m. 7 days a week; 5:30–10:00 p.m. Sun–Thur; 5:30–11:00 p.m. Fri and Sat

Kingfish is a new restaurant named after our sometimes brilliant, sometimes boorish governor Huey P. Long, nicknamed the Kingfish. The governor came into office an outspoken populist and went out shot to death on the steps of the State Capitol building. In between he was a champion of Share Our Wealth, a program to cure poverty and homelessness that, if tried today, would drive the Tea Party and Fox News absolutely apoplectic. He created charity hospitals to provide health care for the poor, erected colleges and schools with free textbooks to fight illiteracy, pushed through massive highway construction, and brilliantly built a series of bridges along the Mississippi so low that large ships coming from the Gulf couldn't get under them and so had to unload here instead of upriver in Memphis or St. Louis, thus giving all the economic benefits to Louisiana.

Chef Greg Sonnier may not be a political boss like his restaurant's namesake, but he can negotiate his way around a kitchen. A James Beard–nominated chef, he was first a protege of Paul Prudhomme at K-Paul's, then won personal acclaim with Gabrielle, a Mid-City restaurant he owned with his wife, Mary, for thirteen years until it became a Katrina casualty. Kingfish's menu is built around local seafood and any number of ways to present a pig, but features the robust layered flavors Chef Greg learned from Prudhomme taken a step (or five) further by Sonnier's passions and, some might say, wit. It starts with appetizers like his crab cake, presented with a protruding claw; in place of eggs mixed in with crabmeat, Kingfish parades a whole fried duck egg. The classic BBQ shrimp, on menus all over town, is here served on a Kingfish-only crunchy sweet-potato waffle shaped like a pirogue (a small flat-bottom boat used by Cajuns on the bayou). Here only can you get your Junky Chick (rotisserie chicken shot up with a Cajun marinade injector) and Shakshuka-gator (alligator sauce piquante by way of Tunisia). "I wanted this menu to be fun," Sonnier says. "I wanted every dish to be unique."

REASON TO GO: If you want your shrimp served in a pirogue, there's only one place to go.
WHAT TO GET: BBQ shrimp served in a pirogue, with a side of Shakshuka-gator.

Lucky Dogs

Entire books have been written about Lucky Dogs (*Managing Ignatius: The Lunacy of Lucky Dogs and Life in New Orleans* by Jerry Strahan). Ignatius P.

Reilly, the emblematic though fictional hero of *Confederacy of Dunces,* was a Lucky Dog cart vendor until he ate himself out of a job. Since 1947, distinctive hot-dog-shaped carts, which have been considered for historical site status, have set up at corners in the French Quarter. They are the only licensed and approved food vendors in the Quarter. Lucky Dogs claims to have sold twenty-one million hot dogs, give or take

Lucky Doggy style

a million. All have been served by vendors in red-and-white-striped jackets, many of whom seem to be on the final caboose of their employment train before attempting petty larceny or pole dancing. The eccentric salesmen only add to the luster of their links. An unidentified French Quarter policeman ate thirty-two dogs at once and has held the record since 1998. Feeling competitive?

• SNACKS • SNACKS • SNACKS • SNACKS • SNACKS • SNACKS •

♔ MR. B's BISTRO

201 Royal St. • (504) 523-2078

HOURS: 11:30 a.m.–2:00 p.m. Mon–Sat; 5:30–9:00 p.m. nightly; 10:30 a.m.–2:00 p.m. Sun jazz brunch

Mr. B's, a Brennan restaurant, has been chosen by *Food & Wine, Gourmet,* and other magazines as having the best barbecued shrimp and best gumbo ya-ya in New Orleans and as the city's best business lunch spot. Our Appendix A judges also chose Mr. B's as Best Business Lunch. Internationally known Paul Prud-homme and local legend Gerard Maras helped open Mr. B's Bistro in 1979. The Brennans had a hunch that the public would support a laid-back alternative to their higher-end restaurants, Commander's Palace and Brennan's. Mr. B's is definitely not casual, however. It has the feel of a club where business deals are made and legal documents signed. They are best known for their barbecued shrimp, which comes with garlic-enriched butter, a hot towel, and a bib to protect a businessman's tie. They also serve one of the better gumbos in town.

Cindy Brennan runs the restaurant and Chef Michelle McRaney runs the kitchen.

REASON TO GO: Find some business that needs attention and go have lunch.
WHAT TO GET: One or both of their signature dishes, gumbo ya-ya and barbecued shrimp.

MURIEL'S

801 Chartres St. • (504) 568-1885 • $$$
HOURS: 11:30 a.m.–2:30 p.m., 5:30–10:00 p.m. 7 days a week

Muriel's interior

Many French Quarter restaurants are haunted by tourists. Muriel's is haunted by Pierre Antoine Lepardi Jourdan. Pierre built his dream house, now used as Muriel's, and then crushingly lost it in 1814 when he wagered his beloved home in a poker game. Before having to vacate the premises, he committed suicide on the second floor. The current waitstaff sets a place for Pierre on the second floor every night. Pierre's ghost is said to move furniture around and now and again hurl glasses against the wall.

While this all might make Muriel's seem like a tourist trap for Goth kids, it is actually a classic and sophisticated Creole restaurant with a wrenchingly beautiful view of Jackson Square from the second-story balcony. The interior rooms on both floors are opulently furnished with gold leaf or deep red walls. The Chart Room has a massive dark wood bar.

More than the beautiful rooms and, yes, even more than Pierre, the food should be the #1 reason to go. Muriel's does classic Creole dishes, often with their own spin, like a sautéed redfish amandine with rich sweet-pea mashed potatoes or filet medallions drizzled with cabernet demi-glace and blue cheese wontons.

REASON TO GO: Fine dining in a beautiful setting . . . and a ghost.
WHAT TO GET: A table on the second floor for a great view of Jackson Square . . . and a ghost.

NAPOLEON HOUSE

500 Chartres St. • (504) 522-4152 • $$
HOURS: 11:00 a.m.–5:30 p.m. Mon; 11:00 a.m.–10:00 p.m. Tues–Thur; 11:00 a.m.–11:00 p.m. Fri and Sat

Where I'd be hard pressed to choose just one place to get the best gumbo, I have zero hesitation naming the best surroundings in which to eat it. The Napoleon House was the former home of Nicholas Girod, our third mayor. It was set aside for Napoleon Bonaparte to come live and basically rule as king of New Orleans. There was a local plot to rescue the French leader from exile in St. Helena. He never made it. His loss. It now looks like it hasn't been touched in all the years

Napoleon House interior

since. If you think photographs of Havana, Cuba, or Venice, Italy, are beautiful (as I do), Napoleon House is the most beautiful place to eat and drink in the city. Its sagging, cracked plaster walls, courtyard, and steps make it the epitome of "faded splendor." The menu is an eccentric mix of comfort foods: panini focaccia, hummus tahini, tapenade and feta, a Reuben, and what many think is the best muffuletta in New Orleans.

Esquire magazine wrote that the Napoleon House might be the best bar in America. They are best known for a cucumber-garnished Pimm's cup, a nineteenth-century gin-based drink.

REASON TO GO: A feast for the eyes.
WHAT TO GET: Strange bedmates of a muffuletta and a Pimm's cup.

NOLA

534 St. Louis St. • (504) 522-6652 • $$$
HOURS: 11:30 a.m.–2:00 p.m. Thurs–Sun; 6:00–10:00 p.m. 7 days a week

Emeril Lagasse opened NOLA to serve as a casual alternative to Emeril's in the Warehouse District. Of his three New Orleans restaurants (Delmonico Steak House in the Garden District being the third) NOLA serves his boldest-flavored dishes. As a transplant from Fall River, Massachusetts, Emeril has definitely embraced the New Orleans credo, "Anything worth doing is worth overdoing." Please know in writing that I do not mean your meal will be overcooked nor overly fussy and architectural. His food won't levitate. You can't, or at least shouldn't, eat the menu. Go to Chicago for that. Dishes at NOLA will have an abundance of (artfully) assembled flavors. Why have mere oysters when you can try his almond-crusted oysters with bacon brown sugar glaze, melted Brie, and rosemary fennel apple slaw? Why eat mere duck, when NOLA serves hickory-roasted duck with whiskey caramel glaze, buttermilk cornbread pudding, haricot vert fire-roasted corn salad, natural jus, and candied pecans?

REASON TO GO: Lively crowd with even more lively flavors.
WHAT TO GET: When it's on the menu, I'm a sucker for his plank fish—the freshest fish of the day, set on a cedar plank with a variety of ingredients and then blowtorched to perfection.

THE OLD COFFEE POT

714 St. Peter St. • (504) 524-3500 • $$

HOURS: 8:00 a.m.–10:30 p.m. Thur–Mon; 8:00 a.m.–2:30 p.m., 5:30–10:30 p.m. Tues and Wed

The Old Coffee Pot has been around since 1894. Their website claims they are "known to serve the best breakfast in New Orleans." By whom this knowledge is held is not specified. I do know it is absent from Appendix A's list of the Best Breakfast Spots, having not received a single vote as a top twelve from any judge. In their defense, the Old Pot is one of the last places in New Orleans still serving calas, spelled callas on their menu. Calas are made from rice mixed into a sugary egg batter, then deep-fried and dusted with confectioner's sugar. It's like a sweeter and creamier hush puppy. Calas came to New Orleans with the slaves from Ghana. Back in the 1700s, slaves were given one day off each week, usually Sundays. After church, slave women would roam the streets of the French Quarter with calas-filled baskets perched on their heads, chanting *"Belles calas! Tout chauds!"* ("Beautiful calas! Very hot!"). When the Spanish took control of Louisiana in the 1760s, they introduced *coartacion*, a practice that gave slaves the right to buy their freedom. Selling calas was a key way to earn money, giving the vendors the chance to buy freedom for themselves and their families.

The Old Pot does a reasonable crawfish étouffée and shrimp Creole, plus a gilding-the-lily overkill, the Fleur-de-Lis, which is chicken with grilled Gulf shrimp, topped with crabmeat, and a dressing of shrimp and crawfish on a bed of asparagus. Guy Ferry (the name Fieri is about as real as his hair) visited here for his TV show and posts the Old Pot on his website, giving it his Flavor Town Congeal of Approval.

> **REASON TO GO:** Calas, though they spell it callas.
> **WHAT TO GET:** Calas, though ask for callas.

OLIVIER'S

204 Decatur St. • (504) 525-7734 • $$

HOURS: 8:00 a.m.–10:00 p.m. 7 days a week

Alfred Hitchcock never won an Oscar. Wright Morris won two National Book Awards but today his novels are taught in no classrooms and won't be found on any bookstore's shelves. Sometimes the Gods of Fame are not fair. Olivier's has been serving food for nearly forty years—their dishes come from family recipes five generations back, beginning with Gramma Gaudet—and yet you've probably never heard of the restaurant unless tipped off by an intelligent concierge. Olivier's deserves to be a "name" restaurant. Their traditional Creole cuisine and setting are elegant without being fussy. Chef Armand Olivier's very gregarious but not pestering family members will accent a meal that rivals those served in the more renowned restaurants that dot the Quarter.

> REASON TO GO: To eat at a restaurant that's worthy of being mentioned in the same breath as Antoine's, Tujague's, and our other renowned restaurants, but never will be.

PALACE CAFÉ
605 Canal St. • (504) 523-1661 • $$$
HOURS: 11:30 a.m.–9:30 p.m. 7 days a week

Palace Café remains one of the last remnants of the old Canal Street, the city's Grand Boulevard, formerly lined with balconied and gilded movie palaces and large department stores, and the street crowded with locals and tourists.

Palace is a beautiful tribute to yesteryear in both look and taste. A spiraling art nouveau staircase will take you from the bistro-feeling main floor to an elegant upstairs dining area with trompe l'oeil paintings and a long above-the-avenue view of Canal Street. There are also tables set outside on the sidewalk, very much like the bistros of Paris. Sadly, the views from the street or the second floor are not as charming anymore, as our current Canal Street is lined with Radio Shacks and Foot Lockers. The fine dining, other than Palace Café, has been consumed by Arby's, McDonald's, and Popeyes.

Dick Brennan's restaurant has maintained a commitment to the past with straightforward tributes to turtle soup and gumbo, closing with Bananas Foster, prepared and flamed at your table. They also have a few twists like panneed rabbit with mustard cream sauce, and a favorite for some is the city's best bread pudding, a brioche bread with white chocolate ganache.

> REASON TO GO: With an active imagination, great views of the formerly grand avenue.
> WHAT TO GET: I'd jump on the white chocolate bread pudding and see if our judges, who didn't pick it as a "Best of," are off their game.

PALM COURT
1204 Decatur St. • (504) 525-0200 • $$
HOURS: 7:00–11:00 p.m. Wed–Sun

The exposed brick walls, bentwood chairs, ceiling fans, and old mirrored mahogany bar make you feel that you've stepped into a nineteenth-century New Orleans restaurant. But in fact, Nina Buck opened Palm Court in 1989. They serve

Lionel Ferbos at Palm Court

crispy fried crawfish tails, Creole gumbo, and shrimp potato cakes as appetizers with red beans and rice, garlic chicken, Shrimp Ambrosia, Oysters Bordelaise, and crawfish pies as entrees. Their #1 draw has not been the food, but a variety of jazz performers each night. From a large band stage with an old Steinway piano, the Crescent City Joymakers, Topsy Chapman and Lars Edegran, Thais Clark, Sam Butera and the Wildest, Juanita Brooks, and the irreplaceable Lionel Ferbos have performed. Depending on his health, Lionel Ferbos performs each Saturday night.

On July 17, 2013, Mister Lionel broke his own record as the world's oldest working jazz musician. As of this writing, the New Orleans trumpeter is 102. He celebrated that night by playing a gig at the Palm Court.

REASON TO GO: To experience the underpromoted pleasure of Lionel Ferbos.

WHAT TO GET: A table with a clear view of the stage.

PELICAN CLUB

312 Exchange Place • (504) 523-1504 • $$$

HOURS: 5:30–9:30 p.m. Sun–Thur; 5:30–10:00 p.m. Fri and Sat

In 1990 owners Richard Hughes and his wife Jean Stinnett-Hughes transformed a neglected nineteenth-century French Quarter town house into an elegant three-dining-room restaurant with a large bar area. Each room has its own ambience, one traditional, another contemporary, created by antique prints and burnished Louisiana cypress in one dining area, contemporary paintings by New Orleans artists and the dramatic black-leather banquettes against cream-colored brick walls in the next.

Their menu is not overly creative, but it's so well prepared that Pelican Club is, for me, definitely a Top 10 restaurant in the city. They offer crab and corn bisque, baked oysters, Gulf fish served whole with crawfish étouffée, crab and shrimp rémoulade over fried green tomato—dishes that can be found in tens, if not hundreds, of New Orleans restaurants, but rarely served so well. Their banana and blueberry bread pudding is noteworthy.

REASON TO GO: To pass through a hundred years of French Quarter history just by walking from one room to the next.

WHAT TO GET: I've had a great meal of just appetizers alone here.

PORT OF CALL

838 Esplanade Ave. • (504) 523-0120 • $$

HOURS: 11:00 a.m.–12:00 a.m. Sun–Mon; 11:00 a.m.–1:00 a.m. Fri and Sat

There's usually a line of people waiting to get into Port of Call. Many swear by it as the best burger joint in New Orleans. One of this book's Appendix A judges, whom I greatly respect, named Port of Call both her best burger joint and best late-night spot. I will never go there again. The two times I ate there the signature thick burgers were so thick that the middle was raw, not rare. And both times the place smelled like urine and disinfectant. That rarely ramps up my appetite. In New Orleans, you get two strikes, not three. There are just too many other options. If you're a burger aficionado my suggestion is you give a nod to Port of Call's pedigree and go there yourself to decide. I just won't be joining you.

R'EVOLUTION

777 Bienville St. (inside the Royal Sonesta Hotel) • (504) 553-2277 • $$$$
HOURS: 1:30 a.m.–2:30 p.m., 5:00–10:00 p.m. Mon–Fri; 5:00–10:00 p.m. Sat and Sun

R'evolution opened in the summer of 2012, a joint venture of award-winning chefs John Folse and Rick Tramonto. In Chef Folse's case I feel I should add "legendary," he being the son of a Louisiana fur trapper who learned how to cook so he wouldn't have to work the swamps, and now widely seen as Louisiana's long-time and leading ambassador for the region's cuisine. Since 1970, he's been a chef overseeing Lafitte's Landing, a destination rural restaurant and an institution as a training and testing kitchen. He's the author of the definitive and authoritative (and fifty-pound) *The Encyclopedia of Cajun & Creole Cuisine*. Chef Tramonto is like-wise a prolific cookbook author and James Beard Award–winning chef, who came to New Orleans having been a star at the hub of Chicago's restaurant scene with his two restaurants, Trio and Tru.

Before opening R'evolution, the two master chefs researched and delved into Louisiana history, exploring the significant culinary contributions. The corn and crab bisque and the crabmeat-stuffed frog legs Chef Folse says come from Louisiana Native Americans. Salumi platters are a tribute to the Italian kitchens. Beer-battered crab beignets presented with four rémoulade sauces and filled with velvety cream cheese from Folse's dairy are a refined riff on French beignets.

The pair also researched and hired a really interesting staff—probably the best educated in New Orleans. Chef de cuisine Chris Lusk has a degree in psychology from Stephen F. Austin University. Executive sous-chef Erik Veney has a bachelor's degree in comparative religions from the University of Virginia. The result as a whole is a very imaginative reinterpretation of classic Cajun and Creole cuisine. In remarks at the ribbon-cutting ceremony, New Orleans mayor Mitch Landrieu called it the most important new restaurant to open here in the last fifty years.

> REASON TO GO: The most important new restaurant to open here in the last fifty years.
> WHAT TO GET: Whatever you choose, you've gotta side-dish it with beer-battered crab beignets.

RED FISH GRILL

115 Bourbon St. • (504) 598-1200 • $$$

HOURS: 11:00 a.m.–10:00 p.m. Sun–Thurs, 11:00 a.m.–11:00 p.m. Fri and Sat

Ralph Brennan's Red Fish Grill has very good food in a very cool setting. It's spacious with etched floors, stained glass, and nautical-themed decor, including a beautifully weathered wall with a massive, peeling-paint redfish, and a school of whimsical wire fish stationary-swimming across the ceiling. Chef Austin Kirzner cooks up a wide variety of the freshest Gulf fish available, plus alligator sausage and seafood gumbo, finished off with his double chocolate bread pudding.

Red Fish Grill has been named New Orleans's best seafood restaurant four years in a row by *Where Yat* magazine.

> REASON TO GO: Heated fish in a cool setting.
> WHAT TO GET: When in Rome (and in season), the redfish.

THE RIB ROOM

621 St. Louis St. • (504) 529-7045 • $$$$

HOURS: 11:30 a.m.–2:00 p.m., 6:00–9:30 p.m. 7 days a week

Inside the Omni Royal Orleans Hotel, the Rib Room has been a high-profile restaurant for fifty years. It appears not much has changed in those fifty years. The Rib Room specializes in large blocks of full-bodied red meat accompanied by bowls of horseradish and slabs of butter, served in a mahogany and brass setting. It's the kind of place you go on an expense account or to celebrate special occasions. If the Rib Room was the kind of place that hung signed pictures of celebrities who ate there, which it is not, you'd see head shots of Louis Armstrong, Luciano Pavarotti, Muhammad Ali, Jane Fonda, Robert Redford, Charlton Heston, Paul Newman, the entire Rolling Stones, and Richard "I am not a *cook*" Nixon.

> REASON TO GO: Maybe you'll sit at a table where sat Jane Fonda, Keith Richards, and Nixon (not at the same time).
> WHAT TO GET: Hmmm . . . how 'bout the prime rib?

ROYAL HOUSE

441 Royal St. • (504) 528-2601 • $$

HOURS: 11:00 a.m.–11:00 p.m. Sun–Thur; 11:00 a.m.–12:00 a.m. Fri and Sat

Do exalted grounds make for enticing food? The Royal House sits on what was the original and longtime residence of the noted Tortorici family of New Orleans. Louis Tortorici left his native Italy for New Orleans. Here he founded the Contessa Entellina Society and became the society's first president. The society made a community out of Italian immigrants nostalgic for their language, traditions, and heritage, and also provided dental and medical services. First the Tortoricis converted the main floor of their home into a café, then four years later in 1900, the café developed into a flourishing full-scale restaurant. Tortorici's became the first Italian restaurant in New Orleans and, at one time, the fourth-longest-running restaurant (105 years) in the French Quarter. Let Mick Jagger gorge his lips over at the Rib Room; Tortorici's drew in famed Italian American singers Frank Sinatra and Dean Martin every time they visited the city. I'd toss in some lame joke about a restaurant having rat (pack) regulars, but I'll spare you that.

After Katrina hit, Tortorici's sat empty for a few years before being bought up by a group that also owns French Quarter restaurants La Bayou, Bayou Burger, Chartres House, Pierre Maspero's, and Pier 424, none of which is profiled in *Eat Dat*, and Kingfish, which is.

SOBOU
310 Chartres St. (inside W Hotel) • (504) 552-4095 • $$$
HOURS: 7:00–10:00 a.m., 11:30 a.m.–10:00 p.m. 7 days a week

The Commander's Palace branch of the divided Brennan family opened SoBou in the summer of 2012, taking over the very space that had been occupied by other side of the family, Ralph Brennan's now-shuttered Bacco. It functions as the restaurant for the über-hip W Hotel. The name is short for "South of Bourbon." Chef Juan Carlos Gonzales serves inventive (eccentric) food fusions for über-hip patrons: Cajun queso (pork cracklins with pimiento cheese fondue), crispy oyster tacos, a foie gras burger served with a mini Abita root beer and foie gras ice-cream float, a cone of raw tuna topped with avocado ice cream.

> REASON TO GO: Meals you won't find *anywhere* else.
> WHAT TO GET: Maybe start off slow with something like sweet-potato beignets with duck boudin and foie gras.

SOUTHERN CANDYMAKERS
334 Decatur St. • (504) 523-5544 • $
HOURS: 10:00 a.m.–7:00 p.m. 7 days a week

Yelp.com rated Southern Candymakers as the #3 best place (out of 1,269 places rated) to eat in New Orleans. Number three! It was rated ahead of Commander's Palace, Cochon, Restaurant August—really, ahead of nearly every place mentioned in this book. Now, Southern Candymakers is a perfectly good place to buy *PRAH-leens* (including sweet-potato flavored), turtles, fudge, toffee, and sugar-covered pecans to take home or send to friends. It's also a place to scarf a few *PRAH-leens* right then and there. But, number three? I think that says less about the brilliance of Southern Candymakers and more about the collective stupidity of Yelp and other online communal mosh-pits of anonymous opinions.

STANLEY

547 St. Ann St. • (504) 587-0093 • $$
HOURS: 7:00 a.m.–10:00 p.m. 7 days a week

It took inventive chef Scott Boswell years to find the right location to house his long-term vision for a New Orleans diner, serving all-day breakfast and brunch, burgers and sandwiches, a soda fountain, and homemade ice cream. Stanley was to be the more casual flip side of Boswell's upscale restaurant, Stella!. In 2008 Stanley opened on a much-coveted corner of Jackson Square, at the hub of tourism between the St. Louis Cathedral and Café Du Monde. The space was the former home of La Madeleine French Bakery. Boswell landed it after Starbucks Coffee withdrew its application. Thank God! In place of grande, venti, or trenta half-caff caramel macchiato, Stanley serves a simple but solid cheeseburger, po' boys including a Korean BBQ po' boy, what the menu bills as New Orleans's Best Reuben, and their many Creole-enhanced breakfast-all-day items, such as Beaux Bridge Benedict (with boudin added to the ham), Bananas Foster French Toast, and Eggs Stanley (cornmeal-crusted oysters, poached eggs, Canadian bacon, and Creole hollandaise on a toasted English muffin). Meals can be topped off with a Stanley Split (Chunky Chartres ice cream on a banana with chocolate sauce, whipped cream, toasted walnuts, and a cherry).

REASON TO GO: To keep Starbucks at bay.
WHAT TO GET: Start with Eggs Stanley and bring in the Stanley Split as your closer.

STELLA!

1032 Chartres St. • (504) 587-0091 • $$$$
HOURS: 5:30–10:30 p.m. 7 days a week

One of our renowned food writers considers Stella! the ≠1 best restaurant in New Orleans. Stella!'s chef, Scott Boswell, is supposedly a delightful person and an adventurous chef, has been trained by a list of the top chefs in the world (Jean-Georges, Charlie Trotter, Hiroyuki Sakai, Chin Kenichi, Daniel Boulud, among others), and was absolutely instrumental in the post-Katrina recovery with his $5 burgers being sold on the street . . .

But . . .

The one and only time I ate there, the service was so bad, flipping between dismissive and downright rude, that I have never given the restaurant a second try. My memories are filled with *un*memorable food and a decor that looked like a Swiss ski lodge (i.e., not good), but I assume the terrible service colors my thoughts. My sense is Scott Boswell deserves another try. You go and tell me about it. Opinions and comments can be left at www.eatdatnola.com.

REASON TO GO: To prove me wrong.

SYLVAIN
625 Chartres St. • (504) 265-8123 • $$
HOURS: 5:30–11:00 p.m. Mon–Thur, 11:30 a.m.–2:30 p.m., 5:30 p.m.–12:00 a.m. Fri and Sat; 10:30 a.m.–2:30 p.m., 5:30–10:00 p.m. Sun

Tucked away in an alley in the French Quarter with outdoor tables facing one of the oldest walls in the city in a courtyard where Faulkner once held court, owner Sean McCusker, a transplanted New Yorker, and Chef Alex Harrell, who's been cooking in New Orleans restaurants since 1998, have created a place more *New* New Orleans than neighboring Quarter restaurants. They avoid standards like barbecued shrimp, trout amandine, and baked oysters; there's not even a gumbo. Sylvain does serve beef cheeks, pan-fried pork shoulder, and a brussels sprout and hazelnut salad.

TABLEAU
616 St. Peter St. • (504) 934-3463 • $$$
HOURS: 11:30 a.m.–10:00 p.m. Mon–Thurs; 11:30 a.m.–11:00 p.m. Fri and Sat; 10:00 a.m.–10:00 p.m. Sun

Tableau is a new addition to the Brennan empire. Dickie Brennan opened his three-story restaurant in 2013. Although "opened" is too passive a word for the loving way the restaurant came about and its attention to historic detail. "We're here for one reason," says Dickie. "I read in the paper one morning that Le Petit Theatre was canceling the season and going to close because of finances. We just couldn't lose the oldest community theatre in America." So he worked up a business plan to keep Le Petit open while taking on some of the building's space (and rent) to create a restaurant that would also serve to draw in theatergoers for before-the-play meals.

"We've pulled the original drawings for that building, and it had a full balcony, so we were able to add a full balcony back with Vieux Carré approval," Dickie noted. A restored grand staircase spans three stories of the restaurant, connecting private dining rooms, balcony dining with a view of Jackson Square, and courtyard seating.

The menu, developed by Chef Ben Thibodeaux, has likewise been researched. Tableau offers court bouillon, a traditional New Orleans seafood stew with Gulf fish, shrimp, oysters, and crabmeat in a rich broth served with popcorn rice. Thibodeaux discovered that one hundred years ago, Leidenheimer Baking Company baked a football-shaped sourdough bread, which the restaurant serves today. Other dishes do get contemporary updates. Tableau has a French onion soup, which is traditional, but with new touches, including andouille and Abita Turbodog beer. They create a lineup of ten sauces made daily, including hollandaise, béarnaise, lemon-caper butter, meunière, New Orleans barbecue shrimp sauce, and amandine.

> REASON TO GO: Support the oldest community theater in America by eating very good food.
> WHAT TO GET: Anything, and then have it doused in ten sauces.

TUJAGUE'S

823 Decatur St. • (504) 525-8676 • $$$
HOURS: 5:00–10:00 p.m. Mon–Fri; 11:00 a.m.–10:00 p.m. Sat and Sun

Tujague's is the second-oldest *continuously* open restaurant in New Orleans (since 1856), or so Antoine's says. They'll argue the point. Tujague's will admit "continuously" presents a problem as they were once closed for three hours, "but it didn't work out," they add. Their 140-year-old guestbook includes the signatures of Franklin D. Roosevelt and Ty Cobb, presumably not at the same table. Brothers Steven and Sanford Latter bought the restaurant in 1982. Neither had any restaurant experience, nor had either even been inside Tujague's before the purchase. Sanford, who eventually sold his shares to Steven, saw the purchase as strictly an investment property. Steven envisioned a sort of Cheers for the French Quarter. He lined the rooms with memorabilia and historic photographs of old menus and previous owners from the original Guillaume and Marie Abadie Tujague to Clemence Castet. Miss Clemence ruled the dining room and the kitchen with an iron skillet and fist. Frustrated with her staff, she often brought food from her kitchen to the tables herself. Tujague's is best known for the beef brisket with Creole sauce and the Chicken Bonne Femme, only sometimes on the menu, a classic New Orleans dish that is heavy with garlic and parsley. While they may or may not beat out Antoine's as the oldest restaurant, their long cypress stand-up bar is the oldest, not just in New Orleans, but all of America. Above the bar is the beautiful, massive mirror brought over in one piece by sailboat after having hung in a Parisian bar for a hundred years.

> REASON TO GO: The history and the historic bar.
> WHAT TO GET: Chicken Bonne Femme, if they have it.

VERTI MARTE

1201 Royal St. • (504) 525-4767 • $
HOURS: 24 hours 7 days a week

Verti Marte is a somewhat seedy, claustrophobically crowded, twenty-four-hour corner grocery that does great takeout or delivery food. This is a place to get not a burger or grilled cheese sandwich, but a fried oyster with crispy bacon and melted cheddar, dressed with lettuce, tomato, and mayo po' boy. Verti Marte used to be a regular hangout for Brad Pitt. But after a national magazine outed that fact, he had to stop going there because tourists started camping out at the corner market as though waiting in line for Beyoncé or Super Bowl tickets.

VIEUX CARRÉ SEAFOOD & MEATS

1015 Iberville St. • (504) 265-8462
HOURS: 9:00 a.m.–7:00 p.m. Mon–Sat; 10:00 a.m.–4:00 p.m. Sun

Vieux Carré is not a restaurant, but *the* place to mail yourself or loved ones back home shrimps, oysters, and crawfish, plus Louisiana meats like boudin, tasso, and andouille sausage. James Dore, Blaine Prestenbach, and Craig Walker used their connections with local fishermen and farmers to set up their business in 2012 and ship the best of what we've got in the fastest way possible.

CHAPTER 3

Bywater
and the
Marigny

Bacon is the candy of meat.

—Kevin Taggart

The minute you land in New Orleans, something wet and dark leaps on you and starts humping you like a swamp dog in heat, and the only way to get that aspect of New Orleans off you is to eat it off. That means beignets and crawfish and jambalaya, it means shrimp rémoulade, pecan pie, and red beans and rice, it means elegant pompano au papillote, funky file z'herbes, and raw oysters by the dozen, it means grillades for breakfast, a po' boy with chochow at bedtime, and tubs of gumbo in between.

—Tom Robbins, from *Jitterbug Perfume*

Bywater and the Marigny were plantation land in the colonial era, later sold to New Orleans by Bernard de Marigny de Mandeville to get cash to pay off his gambling debts. You can call him Bernie Mac (but you'd be the first). At first the area was used by New Orleans for the practice of plaçage. French gentlemen would meet young Creole women at a series of ballroom socials, take the women on as mistresses, then educate them, often in Europe, and build them a small cottage in the Marigny—where they would live with the mistresses three months a year and live with their wives, back in the Quarter, nine months a year. Plaçage was an aboveboard, accepted practice. Much later (1984) unwelcome bustle surrounding the World's Fair in New Orleans prompted many long-term French Quarter residents to move downriver, at first into Marigny, then by the '90s the bohemian communities spread down to Bywater. Post-Katrina saw a surge of YURPS (Young Urban Rebuilding Professionals) leave graduate studies or early careers to head to New Orleans and be a part of something important. As New Orleans has grown to become a player in both the film and music industries, artistic types, such as Ani DiFranco, Dave Pimer of Soul Asylum, and Harry Shearer, humorist and the voice of Mr. Burns, Waylon Smithers, Ned Flanders, and many others on *The Simp-*

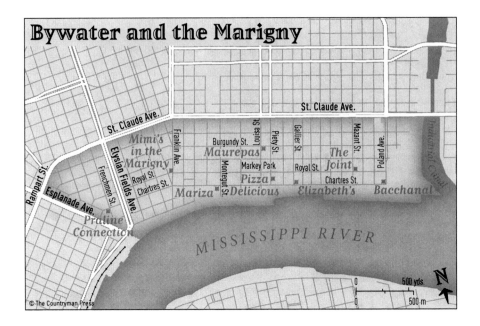

Bywater and the Marigny

sons, joined the YURPS to make Bywater and the Marigny the hippest and hottest neighborhoods in New Orleans (think Williamsburg and Dumbo in New York).

With all this creative energy, the area has also become a center for hot new restaurants.

♛ BACCHANAL

600 Poland Ave. • (504) 948-9111 • $$
HOURS: 11:00 a.m.–12:00 a.m. 7 days a week

Friday lunch among the regulars at Galatoire's is one kind of distinctly New Orleans dining experience. An evening meal out back at Bacchanal, seated under strung lights and tiki torches, listening to live music as the sun sets, is another. Bacchanal opened as a neighborhood wine shop in 2002. The front room is still a wine cellar where you're greeted by exceptionally friendly hipster-clerks, and where you pick up your beverage (wine, water, or carbonated fruit drink) and, if you want, one or more cheeses from the coolers. You should want. An exceptionally friendly hipster-clerk will take your cheese and give you a numbered stand to post on your table. Later, the cheese will be returned to your table, presented on a cheese board with olives, almonds, chutney, and toast slices. Then, you leave the wine room and go out back to a window where exceptionally friendly hipster-clerks will give suggestions and take your food order. They give you another numbered stand to post at your increasingly crowded table. Most menu items are small plates like smoked

Bacchanal's backyard

trout salad with apple, manchego, and buttermilk vinaigrette ($8) or the too-good-to-be-true bacon-wrapped dates, chorizo, pequillo peppers, and roasted tomatoes ($8). Even the larger plates, like an exceptional pork chop served on a bed of arugula, white anchovies, Parmigiano-Reggiano, and balsamic vinegar is only $12. With orders placed and number stands in hand, you then pick out your table either out back or, on oppressively hot nights, upstairs by an indoor bar in air-conditioning. Warning: The upstairs bartender is the lone unfriendly Bacchanal employee. The "Bacchanal Experience" came about after Katrina. The wine store opened its backyard as a dining spot for a variety of chefs displaced from their own flood-damaged kitchens. Now it has a permanent kitchen and its own chef, Joaquin Rodas, making it a classic contemporary bistro in a unique setting. On a clear, warm night, Bacchanal's backyard is the place to be in all of New Orleans.

REASON TO GO: To sit out back and take in a distinctly New Orleans vibe.
WHAT TO GET: Once the vibe sets in, does it really matter? Yes, it does. Get the bacon-wrapped dates.

BOOTY'S

800 Louisa St. • (504) 266-2887 • $
HOURS: 9:00 a.m.–11:00 p.m. 7 days a week

While it may sound like a place on Bourbon Street selling way-too-sweet rum drinks and blaring "Baby's Got Back," Booty's is anything but(t). It bills itself as street food from around the world. The menu is all small plates from $4 to $8. The portions are perfect for each diner to order two and then share. My wife, daughter, and I got the Yuca Mofongo (from Puerto Rico), vegetable kabob with yogurt cucumber dip (from Greece), Kimchi Jeong (Korea), Italian polenta with pesto, pork taco from Mexico, and Japanese ramen noodles, which was nothing like what you ate as a college mainstay, but served with caramelized pork belly and an intensely savory sauce. Each dish was individually great and worked perfectly together.

We drank salted watermelon with lime and a subtle tarragon kick. For dessert we had Booty's tribute to New Orleans's Hubig's Pies, a deep-fried pastry filled with peanut butter, chocolate, banana . . . and bacon. Our feast cost just over $20 per person.

My only complaint has to do with the seating, as in chairs. Booty's is run by twenty-somethings and caters to twenty-somethings. The hard, flat, non-contoured, metal chairs may suit them, but by the end of the meal, my fifty-something butt was sore.

REASON TO GO: Small-plate comfort food from many lands . . . and cheap.
WHAT TO GET: A whole lot of little portions.
WHAT TO BRING: A cushion on which to sit.

THE COUNTRY CLUB

634 Louisa St. • (504) 945-0742
HOURS: 10 a.m.–9 p.m. Sun–Thurs; 10 a.m.–10 p.m. Fri and Sat; brunch 10 a.m.–3 p.m. Sat and Sun; late-night menu available every day until 12:30 a.m.

Housed in a historic Italianate cottage in the Bywater, the Country Club has been a neighborhood secret for over thirty-five years. Chef Maryjane Rosas has worked for Donald Link, but is largely self-taught with a fine intuitive understanding of how flavors work. You can have a wonderful small-plate meal of her house-made boudin balls or Canjiquinha Brazilian pork and corn grit stew, eaten in your choice of the parlor room with the grand hardwood walk-around bar, or by the luscious green-back cabana lounge and pool, or on the breezy front veranda. Depending on your sensibility, I'd probably recommend the veranda. Swimsuits are optional in the pool. Not infrequently completely nude patrons wander from the pool into the parlor to freshen their drinks.

REASON TO GO: Catch a rising star in Maryjane Rosas.

WHAT TO GET: Anything on the veranda. It's "safe" on the veranda.

👑 ELIZABETH'S

601 Gallier St. • (504) 944-9272

HOURS: 8:00 a.m.–2:30 p.m. Mon–Sun; 6:00–10:00 p.m. Mon–Sat

A *New York Times* review best summed up the appeal of this out-of-the-way but essential New Orleans joint: "The thing to love about Elizabeth's is that somebody there tried to make bacon better."

That somebody was Heidi Tull, another in the long history of expat Yats (people who pass through New Orleans, get seduced, and move here—people like Tennessee Williams, Brad Pitt . . . and me). Heidi is a Carolina girl, raised in Sumter where New Orleans's only Civil War general, P. G. T. Beauregard, started the war. She received her culinary degree in Charleston and out of school worked in fine restaurants in Savannah, just across the border. But on her first visit to New Orleans, after ravishing several of the city's great restaurants, she told her husband Joe, "I'm not leaving!" And she didn't. She and Joe took jobs with Emeril's NOLA restaurant, and then she went off to the Windsor Court Hotel. Joe stayed on as NOLA's dessert chef for ten years. And finally in '98, Heidi opened her own restaurant, Elizabeth's, in a then funky neighborhood where tourists never ventured. Bywater is still funky, but now tourists go, primarily to eat at her restaurant. Elizabeth's has received rave reviews in publications like *Gourmet* and *Southern Living*.

Her motto was "Real Food Done Real Good," which still hangs on the rusted sign above Elizabeth's corner door at the intersection of Gallier and Chartres. The exterior is plastered with other hand-painted signs, like a folk art painting of a steaming cup of coffee saying, "Eat here or we both go hungry," or another sign with the inscription, "Eat . . . Relax." The interior walls are every bit as plastered with folk art, mostly the "Be Nice or Leave" paintings of Dr. Bob, a mean old cuss of an artist who'd probably be asked to leave most of the New Orleans establishments hanging his art.

The artwork gives the place a roadhouse appeal, but it's the food that's been causing pilgrimages to Bywater by Uptowners and out-of-towners. Elizabeth's serves classic grits and grillades, fried chicken livers with pepper jelly, all-off-the-bone pork belly, banana-enhanced sweet-potato casserole, the Dream Burger, a hamburger with blue cheese and praline bacon, and the two signature items, calas and praline bacon. Calas is a traditional Creole dish: deep-fried, cinnamon-seasoned rice fritters, creamy on the inside and dusted with powdered sugar. Kinda like beignets—only better. Elizabeth's is one of a few (maybe two) New Orleans restaurants still serving calas. But their signature item is the praline bacon—prepared by dragging bacon through chopped pecans and brown sugar with pork fat and then baking it. It's hell on the arteries but heaven for the soul.

Heidi and Joe moved back to their roots in Carolina with the birth of their son. Elizabeth's has since gone through three sets of owners. The first two were wise enough to keep on Chef Bryon Peck. Then, in 2011, Chef Bryon Peck became owner Bryon Peck.

REASON TO GO: It's the best breakfast in New Orleans. Period. Appendix A judges were off by one spot.

WHAT TO GET: The praline bacon and deep-fried calas are musts. The sweet-potato waffle with duck hash is a strongly advised.

FEELINGS CAFÉ

2600 Chartres St. • (504) 945-2222
HOURS: 6:00–9:30 p.m. Wed–Sun

This café has the cozy atmosphere of a French bistro. Former slave quarters have been transformed into the Patio Bar, where diners can enjoy live piano music. On Thursday nights you can take French classes. On any night, you can browse the Green Room, which displays an impressive collection of Marilyn Monroe and Elvis memorabilia.

REASON TO GO: Dine in former slave quarters or gawk at the Marilyn and Elvis collection.

WHAT TO GET: Old-World dishes like oyster en brochette and Gulf fish Nicholas (grilled, with shrimp and creamed spinach). *Une baise-ing Ay!*

Feelings front with . . . a guy

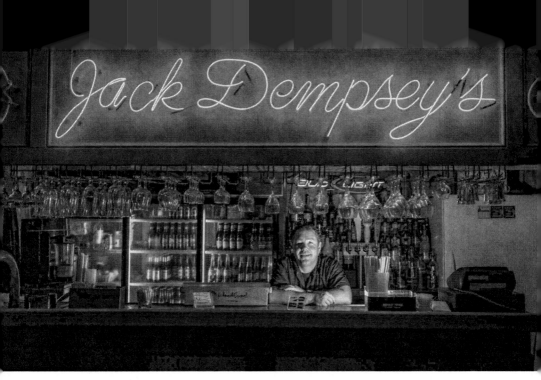

Jack Dempsey's bar

JACK DEMPSEY'S

738 Poland Ave. • (504) 943-9914

HOURS: 11:00 a.m.–2:00 p.m. Tues; 11:00 a.m.–8:00 p.m. Wed and Thurs; 11:00 a.m.–9:00 p.m. Fri; 12:00 p.m.–9:00 p.m. Sat

First off, you need to know the restaurant is not named for the famous prize-fighter, but for a much-loved, old-style crime reporter for yesteryear's *States-Item* newspaper. Dempsey's is a Yat's idea of a great restaurant, enormous piles of food sold at a reasonable price and nearly everything deep-fried. You can order the fried shrimp platter, or the fried oyster platter, fried catfish platter, fried crawfish platter, fried redfish platter, fried frog legs platter, fried boneless chicken platter, fried breaded veal cut, fried soft-shell crab, or, if you must, the rib eye and Dungeness crab (not fried).

> REASON TO GO: To pretend to be an authentic Yat.
>
> WHAT TO GET: How about something fried?

⚜ THE JOINT

701 Mazant St. • (504) 949-3232

HOURS: 11:30 a.m.–10 p.m. Mon–Sat

Many, probably most, people consider the Joint the best BBQ in New Orleans. Of course that's like saying Fred Barnes is the least offensive Fox News commentator. Probably a true statement, but not the highest of praise.

New Orleans is about half a state below the BBQ Belt. You probably need to get up past Opelousas or Ville Platte or across the border into Mississippi before we're talking "serious" BBQ. The last time I ate at the Joint (a Friday night—about 7:30), they were out of both chicken and pulled pork. I said, "I guess I'll have the brisket." In Memphis or Kansas City (or New York City, where Daisy Mae's is the best BBQ I've ever had) being out of chicken and pulled pork, on a Friday night, would have caused overturned chairs and busted-out windows.

But the Joint is an easy, laid-back BBQ joint, with funky art on the walls and five gorgeous, slightly rusted, chip-painted lawn chairs lining the sidewalk. A rambling conversation with the heavily tattooed bartender or the heavily pierced patrons at the next stool is as much a reason to go there as their meats, mostly bought from the legendary Poche's Market in Breaux Bridge, Louisiana, and always slow cooked in the smoker, under an enlarged carport out back.

REASON TO GO: Even if they only have brisket left to sell, it's the best BBQ brisket in New Orleans.

WHAT TO GET: Well . . . let's wait and see what dey's got left.

♕ MARIZA

2900 Chartres St. • (504) 598-5700 • $$$
HOURS: 5:00–8:00 p.m. Tues–Thurs; 5:00–9:00 p.m. Fri and Sat

Mariza is the newest upscale star of the booming Bywater restaurant scene. Chef Ian Schnoebelen and General Manager Laurie Casebonne are longtime Bywater residents and New Orleans restaurant veterans. Before Katrina, they both worked at Lilette where Schnoebelen was sous-chef and Casebonne worked the front of the house. While there, they began planning their own restaurant. Iris, their first, opened early in 2006. The next year *Food & Wine* named Schnoebelen one of the nation's top ten new chefs. In January of 2013, the pair opened Mariza. The restaurant is placed inside a just-opened condo building, previously used as a rice plant. The condos and restaurant are designed to retain as much of the industrial look of concrete and cement walls, tall ceilings, and old woodwork as possible.

The core of Mariza's menu is Italian derived, but loosely so. "I'm not trying to be Italian, I'm just doing my own thing but incorporating a lot of those flavors," Schnoebelen says. While traveling in Italy just before opening Mariza, he took note of the heavily regional focus unique to each city they visited. "Venice, Rome, Florence, Parma—everywhere we went just had the local product. So I'm trying to do that here, too." All the meat on the menu is local. The pork and duck come from Covey Rise and Chappapeela Farms. Two Run Farms provides lamb and beef. The vast majority of the produce is also local, though Schnoebelen jokes, "It's hard to get local celery, but I'm trying to keep it as close as possible."

> REASON TO GO: To experience a new and contemporary, yet authentically New Orleans restaurant in a city embracing but sometimes handicapped by her Creole and Cajun traditions.
>
> WHAT TO GET: Whole roasted Gulf fish served with a fennel and arugula salad in lemon vinaigrette. "That is the style here," Schnoebelen says. "Real rustic and real simple. Just trying to showcase the natural flavors."

♕ MAUREPAS

3200 Burgundy St. • (504) 267-0072 • $$
HOURS: 11:00 a.m.–11:45 p.m. Thurs–Tues; closed Wed

Maurepas Foods, opened in MMXI, was one of the first destination restaurants for foodies dining in the Bywater. The restaurant calls itself "purveyors of robust cuisine." The chef-owner, Michael Doyle, built his reputation at Dante's Kitchen. At Maurepas, Doyle has created a hip setting but kept prices reasonable. The interior has art prints on the walls and Edison bulb chandeliers hanging from a beautiful wood ceiling with antique medallions over a copper bar. His ever-

Michael Doyle in Maurepas

changing menu includes eclectic offerings like goat tacos with pickled green tomatoes and cilantro harissa or mussels with pear cider and king oyster mushrooms. During my most recent visit, their $7 cucumbers with Guajillo vinaigrette, mint, honey, and mushroom cracklins was quite possibly the best vegetable dish I have tasted—ever. The market greens, a stewy version of collards with potatoes and locally smoked ham, for just $3 was a close second best.

Partner Brad Smith is billed as "Chief Intoxicologist." He too makes inexpensive but inventive creations, cocktails like the Gent & Jackass (bourbon, paprika, simple syrup, lemon juice, peach bitters, and basil). I ordered his Tarted Up Mormon (whiskey, lemon, blonde ale, and Espirit de June, a French liquor made from flowers) just for the name, but then drank one of my favorite cocktails. Ever.

REASON TO GO: Really good food (and drinks) at really reasonable prices.
WHAT TO GET: Ibid.

MIMI'S IN THE MARIGNY

2601 Royal St. • (504) 872-9868 • $$
HOURS: 4:00 p.m.–2:00 a.m. Sun–Thurs; 4:00 p.m.–4:00 a.m. Fri and Sat

Mimi's is a bar known for live music when they are, on and off again, allowed to host performances and DJ nights like Soul Sister's Hustle Party when they are not. Owner Mimi Dykes is constantly battling the city about her lack of live-entertainment permit. The bar has been voted New Orleans's best in both the *Gambit* and *Where Yat*. But more than a neighborhood house party, Mimi's is also known for having great food on again and on again, all the time. Heathcliffe

Heathcliffe Hailey working the kitchen

Hailey works the kitchen (as shown above) to create Spanish tapas that go way, way beyond anything that could be considered bar food.

His sherry-braised mushroom manchego toast or his Gambas al Ajillo, which has three Gulf shrimp, thinly sliced garlic, parsley, and a touch of spinach, with more than a touch of butter and white wine, is served until 4 a.m. on weekends, 2 a.m. every other day.

REASON TO GO: To quote a *Gambit* review, "dance your ass off, and feed your soul."

WHAT TO GET: Patatas bravas.

NEW ORLEANS CAKE CAFÉ & BAKERY
2440 Chartres St. • (504) 943-0010 • $
HOURS: 7:00 a.m.–3:00 p.m. 7 days a week

Steve Himelfarb, aka "The Cake Man," began by selling slices of his chocolate cake door-to-door across the city. Over the years, he developed a loyal following of customers who buy cake by the slice, some several times a week. "I made the same chocolate cake every day for four years," he said. "It was very Zen-like to repeat that daily. With repetition comes perfection."

Steve briefly set up a retail front in the French Quarter that was Katrina'd out of existence. When La Spiga, a noted bakery in the Marigny, chose to shut its doors, he leapt at the opportunity. Himelfarb signed the lease on August 29, reclaiming a tragic date. "We have something much better to remember that date for now," he says. The New Orleans Cake Café & Bakery now serves breakfast and lunch in addition to baked goods. The French toast with fresh challah atop homemade orange-pecan syrup is as good as it sounds, as well as the shrimp and organic grits with sautéed tomato and onion. But what says New Orleans, city of excess, more than a boozy cupcake flavored with Champagne or mimosa, or the decadent Sazerac cupcake with whiskey buttercream frosting?

REASON TO GO: Cake.

WHAT TO GET: Sazerac cupcake with whiskey buttercream frosting.

PIZZA DELICIOUS

617 Piety St. • (504) 676-8482 • $

HOURS: 11:00 a.m.–11:00 p.m. Tues–Sun; closed Mon

When people used to ask where to get good pizza, I would answer in my snotty, ex–New Yorker refrain, "Chicago or New York." I'd tried all the local Reginelli's, Theo's, Rocky's, Slice, Naked Pizza, Louisiana Pizza Kitchen, Magazine Pizza, and Big Pie brands that at least one person or publication had tabbed "The Best" and none was better than "just okay." Pizza Delicious has changed all that. Transplanted New Yorkers Mike Friedman and Greg Augarten met at Tulane. Both had fallen in love with New Orleans but missed their native "real" pizza.

"We'd always be excited when a new pizza place would open, hoping that maybe it would be 'the one,' but it never really was, sadly. We were looking for love in all the wrong places," Friedman recalls. The two decided to do it themselves, even though neither knew anything about making pizza. Said Friedman, "We just decid-

Expat-pizza-Yat makers Mike Friedman and Greg Augarten

ed to make pizza one night ourselves. It was our first time. We found a good dough recipe in a cookbook and gave it a try." They began experimenting with recipes in a community kitchen in Bywater. "There was a lot of trial and error based on information that we gathered online. We'd take a recipe, try it, and say 'This doesn't work,' or 'It's too dry,' or 'Too crackery.' And while we weren't experts in making pizza, we were definitely experts in eating it."

A Kickstarter campaign allowed Pizza Delicious to grow from a popular but one-night-a-week place, where they sold slices out of a window in a house, to a full-time, brick-and-mortar pizza parlor. The cast of HBO's *Treme*, mostly from New York and Baltimore, held a blind taste-test pizza competition. Pizza Delicious beat out Patsy's in East Harlem, an unnamed neighborhood Bronx pizzeria, Matthew's in Baltimore, and Bagby's in Baltimore. New Orleans finally has an answer to the question, "Where should I go for good pizza?"

REASON TO GO: The only place in New Orleans to get pizza.
WHAT TO GET: Wadda you, a comedian? Da pizza, ya jamoke.

PRALINE CONNECTION
542 Frenchmen St. • (504) 943-3934 • $$
HOURS: 11:00 a.m.–10:00 p.m. 7 days a week

Cecil Kaigler and Curtis Moore's congenial Praline Connection (in New Orleans pronounced *PRAH-leen*, never *PRAY-leen*) has been the city's premier soul food (with a heavy dose of Cajun-Creole) restaurant since it opened in 1990. In the heart of the blues and jazz clubs along Frenchmen Street, Praline Connection serves a full menu of traditional classics: fried chicken, stewed chicken, fried chicken livers, smothered pork chops, collard greens, filé gumbo, sweet-potato pie, and crowder peas. It is the only restaurant in New Orleans that makes fresh crowder peas every day.

REASON TO GO: The closest thing New Orleans has to soul food (other than Two Sisters—see chapter 4).
WHAT TO GET: Something smothered or fried . . . with greens.

SIBERIA
2227 St. Claude Ave. • (504) 265-8855 • $
HOURS: 5:00 p.m.–12:00 a.m. 7 days a week

Siberia is a dive bar on Dive Bar Row, i.e. St. Claude Street, which was formerly Crap Street until a church petitioned a name change . . . seriously. Other dive bars include the Hi-Ho Lounge, the Allways Lounge, and the five-time national "Best Dive Bar" champion, the Saturn. Siberia has live music and hosts events like Hades

Hubig's Pies

Since a fire in the summer of 2012 destroyed Hubig's factory on Dauphine Street in the Marigny, New Orleans has been in pie withdrawal and anxiously awaiting the rebirth of the local legendary snack food. A Hubig's pie and a cup of coffee were the daily breakfast for (probably too) many. The loss of Hubig's has inspired musical tributes. Dave Jordan wrote a tune mourning the loss for his album, *Bring Back Red Raspberry* (named for his favorite flavor). During a New Orleans City Council meeting, the permit for the new Hubig's factory came up on the agenda, prompting calls for lemon and coconut pies before taking a vote.

Until the fire, Hubig's pies were available in virtually every drugstore, gas station, hardware store, and grocery store checkout line in New Orleans, all freshly wrapped in their distinctive waxy white packages with the chubby cook mascot, Savory Simon. The pies had been delivered fresh to more than one thousand local stores each morning. The New Orleans Parish Jail was their #1 customer. I wouldn't exactly say a Hubig's pie is a culinary masterpiece, but they do satisfy a craving the same way over-the-counter foods like frozen slushies or Ding Dongs can fulfill a momentary need.

Hubig's started in Forth Worth, Texas, around the time of World War I. The Great Depression saw all of their bakeries close their doors except the one location at 2417 Dauphine Street in Bywater, opened by Simon Hubig in 1922. The pies are hand-stamped with the flavors of Apple, Lemon, Peach, Pineapple, Chocolate, and Coconut. Seasonally, there are also Sweet Potato, Blueberry, Strawberry, Cherry, and Banana. The new location will be on Press Street. When they're back, the best way to eat a Hubig's is after ten seconds in the microwave.

Night, the International Noise Conference, and Bits & Jiggles (comedy and burlesque). The reason for its inclusion here is Kukhnya, an eclectic Eastern European restaurant inside the bar where you can get a pol-boy (Polish po' boy), several types of blinis, and both rampushki (garlic cheese rolls) and kapusta (spicy cabbage roll).

REASON TO GO: Bits & Jiggles.
WHAT TO GET: The best kapusta in town.

SUIS GENERIS

3219 Burgundy St. • (504 309-7850) • $$
HOURS: 6:00 p.m.–1:00 a.m. Wed–Sat; brunch 10:00 a.m.–3:00 p.m. Sat

The name Suis Generis translates "something that came from nothing." What kind of something Ernest Foundas and Adrienne Bell have created from nothing is open to debate. Bar? Restaurant? Art installation? Salt and pepper shakers are attached to Hot Wheels cars; the high ceiling sports a giant honeycomb composed of red plastic Solo cups; the three booths running down one wall each feature a glass-enclosed faux burning fireplace log, and there are Barbie Doll lights.

Suis Generis's menu is equally eclectic and changes daily. Their website justifies the ever-evolving entrees with the question, "Do you wear the same clothes all year?" There's a smorgasbord of global influences. Small-plate entrees have included pork belly with cardamom and garbanzo puree and a Greek loukaniko sausage. Thursday is taco night with homemade taquitos. As intoned on the website, "Come on an adventure" and "Rock your taste-buds. Soak in the groovy vibe. Feed your soul."

REASON TO GO: Flash back to an era that never was.
WHAT TO GET: Hey man, whatever they're serving. That's cool.

THREE MUSES

536 Frenchmen St. • (504) 252-4801
HOURS: 4:00–10:00 p.m. Mon and Wed (closed Tues); 4:00–11:00 p.m. Thur–Sun

Three Muses is focused on three things equally—food, drink, and music. Chef Daniel Esses serves Asian-inspired small plates. Here you can try dishes like lamb sliders with tomato chutney and herbed goat cheese, jumbo lump crabmeat cannelloni with vodka sauce, or sesame-crusted fresh fried chicken strips with Thai peanut sauce. Or you can slide a little more local with house-made fried pickles or pork belly braised in NOLABrew's Brown Ale. Chef Esses's two partners are mixologist Christopher Starnes and hostess and noted jazz singer Miss Sophie Lee.

CHAPTER 4

TREME

Start with butter. There's no substitute for butter.

—**Leah Chase**

Honey, and I just love me some red beans. This is a red bean city here.

—**Willie Mae Seaton**

Treme is maybe the most interesting, but probably the least visited neighborhood. Tourists are often afraid to venture into a predominantly black neighborhood with housing projects. Fact is, you're more likely to get mugged in the Garden District, but Sandra Bullock lives there and it's named "Garden," so you'll forever see tourists walking the Garden District clutching self-guided tour maps and gawking at the houses, like 1420 First Street where Peyton and Eli learned to chuck a football.

Rich in history, Treme is the birthplace of jazz. The word "jazz" itself comes from Treme's Storyville section. Alderman Sidney Story had studied the port cities in Europe and concluded the best way to control prostitution and associated crimes was to make a legal but confined red light district. The prostitutes of New Orleans famously wore jasmine perfume. Customers coming away from "transactions" were said to smell like they were "jazzed." At one time, getting jazzed in Storyville was equal in popularity to the swamp tours of today. Legally paid-for fornication with strangers, like feeding marshmallows to gators, was something tourists just couldn't get back home. The U.S. government eventually shut down Storyville in 1917, prompting New Orleans mayor Martin Behrman to utter, "You can make it illegal, but you can't make it unpopular."

In addition to boogie-woogie and boobs, Treme is one of the most important African American neighborhoods in the country. A century before the Harlem Renaissance, Treme was a center of black culture and politics. The 1860s civil rights movement was the first in America. Even during slavery, Treme was primarily populated by free men of color. Paul Trevigne edited the oldest black-owned *daily* newspaper, *The Tribune*, and Treme's St. Augustine Church is the oldest African American *Catholic* church.

I've profiled only four restaurants in Treme. Three are as close to *musts* as any in the city.

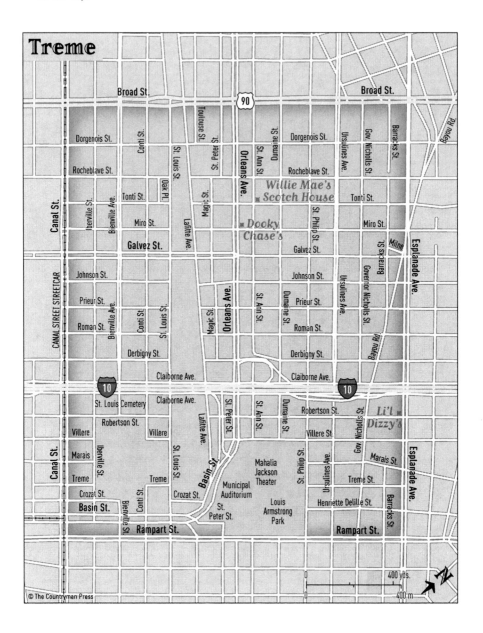

Lolis Eric Elie

Lolis would damn me to hell, or at least cringe uncomfortably, if I wrote that he was "Mr. Treme" or the "unofficial mayor of Treme." He is the personification of understated elegance. His mother was a professor, his father a civil rights attorney. Lolis has a master's in journalism from Columbia University and an MFA from Virginia. Columbia named him "alumnus of the year" in 2012. He has become a recognized expert on New Orleans food and culture and probably could have written a much more thorough *Eat Dat*, but with less bad wordplay or eye-rolling attempts at humor.

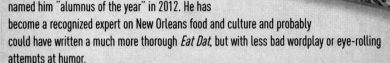

Lolis was a longtime, thrice-weekly columnist for the *Times-Picayune*. He's authored two books, *Smokestack Lightning: Adventures in the Heart of Barbecue Country* and the 2013 *Treme Cookbook* and was co-producer and writer of the documentary based on his barbecue book. He was editor of *Cornbread Nation 2: The Best of Southern Food Writing*. His own essays have been anthologized in *Best Food Writing: 2008, Best African American Essays: 2009, Streetlights: Illuminating Tales of the Urban Black Experience*, and *That's What I Like (About the South)*. A frequent contributor to the *Oxford American*, his work has also appeared in *Gourmet*, the *Washington Post*, the *New York Times*, *Bon Appétit*, *Downbeat*, and the *San Francisco Chronicle* among other publications. Lolis has appeared on air for *CBS News Sunday Morning* and often on National Public Radio programs. Lolis wrote and co-produced and starred in the PBS documentary *Faubourg Treme: The Untold Story of Black New Orleans*, which has won multiple awards as Best Documentary. He was a writer for the HBO series *Treme* and currently writes for the Showtime series *Hell on Wheels*.

Beyond all that he is a passionate spokesperson for his city and her food. He doesn't merely want to set the historical record straight for gumbo recipes or Creole influences, as highlighted in *Eat Dat*'s chapter 1, he wants to convert readers to his vision that food is more than mere nourishment. While writing a piece about the catfish at Barrow's restaurant, Lolis recalls, "I didn't have a particular sense of myself as a food writer, but I was. I realized food was evocative of place." Food is identity, nowhere more so than in New Orleans.

Mr. Okra

Arthur Robinson, mka (mostly known as) Mr. Okra, has been peddling his fruits and vegetables for over thirty years. His means is a battered, chugging Ford pickup truck packed with fruits and vegetables, decorated in folk art painted by Dr. "Be Nice or Leave" Bob, and roving the streets of Bywater, Treme, and Mid-City seven days a week—unless he doesn't feel well or his truck has one of its frequent breakdowns. His calling card is his deep, bullfrog voice, bellowing what he has to sell each day from the truck-mounted PA system.

Years ago he was known as "Li'l Okra" when he worked with his dad, the original Okra Man. He sold produce and random meats at first from a wheelbarrow, then from a horse and buggy. Arthur took up other vocations. He worked at a service station and shipped off for a year as a crewman on a freighter. Returning to New Orleans, he ran his own tire shop, servicing eighteen-wheelers. But eventually he settled into his dad's business, his colorful truck replacing the wheelbarrow and buggy.

Back in the day, New Orleans had many vendors working the city streets, like the ice man, the coffee man, and the charcoal man, who brought their goods or services directly to customers' doors. The calls of itinerant hawkers and bootstrap entrepreneurs used to echo in the air. Now there's just Mr. Okra.

He has become a mobile city icon. Residents passing by his truck in their cars or on bicycles will mimic Mr. Okra's "I got orrrr-angesss. I got banaaa-nasss." His banter has been featured on numerous albums by local bands, plus "Squirm," a song by Dave Matthews Band. He was the subject of the 2009 documentary *Mr. Okra*. Said the film's director, T. G. Herrington, "He's so iconic and such a part of the fabric of my community. After the first screening in New York, people walked up to us and said, 'This makes me want to move to New Orleans. I want to know people like Mr. Okra.'" The Mayor's Office bestowed upon Mr. Okra an honorary "Ambassador to New Orleans" commendation.

Of all of this attention, Mr. Okra says, "I'm a celebrity, but I'm a broke celebrity."

♕ DOOKY CHASE'S

2301 Orleans Ave. • (504) 821-0600 • $$

HOURS: 11:00 a.m.–3:00 p.m. Tues–Fri; 5:00–9:00 p.m. Fri

Owner and chef Leah Chase, now into her nineties, can still be seen going table-to-table. She famously approached President Obama's table when he visited her restaurant on the campaign trail. He got a double barrel of "Oh no you don't!" from Miss Leah as he raised a bottle of hot sauce toward her gumbo. Many consider her gumbo z'herbes, a meatless gumbo created for Catholics to eat during Lent, to be *the* best gumbo in New Orleans. Our A-list critics voted her fried chicken *the* best, surprisingly bumping Food Network favorite Willie Mae's Scotch House to second place. Leah Chase, aka the Queen of Creole, has been working the restaurant since 1957 (the restaurant's been there since '41). "I thought I was going to be the cute little hostess," she recalls, but was shoved back into the kitchen. Prior to working in the kitchen, Leah's training to be a world-renowned chef had been managing two amateur boxers and becoming the first woman to mark the racehorse board for local bookies. Since then, this largely self-taught Creole chef has won practically every award. She's been inducted into the James Beard Foundation's Who's Who of Food & Beverage in America. She was honored with a lifetime achievement award from the Southern Foodways Alliance. She has honorary degrees from Tulane, Dillard, Our Lady of Holy Cross College, Madonna College, Loyola, and Johnson & Wales University. The Southern Food and Beverage Museum has a permanent exhibit named after her.

In addition to some of the best food in New Orleans, Dooky Chase's also has a storied history. During segregation, blacks and whites could not eat together— except at Dooky Chase's. Miss Leah knew no one would be arrested at her restaurant or a riot would break out. Therefore, all civil rights meetings in New Orleans took place inside. Her walls are also lined with one of the best collections of African American art in the country. She's been collecting paintings since the '50s.

As a self-taught chef, Miss Leah never measures an ingredient. She does measure the results and has very strong opinions about the basics of Creole cooking, never hesitating to pronounce about the dishes of others, "That's not Creole." The gumbo at the Dooky Chase's Restaurant contains crab, shrimp, chicken, two kinds of sausage, veal brisket, ham, and the perfect roux. "Not a real dark roux," she says. "That's more Cajun." She steadfastly holds that the roux must be the perfect color and texture and that the cook has to stand guard at her pot to make that happen. "Don't give me that sticky, gooey stuff." Miss Leah has many other rules: Onions and seasoning must be cut very fine. They cannot float. Beans can't float either. Okra has to be cooked down, i.e. to death. Cabbage has to be smothered. And for God's sake, onions and garlic and green peppers, the holy trinity, had better be in there.

TREME

Miss Leah Chase, the Queen of Creole

REASON TO GO: As much (or more) an essential New Orleans restaurant as Commander's Palace or Galatoire's.

WHAT TO GET: The lunchtime buffet can get you eggplant casserole, mac 'n' cheese, dirty rice, fried catfish, spicy sausage, and great fried chicken.

LI'L DIZZY'S

1500 Esplanade Ave. • (504) 569-8997 • $$
HOURS: 7:00 a.m.–2:00 p.m. 7 days a week, 4:00–8:00 p.m. Thurs–Sat

If you watched HBO's series *Treme*, you've seen Li'l Dizzy's. In David Simon's nearly obsessive need to make sure viewers in-the-know knew he was in-the-know about New Orleans, there was a scene filmed in Li'l Dizzy's, a local in-the-know kind of place, about every other episode. Owner Wayne Baquet's restaurant roots run three generations deep. His dad ran Eddie's. His sister opened up Paul Gross Chicken Shack. Wayne has opened a total of eleven restaurants and ran Zachery's in Carrollton for thirteen years. All of the family restaurants were known for their fried chicken. After forty years in the restaurant business, Wayne sold Zachery's to take a step back, immediately felt restless, and stepped back in, opening Li'l Dizzy's in 2004. The Creole filé gumbo served at Li'l Dizzy's is the same gumbo that his family has been serving for decades. It starts with a premade, seasoned, dry roux mix that Wayne and his father developed so that they could reproduce the essence of their gumbo anywhere they ventured.

REASON TO GO: To be in the know.

WHAT TO GET: The $16 buffet is probably your best, most affordable option.

TWO SISTERS KITCHEN

223 N. Derbigny St. • (504) 524-0056 • $
HOURS: 11:00 a.m.–2:00 p.m. Mon–Fri, 11:30 a.m.–3:00 p.m. Sun

Not to be confused with *Court of Two Sisters* in the French Quarter, Two Sisters Kitchen in Treme is soul food, maybe the only "real" soul food served in New Orleans, and really good soul food. The cornbread and small cups of potato salad are brought to each diner as mandatory starters and are as good as what's being served at Mama Dip's (Chapel Hill) or Papa Lew's (Kansas City). We ordered the pork chops, turkey leg, and smothered chicken. All were falling-off-the-bone tender. The very flavorful corn, clearly not from a can, may have been the highlight of the meal.

WILLIE MAE'S SCOTCH HOUSE

2401 St. Ann St. • (504) 822-9503 • $$
HOURS: 11:00 a.m.–5:00 p.m. Mon–Sat, 11:00 a.m.–3:00 p.m. Sun

There's a classic, well-worn cycle for some New Orleans restaurants. Willie Mae's Scotch House is mid-cycle, transforming from beloved local hangout to a place where locals stop going because the lines are too long, jammed with tourists seeking "authentic" New Orleans food where "the locals go." The Food Network and the Travel Channel aired segments on Willie Mae's within six months of each other. Since then, everything has changed. The two TV networks are loaded with shows that highlight locally favorite joints, of course forever destroying that vibe immediately after broadcasting the segment. The difference between those TV shows and a book like *Eat Dat*, where I also seek to highlight local treasures, is

that so few people read books, my reach or influence would be a single peppercorn in Guy Fieri's Flavor Town.

Willie Mae's basically has two items, fried chicken and fried pork chops, from which to build a meal with red beans and rice, white beans and rice, butter beans, green beans, simmered okra, and tomato. While my Appendix A judges have chosen Dooky Chase's fried chicken, many consider Willie Mae's as the best—on the planet. We'll throw down with anyone. Her fried chicken comes from a mysterious recipe she's never revealed. Willie Mae's won an "America's Classic" award from the James Beard Foundation, which recognizes local restaurants that carry on the traditions of great regional cuisine. Months after she received the Beard Award, the restaurant was destroyed by Hurricane Katrina. Three years of volunteer efforts and more than $200,000 in private donations brought Willie Mae's Scotch House back into business. When NPR visited to do a story on Willie Mae's, the radio crew asked Kerry Seaton, current owner and Willie Mae's granddaughter, what was in her secret batter. She responded, "Well, I keep the batter wet. There salt . . . and pepper . . ." They interrupted, "There's gotta be crack cocaine in here somewhere." It's just that good.

REASON TO GO: A fried chicken Holy Shrine.
WHAT TO GET: In line early (before the 11:00 a.m. opening). The place only seats twenty-eight people.

CHAPTER 5

Mid-City
and
Bayou St. John

As bad as it is here [New Orleans right after Katrina], it's better than being somewhere else.

—Chris Rose

All sorrows are less with bread.

—Miguel de Cervantes

The Mid-City and Bayou St. John neighborhoods are home to City Park, which, in addition to the one-hundred-year-old New Orleans Museum of Art and Botanical Gardens, also has an amusement park, paddle-boat rentals, miniature golf, and City Splash, a water park opening in 2015. The Fairgrounds Race Track, down the road from City Park, hosts the Jazz & Heritage Festival, drawing half a million visitors each spring. The Bayou Boogaloo Festival and the VooDoo Experience cling to remaining local events as more and more tourists join them each year. The neighborhoods are primarily paddle-boat and putt-putt blue collar. The restaurants tend to be more affordable, less sophisticated than ones in Uptown, the Garden District, or the French Quarter. Some of the restaurants are beacons to middlebrow taste with what many consider the city's best steak house (Crescent City), best po' boys (Parkway Bakery), ice-cream parlor (Angelo Brocato's), donut shop (Blue Dot), and neighborhood joint (Liuzza's). This was an area hit hard by the flood from Katrina. Many of these restaurants serve as great tales of recovery as well as serving great food.

ANGELO BROCATO'S

214 N. Carrollton Ave. • (504) 486-1465 • $

HOURS: 10:00 a.m.–10:00 p.m. Tues–Thurs; 10:00 a.m.–10:30 p.m. Fri and Sat; 10:00 a.m.–9:30 p.m. Sun

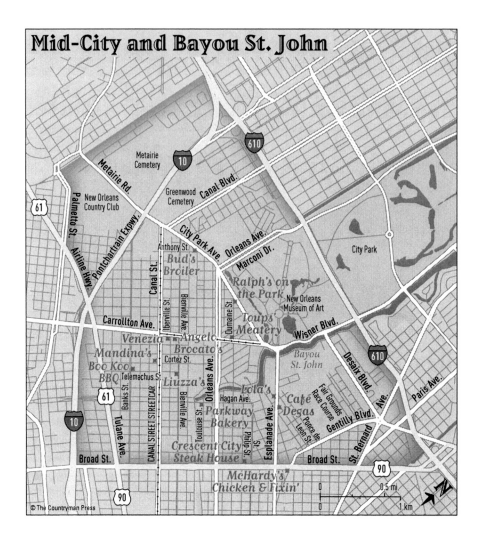

Mid-City and Bayou St. John

New Orleans Country Club · Metairie Cemetery · Greenwood Cemetery · New Orleans Museum of Art · City Park · Bayou St. John · Fair Grounds Race Course

Bud's Broiler · Ralph's on the Park · Toups' Meatery · Venezia · Angelo Brocato's · Mandina's · Boo Koo BBQ · Liuzza's · Lola's · Café Degas · Parkway Bakery · Crescent City Steak House · McHardy's Chicken & Fixin'

Not always, but sometimes when you enter Angelo Brocato's the place is pure magic. The magic is not only their original Sicilian-recipe gelatos, which are all excellent and include two types of Pistachio (they are very Sicilian), Baci, Torroncino, and a great seasonal Louisiana Strawberry (much sweeter than traditional strawberry); it's not only their other traditional Italian desserts like Zuppa Englese, Cassata, Italian fig cookies, spumoni, and cheesecake (I think the best in New Orleans); and it's not only for the cozy old-world feel created by slowly turning ceiling fans, an archway of lightbulbs over the serving counter, rows of apothecary jars filled with candies, glass-topped bistro tables, and century-old portraits of Angelo himself on the wall. No, the true magic is produced by their customers. On certain

Third-generation staff at Angelo Brocato's

nights, the parlor is filled with families with kids blended with heavily tattooed and pierced hipsters and topped with eighty-year-old Italian men, shuffling up to the counter using canes or walkers to have their mini-cannolis and double espresso as they've been doing since Jesus was a juvenile. On such nights, you feel like you've been cast as an extra in *Cinema Paradiso*.

The original dream began in Palermo, Italy, where a young Angelo Brocato began an apprenticeship in an elegant ice-cream parlor and where he learned their special recipes. He immigrated to New Orleans and worked on a sugar plantation, trying to save enough money to open his own parlor. In 1905, he opened Angelo Brocato's Ice Cream Parlor, a replica of Palermo's finest emporiums, and one of the city's first sit-down parlors.

A century later, the business is still run by his family and everything is hand-made daily on the premises. When you order the cannoli, the cone-shaped shell is spoon-filled with a ricotta cheese and sugar mixture right there in front of you and dipped in crushed pistachio nuts.

REASON TO GO: The sweets and the even-sweeter setting.

WHAT TO GET: Leave the diet, take the cannoli.

BETSY'S PANCAKE HOUSE

2542 Canal St. • (504) 822-0214 • $

HOURS: 5:30 a.m.–2:00 p.m. Mon–Fri; 7:00 a.m.–2:00 p.m. Sun

Betsy's is a no-frills Mid-City institution, open for early-morning breakfast and lunch. The low prefab acoustic ceiling tiles, fluorescent light boxes, and an odd assortment of paintings and yellowed clippings pinned to the wall give it an air of a roadside truck stop more than a New Orleans destination. This is where then mayor Ray Nagin brought then president Bush on the one-year anniversary of Katrina, which seems somehow fitting for this less-than-dynamic duo. The food's not that good, but people keep re-electing to come.

REASON TO GO: To hang out in a place where a lot of locals hang out.

WHAT TO GET: Something you can finish while you're there because Betsy's actually charges for takeout containers.

BLUE DOT DONUTS

4301 Canal St. • (504) 218-4866 • $

HOURS: 6:00 a.m.–4:00 p.m. Tues–Fri; 6:00 a.m.–3:00 p.m. Sat and Sun

In what sounds like the beginning of a joke, three cops opened a donut shop. Officers Dennis Gibliant, Ronald Laporte, and Brandon Singleton added to the joke by opening Blue Dot Donuts on April Fool's Day. They have offered more than fifty flavors of donuts (not all at once). Customer favorites include maple bacon bars, peanut butter and jam, red velvet with cream cheese, and huge apple fritters. The menu forever continues to expand. "To us it's a donut shop, but it's also a donut bakery," says Gibliant. "It's here to be creative." There's even thought of a seafood donut, though, thankfully, not yet executed.

REASON TO GO: How often do you get to eat at a donut shop *owned* by cops?

WHAT TO GET: The maple bacon bars are the bomb.

BOO KOO BBQ

3701 Banks St. • (504) 265-8997 • $$

HOURS: 11:00 a.m.–3:00 p.m., 5:30 p.m.–1:00 a.m. Mon–Sat; 11:00 a.m.–10:00 p.m. Sun

Boo Koo BBQ is a pop-up with a window at the back of Finn McCool's Bar. The bar is one of those classic smoke-filled, dog-strewn Irish bars with at least two TVs forever blaring rugby and soccer matches. For these reasons, I suggest going to Boo Koo on a sunny day when you can eat at one of the picnic tables outside and away from the smoke, the dogs, and sporadic yelling of *"gooooaaalllll!"* They excel at more-than-bar-food dishes like Cajun *banh mi*, filled with smoked pulled pork and boudin and topped with pickled carrot and daikon radish. The Limerick is an eight-ounce Angus beef burger with bacon and a fried egg. Da Mutha Load nachos are smothered in an almost-too-much layer of barbecued pulled pork, brisket, smoked chicken, boudin, cheddar cheese, sour cream, and jalapeños.

REASON TO GO: *Goooooddd!!!* bar food.

BUD'S BROILER

500 City Park Ave. • (504) 486-2559 • $
HOURS: 24 hours 7 days a week

Shannon Wright, inside her dream castle

Alfred "Bud" Saunders came to New Orleans from Austin, Texas, in 1952, armed with what would become locally famed and passionately guarded Hickory Smoke Sauce. Bud's signature item is the quarter-pound ground chuck grilled over real charcoal and served six different ways on toasted buns. As stated in the menu, "High quality meat and glowing charcoal makes the difference." Their other menu items are hot dogs, a shrimp po' boy, and chili-cheese fries, plus a pink lemonade so sweet your teeth hurt.

After Bud retired in 1980, his wife took over, then longtime employee Joseph Catalano, and then Katrina shuttered Bud's for four years. Billy and Shannon Wright became the new owners in a storybook way. They felt a civic obligation to reopen Bud's Broiler. As Billy put it, "There were five time-tested New Orleans icons in Mid-City that the storm took away: Rock 'n' Bowl, Mandina's, Brocato's, Parkway Bakery, and Bud's. With our reopening, they're all back. So in a sense this is the icing on the cake for Mid-City."

As a child, Shannon (then) Prince rode her bike through the streets of her Mid-City neighborhood imagining the great things she would someday accomplish. Her friends had more typical dreams of becoming an astronaut or movie star. Shannon wanted to own and run a Bud's Broiler. In April 2009 her dream became a reality. Shannon and Billy had discovered while dating they had each looked into buying the Bud's franchise independently. "Everything in our life is almost parallel. She wanted to buy Bud's, I wanted to buy Bud's," said Billy. "I got married to Shannon and Bud's at the same time." Shannon and Billy even share a favorite Bud's burger, one they've both been eating since they were kids: the No. 6, with lettuce, tomato, pickle, mayonnaise or mustard, and cheddar cheese. Like fated lovers, the couple intones, "We're both No. 6s."

REASON TO GO: A classic neighborhood joint since 1956, damaged by Katrina, with a fairy-tale ending.
WHAT TO GET: The Number 6.

BUTTERMILK BAKERY
1781 N. Dorgenois St. • (504) 252-4538 • $
HOURS: 6:00 a.m.–6:00 p.m. 7 days a week (except when it's closed)

The old McKenzie's bakery chain had a cult following in New Orleans. Although it closed in 2000, you can still buy McKenzie's night-lights, jewelry, coffee mugs, etc. It invokes such nostalgia there's even an "I miss McKenzie's" Facebook page. Their most beloved offering was Buttermilk Drops (what other cities might call donut holes). Many local bakeries have tried to duplicate the McKenzie Buttermilk Drops. Traditionalists feel baker Dwight Henry at his Buttermilk Bakery has come the closest. Cast as the father in the indie film *Beasts of the Southern Wild*, Dwight Henry is now better known as the winner of the Los Angeles Film Critics Award for best supporting actor, and has been nominated for an Oscar and an NAACP Image Award.

REASON TO GO: Eat donut holes with a history, baked by a Hollywood movie star.

CAFÉ DEGAS
3127 Esplanade Ave. • (504) 945-5635 • $$$
HOURS: 11:00 a.m.–3:00 p.m., 6:00–10:00 p.m. Wed–Sat; 10:30 a.m.–3:00 p.m., 6:00–9:30 p.m. Sun

Café Degas was named after the nineteenth-century French impressionist Edgar Degas, who came to New Orleans in 1872 and stayed just down the street at 2306 Esplanade Avenue. Jacques Soulas is also a French painter, but a restaurateur as well. He came to New Orleans in 1980 and with friend Jerry Edgar created a restaurant reminiscent of a real French bistro, built around atmosphere with very good food. The café has a casual patio feel because diners sit on a wooden deck with a large pecan tree thrusting through the middle of the room and plastic flaps used as walls. On sunny days or comfortable evenings the flap/walls are peeled back, making the dining area blend right into the outside neighborhood.

Café Degas specializes in classic French bistro food: steak frites au poivre, Parmesan-crusted veal medallions, seared duck breast with mushroom spaetzle, sautéed liver with bacon and caramelized onions, or a basic salad Niçoise.

> REASON TO GO: On a sunny day or pleasant evening, when the flaps are pulled aside, it's as though you were dining at a bistro table set out on a Parisian street.

CAFÉ MINH

4139 Canal St. • (504) 482-6266 • $$
HOURS: 11:30 a.m.–9:00 p.m. Mon–Thurs; 11:30 a.m.–10:00 p.m. Fri; 5:00–10:00 p.m. Sat

One local food critic called Café Minh the Commander's Palace of Vietnamese restaurants. I see it more as the Patois of Vietnamese restaurants. Both are silly, less-than-helpful statements for visitors who have dined at neither Commander's nor Patois.

Chef-owner Minh Bui left his native Vietnam in a boat with others trying to escape the fall of Saigon. He turned up in New Orleans, worked as a waiter at Commander's Palace, and opened three other less-ambitious restaurants before taking over the former Michael's Mid-City Grill with his wife, Cynthia VuTran, who is also a Vietnamese chef, and turning it into Café Minh. Their dishes fuse French, Vietnamese, and Creole cuisines.

Located on Canal Street between a drive-through bank and Doggy Dog Day Care, the interior, with high ceiling, tables covered in white cloth, and fresh flowers, is unexpected. The larger surprise is the sophisticated menu. This is no *banh mi* and pho place. Appetizers include Beggar's Purse (my favorite), a mini-crepe filled with shrimp and pork and served with spicy soy sauce; homemade cornmeal-crusted Gulf shrimp; or oyster Caesar. Entrees include blackened jumbo scallops, served atop field greens with orange segments and tossed with triple sesame vinaigrette, and their two signature dishes, Lacquered Duck, an entire half of a smoked five-spice duck served with mung bean sticky rice and natural au jus, plus Minh's Bouillabaisse, which is poached mussels, shrimp, scallops, and fish with angel-hair pasta in a light seafood saffron broth.

> REASON TO GO: Way beyond pho and *banh mi* Vietnamese food.
> WHAT TO GET: I'd start with the Beggar's Purse and go to the Lacquered Duck, but you may be more of a Commander's Palace Vietnamese type.

CRESCENT CITY STEAK HOUSE

1001 N. Broad St. • (504) 821-3271 • $$$

HOURS: 11:30 a.m.–9:30 p.m. Tues–Fri; 4:00–10:00 p.m. Sat; 2:00–9:00 p.m. Sun

This is a classic old-fashioned steak house, serving the same menu since it opened in 1934. Founder and owner John Vojkovich, an immigrant from Croatia, was the first to bring prime beef to New Orleans. Crescent City serves steak and only steak; your choice of rib eye, filet (wrapped in bacon), strip sirloin, T-bone, and enormous porterhouse meant for two or three people. All meats have been dry-aged on the premises. Steaks come to your table sizzling in butter, a Crescent City Steak House style that has become the tradition in New Orleans. Side dishes like sautéed spinach, peas, mushrooms, and broccoli au gratin are served à la carte. The potatoes—au gratin, french fries, German fries, Lyonnaise, Braebant, cottage fries, and shoestring—are all hand cut, individually prepared, and almost as much a signature item as the steaks.

Slowly turning overhead fans and antique chandeliers grace an old pressed-tin ceiling. There are small curtained private booths to the side of the dining floor where one can imagine business deals were done decades ago, or perhaps rubouts and hits were issued. *Playboy* magazine tagged Crescent City one of the top ten steak houses in America.

REASON TO GO: Steaks sizzling in butter.

WHAT TO GET: A side booth with curtain.

♛ CRESCENT PIE & SAUSAGE COMPANY

4400 Banks St. • (504) 482-2426 • $$

HOURS: 11:00 a.m.–10:00 p.m. Mon–Sat; 9:00 a.m.–2:00 p.m. Sun

Crescent Pie & Sausage opened in December 2009, having been highly anticipated for years. Co-owners Jeff Baron and Bart Bell had built a reputation and loyal following as smoker-toting road warriors, serving food on the festival and outdoor-event circuit. They were nearing their dream of having a brick-and-mortar place when the building they had chosen on Banks Street collapsed under Hurricane Gustav in 2008. And here you thought it was just Katrina. Baron and Bell had to make a new, if temporary, plan. They opened a breakfast joint called Huevos (closed in 2011) in an available but much smaller space next door. They also immediately started planning for their new location, built from scrap (literally). The result is a beautiful tree house of a restaurant, elevated with a large outdoor deck and a cypress-clad interior, built by salvaged wood from the original building. It feels like a rustic Southern bistro. Worth noting are the black-and-white photographs on

Gigi dishin' it up at Crescent Pie & Sausage

the wall of local music legends. They are all taken by Rick Olivier, the photographer for this book.

Product placement: You can view Rick's work and buy his prints at www.rickolivier.com.

Chef Bart Bell grew up in Cajun country and that has completely informed his cooking. As a kid he ate jambalaya that changed with the seasons. Duck, venison, turkey—whatever was outside in the yard or came back from a recent hunt made it into the pot. Bad Bart's Black Jambalaya, the notedly dark, richly spiced jambalaya served at Crescent Pie & Sausage Co., and considered to be among the best jambalaya in New Orleans, is loaded with braised pork, or chicken, or andouille, chaurice, or smoked sausage depending on what Bell has been cooking that day. Chef Bart has no formal training. He started cooking in the college kitchen to help pay tuition. "I changed majors a hundred times," he recalls. "The one thing I didn't change was cooking and enjoying my job." Then, as fate and the Food Network would have it, he saw Emeril on TV one day, causing a culinary kensho. "I was like: 'That's in New Orleans. I have friends in New Orleans. I'll go there and get a job.' So I got a job at Emeril's Delmonico's under Chef Neal Swidler, and he's a cool fucking guy. We're still good friends. He made being a chef really cool."

Crescent Pie & Sausage's menu is stated right in the restaurant's name. Chef

Bart has a passion for, perhaps obsession with, house-made sausages. They offer daily "Little Smokies," smoky junior-sized kielbasa slathered in barbecue sauce; more lively than your average boudin; coarse-ground and spicy Merguez served unadorned or as spicy sausage po' boys topped with melted peppers and bratwurst riding a mound of pickled cabbage and German-style potato salad. For $4, you can order "A Link," a single (one) link from their daily selection.

The pies are not the sweet-potato or the blueberry kind, but a rural Louisiana version of empanadas. They're filled with a variety of spicy meats, spicy crawfish, a creamy not spicy duck confit, and vegetables like collard greens and mushrooms. And yes, they have pizza pies. In addition to the more "normal" margherita and sausage and peppers, you'll also find duck and Brie pizza and the Mid-City Slammer—andouille, grilled chicken, house-smoked coppa, cheddar, mozzarella, and red sauce.

REASON TO GO: To have your own culinary kensho.
WHAT TO GET: The jambalaya and a pie. I'm not sure which you'll consider to be the side.

KATIE'S

3701 Iberville St. • (504) 488-6582 • $$$
HOURS: 11:00 a.m.–9:00 p.m. Tues–Sat; 9:00 a.m.–3:00 p.m. Sun; 11:00 a.m.–3:00 p.m. Mon

In 1984, when the sagging oil industry flattened his career, Leo Leininger created his fresh start by opening Katie's on a backstreet in Mid-City. Mr. Leo passed away in 1987, leaving his family to build the burgeoning neighborhood joint. Experienced restaurateur Scott Craig bought Katie's in '94 and had the good sense to install his momma, Mary, at the front door, where she became known as "The Hostess with the Mostess" while Scott and his brother David worked the kitchen. Ten years of success were washed away by the seven feet of water that came with Hurricane Katrina. It took more than four and a half years for Katie's to reopen. Short on insurance, to help pay for the restaurant's recovery Scott sold honorary tables and places at the bar to his loyal or loaded customers. Today, you can see their names on brass plaques as you dine at "their" tables. When Katie's finally did reopen, the menu had been reworked nearly as much as the interior. A very broad menu of steaks, seafood, Italian, gumbo, po' boys, cheeseburgers, and muffulettas is highlighted by their signature items like The Barge, an entire French bread loaf overstuffed with fried shrimp, catfish, and oysters (serves four people), and The Boudreaux, a pizza with cochon de lait, roasted garlic, fresh spinach, red onions, scallions, and garlic butter cream reduction. However, if you're just in town for a few days, don't make the same mistake as Food Network's oafish host, Guy Ferry (that's Fieri's real name). He devoted an *Off the Hook* segment to Katie's when he was half a block from the better Liuzza's.

REASON TO GO: The line's too long at Liuzza's.
WHAT TO GET: If with a group, The Barge. If alone, join a table, as accepted, even encouraged, by locals.

♛ LIUZZA'S

3636 Bienville St. • (504) 482-9120 • $$
HOURS: 11:00 a.m.–4:00 p.m. Mon; 11:00 a.m.–10:00 p.m. Tues–Sat

Hurricane Katrina turned out to be the least of the problems for owner Michael Bordelon. After closing the refurbished Liuzza's one night, Bordelon was struck by a speeding drunk driver. He spent a week in a coma and a month in the hospital, and rehabilitation continues for the brain trauma he suffered. A week after the wreck, Shanette Bordelon Elder, Michael's sister and co-manager of the restaurant, died of cancer at age fifty-nine. The neighborhood pulled together to create a fund-raising Liuzza Palooza. The festival was located a block from the restaurant where signature small dishes were served (like Drago's famed charbroiled oysters) and top musicians played (like Rockin' Dopsie and the Zydeco Twisters and the Creole String Beans), along with cooking demos and kids' activities. Liuzza Palooza drew four thousand people and raised $130,000.

Product placement: Rick Olivier, who took the photographs for this book, is also the lead singer for the Grammy-nominated Creole String Beans. You can visit them at www.creolestringbeans.com.

Founded in 1947, Liuzza's has changed hands several times from the original namesake owners. It has remained through all the changes a beloved cash-only, comfort-food neighborhood joint, where drinks are served in large frosted mugs. They do a decent po' boy, but are better with their fried pickles, Spinach Lougia (spinach with garlic, olive oil, and chicken stock), Crawfish Telemachus (crawfish cream sauce over pasta), or Eggplant St. John (eggplant medallions and pasta topped with shrimp and artichoke sauce). More years than not, Liuzza's is chosen as "Best Neighborhood Restaurant" in the *Gambit* Weekly Poll. Liuzza's is also where the John Goodman character in HBO's *Treme* chose to have his last meal before committing suicide.

REASON TO GO: A classic New Orleans neighborhood joint where 90 percent of the customers will be local.
WHAT TO GET: John Goodman had the gumbo for his last meal in *Treme*. You might want to choose the Eggplant St. John instead.

LIUZZA'S BY THE TRACK

1518 N. Lopez St. • (504) 218-7888 • $$
HOURS: 11:00 a.m.–7:00 p.m. Mon–Sat

What few visitors could guess and most locals don't know is that the two Liuzza restaurants (about fifteen minutes apart) have not been affiliated for decades. Jack Liuzza opened a combination grocery store, bar, and bookie joint by the Fair Grounds Race Track (the oldest *continuously running* horse track in America) in 1936. His grandson, also named Jack, converted it into a grill in 1965. Then, in 1996, Billy Gruber bought the restaurant. Over the years, the Gruber family has run a number of New Orleans cafés. Billy's Creole gumbo is a special (and secret) recipe, one that's a nod to his mother's Boudreaux Cajun heritage. Starting with a nearly black roux, Billy layers locally made sausage, cooked-to-order seafood, and a (secret recipe) mixture of thirteen seasonings. They also serve garlic- and horseradish-spiked roast beef, slowly simmered corned beef, (secretly seasoned) sausage, and a renowned barbecued shrimp po' boy, served in a hollowed-out length of Leiden-heimer's French bread literally overflowing with sautéed shrimp and the restaurant's own (secret version) of the rich, peppery, butter-infused New Orleans BBQ sauce.

For two weekends a year during Jazz Fest, Liuzza's by the Track becomes a New Orleans version of the Churchill Downs infield during the Kentucky Derby. After-party throngs inhale cold Abita drafts with Liuzza's victuals.

I'm so proud I got through this entire profile without writing, "chomping at the bit" or "winner's circle."

REASON TO GO: Pull up a stool at a former bookie joint by the track with a menu that includes at least four secret recipes.

WHAT TO GET: Creole gumbo or BBQ shrimp po' boy and a cold one.

LOLA'S

3312 Esplanade Ave. • (504) 488-6946 • $$$
HOURS: 5:30–9:30 p.m. 7 days a week; till 10:30 p.m. Fri and Sat

It's peculiar that in a city once owned by Spain there aren't more Spanish restaurants. There are at least three French-influenced restaurants per block. And New Jersey never owned us, yet there are ten Subways in the area.

Angel Miranda opened his first Spanish restaurant, Altamira, in the Warehouse District in 1980, or ten years before Emeril's joined the neighborhood. The restaurant closed a few years later. His second attempt was in '94 when he opened Lola's, named after his mother, on Esplanade where once the wealthy Spanish citizens lived with well-to-do Creoles along what was called "millionaire's row." This time his restaurant was *un gran éxito*.

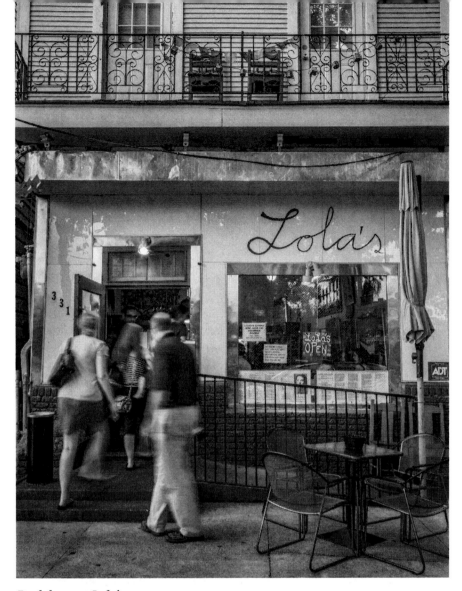

Rush hour at Lola's

Lola's serves authentic Spanish food (not Mexican, not South American, not Latin Isles). They serve a great paella and even greater pisto. Pisto is a portobello mushroom stuffed with eggplant, peppers, onions, squash, tomatoes, and garlic and served with black beans, rice, and asparagus. Paella, as you probably know, is a garlic and saffron rice dish teeming with shrimp, fish, calamari, scallops, mussels, and vegetables. To say that Lola's dishes are garlic-friendly is a gross understatement. More than friends, I'm pretty sure they're having sex.

Personally, I think Lola's serves the best Spanish meals I've ever had. If I were a native of New Orleans, that might not be saying so much. But I lived nearly three decades with easy access to a ghetto of great Spanish restaurants in Newark, New Jersey. I've eaten at Sagres, Casa Vascas, Forno's, and Coimbra. Lola's is better.

REASON TO GO: Best Spanish restaurant in New Orleans (or Newark, New Jersey).

WHAT TO GET: I'd start with the garlic mushroom or garlic shrimp, then have the garlic soup (no joke, it's great). For entrees, there's shrimp pasta with garlic, Caldereta (a lamb stew with garlic), or the straight-up garlic chicken. Sadly, none of the three dessert items, flan, a chocolate chuflan, or homemade almond-nougat ice cream, has a pinch of garlic.

MANDINA'S

3800 Canal St. • (504) 482-9179 • $$$

HOURS: 11:00 a.m.–9:30 p.m. Mon–Thur; 11:00 a.m.–10:00 p.m. Fri and Sat; 12:00 p.m.–9:00 p.m. Sun

As was the case with seemingly half the neighborhood restaurants in New Orleans, Mandina's started out as a corner grocery, this one run by Sebastian Mandina, an immigrant from Salaparuta, Sicily. His sons, Anthony and Frank, who had been born on its second floor, converted the family business to a full-scale restaurant. Anthony's son Tommy took over in 1975; he too had been raised in the apartment above the restaurant. Tommy is now semi-retired while his daughter, Cindy, runs the restaurant today thanks, in part, to Harry Connick Jr. Cindy had been working at the restaurant since she was eight years old and bussing tables. She started writing checks to vendors when she was eleven. Becoming the fourth generation to run Mandina's was about the furthest thing from her dreams and desires when she got her master's in business administration from Loyola. But then, she was leafing through an in-flight magazine during a trip to Hawaii when she was stunned to read Harry Connick Jr.'s comments about her family's restaurant. He said their dishes were those "you can get anywhere. It just tastes better there." The article woke Cindy up to the realization that Mandina's was part of the soul of New Orleans and more than an old pink-painted joint. "I always thought of Mandina's as just a neighborhood restaurant," Cindy said. "Dad went to work. Mom was home raising the kids. Dad came home. That was it. Who knew?"

Katrina took a toll on the place. When the contractor started to peel back some outside damage for repair, he realized the seventy-two-year-old restaurant was in much worse shape than he'd thought. He said, "It was only standing because of grout, God, and gravity." Tommy Mandina was ready to throw in the towel, in spite of the protests of his regular customers. "I'm done," he said. "This is going to be too hard and take too long." That's when Cindy said, "I want to do it."

Cindy oversaw Mandina's return to being a place frequented by both natives and tourists. Noel Cassanova, a regular for sixty years, characterized the clientele: "At the bar, you had the bookmaker standing next to the district attorney standing next to the guy who runs the hospital. Later on at night, you'd have a couple of police captains in there. It was unbelievable." Once again, people are lined up outside for their it-just-tastes-better-there Catfish Meuniere, Trout Amandine, grilled shrimp over pasta Bordelaise, or the more casual po' boys and muffuletta. Don't worry, the line outside moves quickly, which is surprising because most of the waiters inside decidedly don't. You can choose to wait at the bar, where they don't have jiggers, they just pour. I'm not sure he's still there, but if you're lucky, Nubby the one-armed bartender will serve you.

REASON TO GO: "It just tastes better there." —Harry Connick Jr.

WHAT TO GET: Aim high with the Trout Amandine or aim less high with a roast beef po' boy.

♛ McHARDY'S CHICKEN & FIXIN'

1458 N. Broad St. • (504) 949-0000 • $

HOURS: 11 a.m.–6:30 p.m Mon–Sat; 11 a.m.–3:30 p.m. Sun

It's with a tip of the toque to Judy Walker that McHardy's is included in this book. I had never heard of McHardy's until Judy, food editor of the *Times-Picayune*, had it on her best fried chicken list for my Appendix A. In a town with Dooky Chase's, Li'l Dizzy, Fiorella's, and Willie Mae's Scotch House, that's saying something. So I had to stop by this takeout fried chicken stand located in an area few tourists—or locals—will just happen by.

The chicken was as advertised. Personally, I may still lean toward Willie Mae's, but McHardy's gives everyone else a run for the money. The money required at McHardy's is far less. My family ordered the ten-piece chicken, fried shrimp, red beans and rice, coleslaw, potato salad, and lemonade (all made in house). We got change back from $20.

The always-on-the-premises owner, Kermit Mogilles, is as much a reason to go to McHardy's as their fried chicken. He can passionately talk to you about the different parts of a chicken, from drumette to wing tips, about the education system in New Orleans, about the inequity of wealth in America, and he's clearly a devotee of Tom Fitzmorris's Nomenu.com, correctly quoting the 1,359 restaurants cited in Nomenu that week. Kermit is most passionate when talking about how McHardy's prepares its chicken.

In the large, rear prep room, employees inspect each chicken upon delivery, trimming the yellow ribbons of fat, seasoning the meat before it's battered and sent to the fryers up front. "We marinate the chicken once and then again in another solution so the seasoning permeates all the way through to the bone," he said. "It goes through four or five different steps before it hits the oil." The result is chicken that is highly seasoned without being spicy, always fresh, and exceptionally lean, giving each piece more crunch and less grease.

You can buy the five-piece box for only $3.14 or the suitcase-sized hundred-piece for $62.80. At Mardi Gras time they sell a lot of the hundred-piece boxes for parade viewers, averaging about three thousand pieces a day and opening up the restaurant at 5:00 a.m. to serve the Mardi Gras surge.

What Kermit did not tell me, and I had to read about later, was the resilient history of McHardy's. They were looted after being flooded following Hurricane Katrina. Kermit also lost his Gentilly home to the flood. But he and his wife, Albi, repaired the restaurant and with the help of family members reopened in January 2006. Five months later, a fire from a power surge devastated the restaurant once again. As the ruins smoldered, he told people that perhaps this was the end for McHardy's. It was then that Melvin Jones, a friend who runs a local ministry for people overcoming addictions, showed up on his doorstep with a small army of ex-addicts who happened to have professional building skills.

Great fried chicken and a great storytelling owner make McHardy's a place to go. The restaurant's rebirth and then two-dat rebirth make it emblematically New Orleans.

This is a city that was 80 percent burned down in 1788 and 80 percent under-water in 2005. It has survived the oil bust of the 1980s and the BP oil spill in 2010. New Orleans is a city filled with people like Kermit Mogilles who, when knocked to the ground, get up and get on to the next parade or festival.

REASON TO GO: Great fried chicken, ebullient owner, emblematic New Orleans tale.

WHAT TO GET: The choice is . . . five-piece or hundred-piece?

NEYOW'S CREOLE CAFÉ

3340 Bienville St. • (504) 827-5474 • $$

HOURS: 11:00 a.m.–9:00 p.m. Mon–Thurs; 11:00 a.m.–11:00 p.m. Fri and Sat

The name Neyow's takes some explaining. It's pronounced *neo's*, and it is the owners' tribute to their favorite dog breed, the Neapolitan mastiff, filtered through some Yat-bonic spelling. A variety of dog photos lines the walls. The staff have dogs embroidered on their duds. Other than the dog thing, Neyow's is a classic

New Orleans neighborhood joint. The building was a branch of a local pizza chain that never reopened after Hurricane Katrina. The menu features pork chops and chicken, lots of fried seafood (their catfish is right up there with the best we've had in New Orleans), red beans, po' boys, and a robust gumbo loaded with hot sausage, smoked sausage, and cubes of pork that more than represents. Where nearby neighborhood icons like Liuzza's and Mandina's lean toward a Creole-Italian tradition, Neyow's is a superior delivery of the city's black Creole style.

REASON TO GO: A variation on the classic Creole neighborhood joint.

WHAT TO GET: Can't recommend the catfish enough.

NORMA'S SWEETS BAKERY

2925 Bienville St. • (504) 309-5401 • $

HOURS: 7:00 a.m.–8:00 p.m. Mon–Sat; 7:00 a.m.–6:00 p.m. Sun

Norma's is a Latin American grocery that has a butcher in the back with bins of hot chicharones (basically Latin American cracklins), a bakery with Mexican pastries and guava-filled king cake, piñatas hanging from the ceiling, and the #1 reason I include them in the book, a takeout counter selling freshly homemade empanadas, pasteles, a variety of tamales, Cuban sandwiches, and lesser known vigoron, a Nicaraguan dish of boiled yuca and chicharones.

The staff is always very welcoming and will explain behind-the-counter items with which you have zero familiarity.

PARKWAY BAKERY & TAVERN

538 Hagan Ave. • (504) 482-3047 • $

HOURS: 11:00 a.m.–10:00 p.m. Wed–Mon; closed Tues

For serious po' boy aficionados there isn't just one best po' boy place, but separate stops required to eat the best roast beef po' boy, then the best shrimp po' boy, best oyster, catfish, meatball, duck debris, soft-shell crab, etc. One po' boy eatery has forty-five different types. For those of you without the time, interest, or digestive system to consume forty-five po' boys, Parkway Bakery & Tavern is considered by many to be the best across-the-board po' boys in New Orleans. The Appendix A judges chose it for "Best Po' Boys" by a comfortable margin.

Parkway has been a neighborhood landmark since 1911. German baker Charles Goering ran Parkway Bakery for the first eleven years, then Henry Timothy purchased it with the intent of continuing to run it as the neighborhood bake shop until he added the recently invented "poor boy" sandwich in 1929 to feed the workers at the nearby American Can Company. A flood briefly closed the bakery

Jay Nix, Parkway's savior

in 1978. A more devastating setback occurred when the American Can Company closed in 1988, taking much of Parkway's business with it. They reduced the bakery hours, and then in 1993 closed the doors of Parkway for good.

Jay Nix lived next door to Parkway. He saw the bakery as a cornerstone of the neighborhood, and hated to see it vacant. So, in 1995, he bought it, with no intention of reopening the bakery, but to use the space as storage for his contracting business. Nix kept encountering people with stories to tell about growing up with the bakery. In 2003, Nix finally decided to follow the voices on the street and rumblings in his heart to reopen the Parkway Bakery. Nix's nephew, Justin Kennedy, moved to New Orleans also in 2003, and jumped in as the untrained but enthusiastic chef. "The first day we opened, people were lined up," Justin remembers. "It's just been amazing how close the people are to this place. It's more than a sandwich shop here. People come here and even before they buy a sandwich, before they eat their roast beef, they walk in the door and you can tell they're happy already."

While waiting in line, you can admire the eclectic memorabilia hung on the walls: old campaign posters for Lindy Boggs (Cokie Roberts's mom), ads for the dearly departed Pontchartrain Beach Amusement Park, T-shirts of past city football champs from the 1950s. You can also strike up a conversation with others in line. As Justin notes, "You've got your crooks, you got your artists, your judges, your big businessmen, your sewage and water guys, and your carpenters. They all come here.

We feed a thousand people a day. It's amazing, a whole mix of people. If you want to see New Orleans, just come in here and watch people come through."

REASON TO GO: The most locally loved po' boy place in New Orleans.
WHAT TO GET: Any of a number of po' boys, but do get the sweet-potato fries . . . and a Barq's.

RALPH'S ON THE PARK

900 City Park Ave. • (504) 488-1000 • $$$
HOURS: 5:30–9:00 p.m. Mon–Sat; 11:30 a.m.–2:00 p.m. Tues–Fri; 10:30 a.m.–2:00 p.m. Sun

Ralph's on the Park was constructed in 1860 by a French immigrant who tended cattle in City Park and, while the bovines grazed, had the big idea of a coffeehouse and concession stand for people strolling the the expansive greens or canoeing Bayou St. John. In 1869, just after the war (Civil), it became a full-scale restaurant. Over the years, ownership has passed through the most renowned restaurant families of New Orleans, including the Antoines and the Tujagues, and since 2004 Ralph's has been part of the Brennan's mini-empire.

The restaurant is sort of our Tavern on the Green or Sutro's Cliff House, an upscale restaurant that draws customers equally for the view and the food. From either the huge first-floor windows or the balcony on the second floor, diners have a broad view of the park's beautiful three-hundred-year-old live oak trees and the swampy bayou. Inside there's the view of the two huge, wall-sized paintings by Tony Green, who describes himself as "artist, musician, firebrand." Both paintings depict festive events held at the restaurant's location: "The Tenth Grand Festival and Fête Champêtre" (1890s) and "The Ball of the Two Well-Known Gentlemen" (1910–1917).

The menu has been upgraded significantly since the Brennans took over, first by the inventive master chef Gerard Maras, and then his established creative style passed on to current chef Chip Flanagan. They do small plates like the butter-poached alligator tart and the rib-eye-wrapped scallop, and the icky-sounding but delicious foie gras peanut butter and jelly sandwich, as well as more "normal" (for New Orleans) Cajun Scotch egg (hard-boiled, covered with boudin, then fried), citrus-glazed lamb spareribs, and cauliflower soup with a mini crab cake. Most dishes add just a little twist to expectations. This includes desserts like the mint chocolate pot de creme or the stuffed peach sno-ball.

REASON TO GO: The view.
WHAT TO GET: When in Rome . . . go ahead, try the foie gras peanut butter and jelly sandwich.

Barq's Root Beer

Edward Charles Edmond Barq (you can call him Eddie B, if you must) was born in New Orleans's French Quarter in 1871. His father died when Ed was two years old, sending his family to Nice, France. There, his bilingual mother taught wealthy expat-sans-Yat American kids. In France Ed learned the art of creating chemical flavors from masters in Paris and Bordeaux. Later, to avoid being

drafted into the French military, Ed returned to New Orleans with his brother, Gaston. In 1890 they opened Barq's Brothers Bottling Company in the French Quarter. The brothers bottled carbonated water with various flavors. The most popular initially was their orange-flavored soda called Orangine, which won the Gold Medal at the 1893 World's Fair in Chicago. Their

sodas had more carbonation and less sugar than the other early sodas like Vernor's (America's first soft drink) and Coca-Cola (the company that likes to think it was the first), but, unlike the others, they had caffeine.

When they created what was to become their signature flavor, the Barqs were forbidden to call it "root beer" because the Hires Company, acting very much like the NFL claiming to hold rights for "Who Dat," sued Barq's. Hires claimed that they owned the rights to the words "root beer" exclusively. The inability to use "root beer" pushed the Barq boys to create their bare-to-the-bones, but delightful, slogan, "Drink Barq's. It's Good." The company did eventually win the right to call their drink what it was, but then almost immediately dropped any root beer references in 1938 when the federal government banned caffeine in root beer. Rather than remove caffeine, Ed Barq simply changed the name of his drink from Barq's Root Beer to a legal Barq's Sr.

Earlier, in 1931, Barq was the first to offer his soda in anything but the traditional six- and eight-ounce bottles. He convinced the Fabachers, a New Orleans brewery family, to sell him clear twelve-ounce bottles that would give his customers "a sense of satisfaction which comes with getting more of a good thing than the price seems to warrant." Eddie B was the Sam Walton of his day. The twelve-ounce bottle remained priced at five cents and was a huge hit.

Barq's decided to franchise his now nationally popular soda. The first franchise came in 1934 in Mobile, Alabama. Three years later sixty-two bottling plants churned out Barq's in twenty-two states. The drink's popularity was bubbling over. The number of franchises peaked in 1950 at about two hundred. Eddie B had become very rich. He invested heavily in real estate and banks, bought a yacht, and opened a car dealership in Pascagoula, Mississippi.

Believing his soda was good enough to sell itself, Barq's always had tiny advertising budgets. The beloved slogan, "Drink Barq's. It's Good," was given to restaurants as a logo on clocks and on the frame of chalkboards where daily lunch specials were handwritten. The logo was also etched on pencils and rulers handed out to schoolchildren.

The inevitable happened in the merger-and-acquisition-happy 1990s. Barq's was acquired by a larger company, Coca-Cola. Almost immediately, committees of business-casual pencil pushers (and pencils without the Barq's logo) met in glass-walled offices to market-test and PowerPoint-present the wonderful "Drink Barq's. It's Good" logo out of existence. They now use "Barq's has bite!"

All was not lost. Barq's executed a clever contract by which Coca-Cola obtained the rights to market and bottle Barq's, but not to make the syrup. By contract, Coca-Cola has to purchase the syrup for the root beer from Edward II's adopted son, Jesse Robinson, in New Orleans. By contract, all bottles sold in Louisiana have a different-colored logo; are imprinted with "Copyright Barq's, Inc." along with the "Copyright Coca-Cola" shown by itself on all other outside-Louisiana bottles; and are not ink stamped "Barq's has bite!" but instead "Drink Barq's. It's Good!"

REDEMPTION

3835 Iberville St. • (504) 309-3570

HOURS: 11:00 a.m.–10:00 p.m. Tues–Fri; 5:00–10:00 p.m. Sat; 11:00 a.m.–
3:00 p.m. Sun

Christian's was one of the major restaurants that didn't return after Hurricane
Katrina. It had an ambience like no other place else in New Orleans, set inside
a century-old church. Maria and Tommy Delaune took over the space and renamed
it Redemption. Then they went looking for a chef. Redemption is a perfect place,
even if in name only, for Chef Greg Picolo to have landed. He'd been the chef at the
Bistro at the Maison de Ville for nearly two decades. The cozy red-walled Bistro had
been a fixture in the French Quarter.

Then it figuratively hit ten miles of unpaved road. First, it was Katrina-closed.
Picolo and a business partner bought the business and reopened a year later, but
in 2009 a fire in the adjacent building forced them to close it again. A third blow
came when a dispute with the landlord over an air-conditioning system led to
another restaurant closure. Three strikes and Picolo was out of there.

Chef Greg Picolo's Redemption menu includes dishes such as the crispy
avocado cup filled with Louisiana crawfish rémoulade, roasted duck breast served
with red onion and yam hash, and stuffed everything—stuffed jumbo shrimp,
seafood-stuffed pave of Atlantic salmon.

> REASON TO GO: It seems every city has one (1) restaurant set inside an old
> church. This is ours.
> WHAT TO GET: Better food than you'll get in the Abbey (Atlanta), St. Bart's
> (New York), or Priory (New Jersey).

TOUPS' MEATERY

845 N. Carrollton Ave. • (504) 252-4999 • $$$

HOURS: 11:00 a.m.–2:30 p.m., 5:00–9:00 p.m. Tues–Sat

Don't ask for their vegetarian specials. Remember, Chef Isaac Toups is carrying
a meat cleaver and he knows how to use it. It's all meat, meat, and meat, from
the small-plate Meatery Board to the à la carte cracklins, rillons, and boudin balls,
and on to the entrees, tri-tip steak, massive double-cut pork chop, and the in-
your-face challenge of the lamb neck. Ordering the lamb neck will require picking
through many small vertebrae to dig out shreds of marrow-laden meat strips. Just
think of it as a meat version of eating pistachios or edamame.

Isaac and Amanda Toups opened their restaurant in 2012. Isaac had spent a
decade with Emeril's restaurants, starting out as a cook at Delmonico's. He'd been

named the *Times-Picayune* "Chef to Watch 2010." Amanda's background is in wine and wine education. She managed W.I.N.O. (Wine Institute of New Orleans) for the enterprise's first four years. The manager, Larry Nguyen, also comes with a pedigree. He was named maître d' of the year by *New Orleans* magazine in 2010.

If you're a meat lover with more sophistication than meat-lover's pizza, Toups' is a nearly perfect restaurant.

REASON TO GO: Meat with a side of meat.

WHAT TO GET: The lamb neck. I dare you. I double dare you.

♕ VENEZIA

134 N. Carrollton Ave. • (504) 488-7991 • $$

HOURS: 11:00 a.m.–10:00 p.m. Wed–Fri; 5:00–10:00 p.m. Sat; 12:00 p.m.–8:00 p.m. Sun

I will admit to being delighted that Venezia surprisingly beat out the better-known Vincent's, Irene's, and all other Italian restaurants in New Orleans (except Mariza's) to be voted #2 on Appendix A's "Best of" list. It is my neighborhood joint where more end-of-week Friday nights than not I'll pick up eggplant Parmesan or spaghetti to go home and carb out in front on the TV. I also feel Venezia deserves its high ranking. Their al dente pasta is simply much better than Vincent's or Irene's or that found in any other New Orleans Italian restaurants.

They opened in 1957, when pizza was just catching on across America. Venezia was one of New Orleans's first pizza places. Their vintage neon sign, "Venezia/Pizza Pie/Italian Food," reveals not much has changed there since 1957. When's the last time you saw a restaurant advertise pizza *pie*?

It has been described as a "red gravy" kind of place, or a neighborhood joint where people bring momma and all the bambinos. On weekend nights, there's usually a family outside on the bench or huddled up at the bar, waiting for a table to open up.

The restaurant is reputed to have been Mafia kingpin Carlos Marcello's closer-to-home substitute for Mosca's, the legendary roadhouse hangout. Venezia is much closer than Mosca's to the Marcello mansion, but we'll never really know if Venezia actually has a shady past or if that's just a story the current management allows to go unchallenged. Never let the truth get in the way of a good story.

REASON TO GO: A great place to settle in and spill red sauce on your shirt and no one will care.

WHAT TO GET: The pizza is good. The pasta is better.

Gerard Maras

One of the greatest chefs in New Orleans hasn't stockpiled awards; has never been on *Chopped*, *Iron Chef*, *Cutthroat Kitchen*, nor any Food Network show; has not even been associated with any restaurant the past ten years. Yet, a recent magazine article called him "The most important chef in New Orleans history." Even given that bit of (over-the-top) hyperbole, Gerard Maras is essentially important to many restaurants and dishes you'll experience here.

Since he arrived in 1981 to work at Commander's Palace, Chef Gerard has, more than anyone, helped shape the new Creole cuisine of New Orleans. The Brennan family immediately recognized his brilliance and creativity and, in short order, let him create the menu for their newest restaurant, Mr. B's. Maras remembers, "Ella hired me as a sous-chef at Commander's and about a month later Emeril joined. Three months later, I left Commander's to open Mr. B's."

GERARD MARAS

Chef Gerard Maras by artist Rise Delmar Ochsner

At Mr. B's, Chef Gerard developed recipes they are still using today for dishes like BBQ shrimp, jumbo lump crab cakes, and pasta jambalaya. He stayed at Mr. B's until 1995, and he then wandered off the restaurant map for the next few years before opening Gerard's Downtown in 1998. During his wanderlust he was doing something that later would change the culinary landscape. Maras began to farm-source ingredients like pea shoots and micro greens he couldn't get anywhere else. As early as the 1980s, he began driving up to Mississippi to meet with farmers such as Dan Crutchfield, who was growing peppers, black radishes, and pink-eyed peas and raising small pigs and rabbits. He was inspired to start farming his own produce on his own land. When he had a surplus of produce, he taught his cooks how to pickle, preserve, and can. While this is now common in any restaurant, it was then revolutionary. The seasonal-driven food in New Orleans restaurants can be traced back to Commander's Palace and its key and creative staff, chefs Paul Prudhomme, Emeril Lagasse, and Maras.

Gerard's Downtown was much more than a restaurant; it became his virtual graduate school for many of today's most acclaimed and talented chefs. If there was a James Beard Award for teaching, Gerard Maras would have a trophy case that rivals the Boston Celtics or New York Yankees.

You can find Chef Gerard's teaching in a lunch sandwich of porchetta with pickled cucumber and pickled red onion at John Harris's Lilette. Harris spent an influential year running lunch service at Gerard's Downtown. More than technique, Maras taught attitude. "One thing Gerard taught me," Harris explains, "was to always try to be overly generous with your staff. So maybe I only need one or two cooks for a shift, but if I have one more and pay them a little more, that breeds loyalty."

Alex Harrell at Sylvain spent six years with Maras. Maras's kitchen demeanor rubbed off on Harrell. "It was Gerard's manner to be a teacher. He loved working with people who maybe didn't have the knowledge, but had the desire to cook. As long as you were willing to learn, he would tolerate a mistake. He had an incredibly calm presence in the kitchen and I never saw him raise his voice," says Harrell. The chicken-liver pâté at Sylvain's is Harris's "cover song" of the duck-liver pâté from Gerard's Downtown.

The crab butter fish en papillote at Borgne is Brian Landry's interpretation of a dish he learned from Chef Gerard, as are the charcuterie offerings at Aaron Burgau's Patois.

Slade Rushing and Allison Vines-Rushing met in Maras's restaurant kitchen, fell in love, married, opened up their restaurant, MiLa, and were 2013 James Beard nominees (Allison had already won the 2004 James Beard for "Rising Star Chef of the Year"). Other star chefs who were schooled by Maras include Corbin Evans, David and Torre Solazzo, Anton Schulte, Ann Weatherford, and Paul Williams.

People with far more discerning palates than I possess say you can recognize Chef Gerard's cooking, even when executed by others, the way you can see Lee Strasberg's method acting all over the work of Marlon Brando, Robert De Niro, Al Pacino, and countless others. Maras comments on his past co-workers, "I see techniques more than recipes. The way, for instance, all of the chefs who cooked for me all cook pork the same way. First you dry-brine it, so the flavors penetrate the meat. Then you sear it. Next, you put it in a very hot oven for a few moments. Finally you pull it off the heat and wrap it in double layer of foil for about fifteen to twenty minutes. What results is a perfectly juicy, just-pink-in-the-center cut of pork. They all do that."

Gerard Maras, a quiet, self-effacing man, a Zen master or Yoda-like figure for the New Orleans food scene, currently has no plans to return to a restaurant: "When I work in a restaurant, I am there twelve to fourteen hours a day on my feet; it's a tough life. It's time to leave all of that to the young." A chef you should know every bit as much as you know Emeril Lagasse or Anthony Bourdain lives without fanfare on his family farm located on the North Shore of Lake Pontchartrain. He still teaches, mostly at the New Orleans Culinary Experience, and mostly for tourists.

Always pass on what you have learned.
—Yoda

Meschiya Lake, Best Female Vocalist winner and Little Gem regular

CHAPTER 6

Warehouse District
and
Central Business District

The city can drive a sober-minded person insane, but it feeds the dreamer. It feeds the dreamer stories, music and food. Really great food.

—**Andrei Codrescu**

If you asked me what kind of food we serve in New Orleans, I'd say we serve New Orleans food.

—**Emeril Lagasse**

C ross Canal Street from the French Quarter and you enter a different world. The street names all change at Canal, from Bourbon to Carondolet, Chartres to Camp, Royal to St. Charles, because back in the day the French and the Americans thought each other were idiots. They certainly weren't going to share a street name. The architecture is likewise completely different. You leave the centuries-old narrow streets lined with French and Spanish villas with cracked plaster and sagging ironwork balconies and enter a neighborhood that looks like a mere decades-old Any City USA. Here are large hotels; the cavernous Morial Convention Center; most of the city's museums (World War II, Civil War, Children's Museum, Contemporary Art Museum, and the Ogden); the gaudy Harrah's Casino; the huge spaceship Mercedes-Benz Superdome; the port to board Carnival, Norwegian, and Royal Caribbean cruise ships; and New Orleans's tallest building, the fifty-story One Shell Plaza. Donald Trump intended to build a seventy-two-story ode to His-selfness, but The Donald learned about The Bedrock. We have none. New Orleans is a swamp. To build a seventy-two-story building would require a profit-devouring deep foundation or Trump Tower New Orleans would disappear into the bog.

There are a few older eating establishments like Ernst Café (1902) and the Pearl Restaurant & Oyster Bar (1920s), but mostly the area was literally warehouses

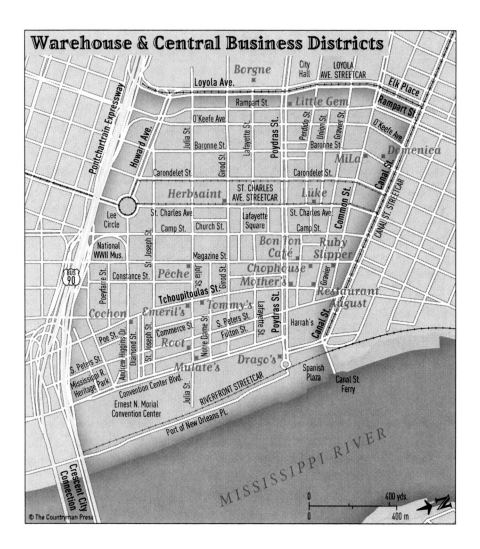

Warehouse & Central Business Districts

until the 1984 World's Fair brought new construction and energy to the area. In 1990 budding star Chef Emeril Lagasse plopped his restaurant at the corner of Julia Street and Tchoupitoulas in the middle of industrial buildings. I give Emeril's success much of the credit for turning the neighborhood into one that is abuzz with tourists today. The area has as many four-star restaurants and award-winning chefs as any in the city.

AMERICAN SECTOR

945 Magazine St. • (504) 528-1940 • $$
HOURS: 11:00 a.m.–9:00 p.m. 7 days a week

Created to serve visitors to the World War II Museum and located adjacent to the exhibits and 4-D movie theater, American Sector says the "food honors the museum's mission." The website also underlines, "The menu is a playful homage to 1940s dishes." That seems to have been their pitch line to the museum when trying to get in. Me thinketh their menu betrays their true intent to do a John Besh restaurant in prime retail space. The menu is locked and loaded with shrimp pies, crispy hog's head cheese with black-eyed peas and a slow-poached yard egg, and the All-American alligator and pork cheek meatballs. Gee! Wasn't that Archie and Jughead's favorite after-school snack?

I'm not saying it's not good. It is. But if you come expecting Johnny Rockets, you'll be surprised when faced with Jacques Roquette.

American Sector has what they bill as "New Orleans's Best Happy Hour" from 3:00 to 6:00 p.m., seven days a week. They serve half-priced beverages and 75-cent barbecue sliders.

> **REASON TO GO:** To honor the soups. They have tomato, rice noodle, and a shrimp and sausage gumbo.
> **WHAT TO GET:** Good ol'-fashioned alligator and pork cheek meatballs.

ANNUNCIATION

1016 Annunciation St. • (504) 568-0245 • $$$
HOURS: 5:30–10:00 p.m. Mon–Thurs; 5:30–11:00 p.m. Fri and Sat

Chef-owner Steve Manning is a Michigander, often seen in his Detroit Tigers cap, who became an expat Yat, falling in love with New Orleans, working for Uptown favorites Gautreau's and then Clancy's. Then he went to New York in '97, trying to spread the love with his Creole restaurant, Bayou, in Harlem. A year before Katrina, he returned to New Orleans for a second long stint at Clancy's. Finally in 2012 he found the right spot, a stone's throw from Cochon, to open his own place.

With over twenty years at Clancy's, it's not surprising that while the ambience is totally different, the menu at Annunciation has many broad-stroke similarities to his former restaurant. Before opening Annunciation, Chef Manning laid out the plan: "We're going to emphasize New Orleans seafood, not so much fried and boiled but Creole seafood. Kind of like Clancy's, because of course that was my food for so long." Many dishes are not adapted but exactly duplicated from his created recipes in his old restaurant. The fried oysters with spinach and Brie is exactly the same as the dish served in Clancy's. To quote Alfred Hitchcock, "Self-plagiarism is style."

Sometimes he'll tweak it a bit. His seared scallops at Clancy's get a little lagniappe, seared with foie gras at Annunciation. His new place also features the Chicken Bonne Femme, a garlic-heavy country dish made famous by Tujague's.

REASON TO GO: Clancy's with less cab fare.

WHAT TO GET: The fried oysters with spinach and Brie and compare it to Clancy's.

BESH STEAKHOUSE

8 Canal St. (inside Harrah's Casino) • (504) 533-6111 • $$$$

HOURS: 5:00–10:00 p.m. Sun–Thurs; 5:00–11:00 p.m. Fri and Sat

As a John Besh restaurant, the quality is first rate. The menu has a New Orleans spin on a traditional steak house, offering dishes like scallop and pork belly with crushed fava bean pesto and morel mushrooms, blackened Chappapeela duck breast with confit, brussels sprout choucroute and Creole mustard, as well as a variety of seafood dishes, and of course steak. Chappapeela is a first-rate duck and pig farm in Husser, Louisiana. Choucroute is a French take on sauerkraut. Don't feel badly; I had to look them up too.

The thirty-day-aged New York strip will set you back $75. The thirty-eight-ounce cowboy steak is $79. So, it's not cheap. My knocks on the steak house are that (a) it's inside Harrah's Casino, meaning you'll be hit with the smell of five packs of cigarettes before you enter the restaurant, and (b) the walls of the restaurant are lined with the ubiquitous Blue Dog paintings of George Rodrigue. Rodrigue is a great local artist, early on painting scenes of Cajun life. And then his dog, Tiffany, died and came back to George in his dreams. Since then, every painting (and there are thousands) has his blue dog staring back at you. It's made the artist a millionaire, but we now have to see the Blue Dog staring back at us everywhere: the Sheraton Hotel, the meridian on Veterans Boulevard, on billboards, postcards, and posters. I personally don't want Tiffany staring back at me as I eat a $79 steak.

BON TON CAFÉ

401 Magazine St. • (504) 524-3386 • $$

HOURS: 11:00 a.m.–2:00 p.m., 5:00–9:00 p.m. Mon–Fri

Bon Ton Café is inside the historic 1840s Natchez Building, and is New Orleans's oldest Cajun restaurant. Owned by the Pierce family since 1953, they serve traditional Cajun food without a hint of Creole sneaking in. Before Bon Ton existed, the now ubiquitous crawfish were dismissed as "mudbugs" and not offered on any menu. Where crawfish is king of Bon Ton, you can also order other Cajun classics like shrimp and crab okra gumbo, étouffée, and grilled Gulf fish topped with grilled Louisiana oysters (or shrimp).

REASON TO GO: To honor the original.
WHAT TO GET: Crawfish.

BORGNE

601 Loyola Ave. (inside Hyatt Regency) • (504) 613-3860 • $$$
HOURS: 11:00 a.m.–10:00 p.m. Sun–Thur; 11:00 a.m.–11:00 p.m. Fri and Sat

Star chef John Besh's latest restaurant is in the Hyatt Regency hotel, a screen pass from the Superdome. In a location seemingly perfect for brats-and-brew tailgate parties before Saints games, Besh offers something quite different. In the kitchen, he has placed the former executive chef of Galatoire's Brian Landry. Besh and Landry both grew up fishing on Lake Borgne. The restaurant is their tribute to coastal Louisiana cuisine, serious about the results but playfully experimental with the ingredients. They offer crawfish croquettes with chipotle rémoulade (only 50 cents during Happy Hour), a ten-clove garlic white shrimp, and a creamy broth of oysters over spaghetti with grated bottarga. Bottarga is not a cheese. It's a suddenly *trés chic* ingredient at hip restaurants in LA and New York and this one in New Orleans. Bottarga is the pressed dried eggs of tuna or gray mullet. Yummy.

Borgne is also the only restaurant I know, perhaps in all the United States, with culinary tributes to Isleños. They are descendants from the Spanish settlers in the Canary Islands who made their way into Louisiana in the 1770s. They now live largely in St. Bernard Parish, just southeast of New Orleans, and have maintained their own culture and distinctive cuisine. If you are ever here in March, the Isleño Fiestas, a celebration of Canary Island food and music, is definitely worth attending. Food tents serve empanadas and paella but also caldo (a soup of white, lima, and green beans), pickled pork, cabbage, and platanos isleños, deep-fried, slightly green bananas wrapped in bacon. Those are not (yet) offered at Borgne. Their drinks menu, however, includes the Canary Island Ice Pick (Ron Miel honey rum, Arehucas rum, mint tea, and fresh lemon) and a hibiscus mojito (Cruzan aged rum, hibiscus, lemongrass, mint, and lime).

REASON TO GO: Where else can you get 50-cent crawfish croquettes with chipotle rémoulade?
WHAT TO GET: The best (maybe only) Isleños-influenced food you'll find.

CAFÉ ADELAIDE

300 Poydras St. (inside the Loews Hotel) • (504) 595-3305 • $$$
HOURS: 6:30 a.m.–9:00 p.m. Mon–Thur; 7:00 a.m.–10:00 p.m. Fri–Sun

Café Adelaide is a Brennan's restaurant, named for Adelaide, patriarch Owen Brennan's younger sister and the bookkeeper for his original Brennan's on Royal Street. The café is located inside the Loews Hotel, and considerably more casual and affordable than their flagship restaurants, Commander's Palace, Ralph's on the Park, and the currently padlocked Brennan's. They do a brisk lunch businesses, being near many high-rise (for us) office buildings. The Brennans have used Café Adelaide as a training ground/stepping-stone for their up-and-coming chefs.

> REASON TO GO: You might be eating the food of the next John Besh or Donald Link.

CAPDEVILLE

520 Capdeville St. • (504) 371-5161 • $$
HOURS: 11:00 a.m.–2:00 p.m., 5:00–11:00 p.m. Mon–Thur; 11:00 a.m.–1:00 a.m. Fri and Sat; 12:00 p.m.–7:00 p.m. Sun

Capdeville, the restaurant and the street, are named after our one-term mayor, Paul Capdeville, who walked the entire way from Greensboro, North Carolina, back to New Orleans after he surrendered following the Civil War. Eight hundred miles by foot, and this was before an endless parade of Hardee's, Denny's, and Chick-fil-A's would have served as his inspiration to keep a-comin' back to New Orleans. Yes, I'm trying to lose my readers, three fast-food chains at a time.

Capdeville, serving mostly burgers to a mostly lunchtime crowd from the nearby office buildings and federal courthouse, could have easily slipped into a BJ's or Rock Bottom–feeling chain, but Chef Marcus Woodham, who doubles as the sous-chef at Patois, saves the day (and evening hours till 11:00 p.m., 1:00 a.m. on weekends). He, unfortunately, can't do much about the vintage concert T-shirts the servers wear, nor the rock music playing in the background. His menu, however, does creative riffs on comfort food. Duck crackling replaces bacon on the burgers. In place of loaded nachos or potato skins buried in cheese and sour cream, Capdeville offers an appetizer of a calas-like fried ball of red beans and rice with pickled pork. Their vichyssoise has a strain of blue cheese. No, wait! Vichyssoise?

CARMO

527 Julia St. • (504) 875-4132 • $$
HOURS: 11:30 a.m.–3:00 p.m., 5:00–9:00 p.m. Mon–Sat

Whether by accident or design, Carmo is a really smart restaurant. Nestled among many large hotels and near the convention center, they offer a predominantly vegetarian menu for tourists just not that into us (our preference for pork, duck fat, and shellfish instead of anything green). Here you can get their Burmese Tea Leaf Salad (fermented tea leaves, dried beans and peas, cabbage, chilies, tomatoes, sesame seeds, crispy shallots, and peanuts), the Esmeralda Salad (quinoa, black beans, corn, peppers, and cilantro, tossed with coconut chili lime vinaigrette and topped with toasted pumpkin seeds and vegan cheese), or their signature Carmo Salad (rice, pineapple, avocado, almonds and cashews, raisins, cucumber, green pepper, smoked vegan ham, and cilantro tossed with citrus mango vinaigrette, served on a bed of organic lettuces). Not exactly what most visitors come here to eat, but Carmo offers a nice alternative on days you wake up with fat, salt, and booze playing chamber music in your stomach.

CHOPHOUSE

322 Magazine St. • (504) 522-7902 • $$$
HOURS: 4:00–10:00 p.m. Sun–Thurs, 4:00–11:00 p.m. Fri and Sat

On one hand, Chophouse is a traditional steak house offering large cuts of beef with à la carte sides like creamed spinach or steamed asparagus and a loaded baked potato. Owner Jerry Greenbaum notes, "We don't do a lot of fancy sauces. We don't disguise our food, because our food is extremely high quality." Chophouse is one of the few steak houses that use USDA Grade Prime on every cut of steak, including filet. They also wet-age their meat for twenty-eight days. Why twenty-eight days and not, say, thirty, I have no idea. What is wet-aging, I have no idea. Sounds like the opposite of dry-aging. They say it gives the beef additional flavor and tenderness.

On the other hand, Chophouse is an untraditional New Orleans steak house. They cook their beef "Pittsburgh-style," meaning charred on the outside. No sizzling in butter as it hits your table. Their stone crab is flown in fresh from Florida. For dessert you can have cheesecake imported from New York's Carnegie Deli. Yet, it's most definitely a New Orleans steak house with at least three seafood entries on any given night. Greenbaum, also not from New Orleans, came here to go to Tulane and, like so many others, fell in love with the city.

The atmosphere is lively. "We don't want you to sit in our restaurant and have to worry about the person next to you hearing everything you say," says Greenbaum.

"We got a buzz in our restaurant; we have live music and a lot of action going on."

REASON TO GO: A lively place with unadorned but delicious steaks and sides.
WHAT TO GET: A Pittsburgh-style steak, topped with Florida stone crab, and New York cheesecake for dessert.

👑 COCHON

930 Tchoupitoulas St. • (504) 588-2123 • $$$
HOURS: 11:00 a.m.–10:00 p.m. Mon–Thurs; 11:00 a.m.–11:00 p.m. Fri and Sat

Cochon, whose name is French for "pig," boasts not one, but two James Beard Award–winning chefs. Donald Link is the star and face of Cochon and his mini restaurant empire. Stephen Stryjewski matched Link's James Beard Awards as the 2011 winner. Their restaurant, voted ≠1 Best Cajun by the Appendix A judges, was nearly revolutionary when it opened in 2007. With notable exceptions like K-Paul's, much of the Cajun food being served in New Orleans could be characterized, as chef Link put it, as "a fried shrimp plate, a fried oyster plate, a fried catfish plate, and a fried combination plate—with fried shrimp, fried oysters, and fried catfish."

Cochon's only combination plate is their boucherie, which includes paper-thin slices of house-made salami, spicy tasso, and pork belly, served with homemade bread-and-butter pickles, pickled jalapeños, and house-made mustard. Other small-plate pork-atizers include their best-in-the-city fried boudin, smoked pork ribs with watermelon pickle, and pork cheeks with baby limas, mushrooms, and peach relish.

Back in 2007 my wife and I lived in Ohio, a state whose culinary contributions were the creation of the popcorn ball (Euclid Beach Park) and the fried baloney sandwich (Waldo). On a trip to New Orleans, we ate at Cochon. Marnie seemed suddenly overcome with emotion. When I asked, "What's up?" she replied, "I'd forgotten what food's supposed to taste like."

Cochon's entrees include smothered pork loin with apples, caramelized onions, and cheddar; smoked ham hock with farro, cucumbers, and English peas; and namesake Louisiana cochon with turnips, cabbage, pickled peaches, and cracklins.

The year the restaurant opened, Link won the James Beard Award for Best Chef South, and Cochon was nominated for Best New Restaurant. The James Beard Foundation again nominated Link in 2012 for Outstanding Chef. The James Beard Foundation even honored Donald Link's cookbook, *Real Cajun*.

REASON TO GO: To make a cochon of yourself.
WHAT TO GET: "One charming motherfuckin' pig. I mean, ten times more charmin' than that Arnold on *Green Acres*, you know what I'm sayin'?"

Donald Link, chef, owner, James Beard Award winner

COCHON BUTCHER

930 Tchoupitoulas St. • (504) 588-7675 • $

HOURS: 11:00 a.m.–10:00 p.m. Mon–Thurs; 11:00 a.m.–11:00 p.m. Fri and Sat; 10:00 a.m.–4:00 p.m. Sun

The Butcher is found around the side of Cochon's building on Andrew Higgins Boulevard. Same buiding, same chefs, they share the bathroom, and you can get some of the same dishes—for less. It's a meat counter where they sell boudin, andouille, Kurobuta bacon, sopressata, guanciale, pâtés, and rillettes, plus packaged foie-gras-enriched butter, house-made pickles, mustards, and hot sauces to take home from behind the counter. But there are also settin' spots where you can pull up a chair, if any are available, and dine inside. They'll even cook it.

For a mere $9 to $12 the Butcher serves best-value-in-New-Orleans sammitches: a buckboard bacon melt, duck pastrami sliders, pork belly on white bread with mint and cucumber, and the house-smoked turkey, watercress, grilled onion, and lemon thyme on pecan bread. Their boudin and pickle appetizer went from $3 to $6 this past year, but remains a steal and I think the best boudin in the city. You can get bottled soda or alcoholic drinks from the Swine Bar.

No reservations are needed or taken. When there's a large convention in town, the midday mass exodus from the nearby Morial Center can make getting a lunchtime table as hard as getting Saints tickets.

REASON TO GO: The best quality-of-food versus price-you-pay ratio in New Orleans.

WHAT TO GET: A $6 boudin appetizer, a $9 sammitch, and a bottled Barq's and you're still under $20, with tip.

DOMENICA

123 Baronne St. • (504) 648-6020 • $$
HOURS: 11:00 a.m.–11:00 p.m., 7 days a week

Located inside the stunning and historic Roosevelt Hotel, John Besh's Domenica is an Italian restaurant with a Jewish executive chef, Alon Shaya. Shaya has been nominated for the James Beard Award as Best Chef in the South. While the restaurant serves other rustic Italian dishes, including a salumi tray and a noteworthy whole roasted cauliflower, they are known for their pizza. If I had a Best Pizza category in Appendix A, I have no doubt the judges would have chosen Domenica (though I personally would lean toward Pizza Delicious). *New Orleans* magazine chose it as Best Pizza in the city. Eaternola.com chose it as the Best Restaurant, pizza or otherwise, in New Orleans. My first visit I had the Calabrese Pizza. It was a little too spicy for me (and I like spicy), but I knew from the practically perfect crust that a second try was needed. I went back two days later and ordered the Cotechino (pork sausage, scallions, and tomatoes) and the Bolzano (roast pork shoulder, fennel, bacon, and sweet onions). Chef Shaya claims what makes their pizza better is they have the only Pavesi wood-fired oven with a rotating stone deck in America. I have no idea what that means, but I do know good pizza. Domenica is good pizza.

REASON TO GO: What most people consider the best pizza in New Orleans.

WHAT TO GET: Pizza, considered by most people to be the best in New Orleans.

DRAGO'S

2 Poydras St. (inside Hilton-Riverside) • (504) 584-3911 • $$
HOURS: 11:00 a.m.–10:00 p.m. 7 days a week

The original Drago's was opened in 1969 out in Fat City by Lake Pontchartrain. Drago and Klara Cvitanovich opened a second location inside the Hilton Riverside Hotel, a stone's throw from the Mississippi River. Their Charbroiled Oysters, topped with Parmesan, butter, parsley, and garlic, has been called "The Single Best Bite of Food in New Orleans." Drago's also serves creative dishes like Shuckee Duckee, two blackened and lean duck breasts surrounded by creamy linguine and oysters, and Cajun Surf & Turf, blackened medallions of rare filet mignon, with oysters and shrimp.

You can now order your own Charbroiled Oysters Kit to make their signature plate wherever you live. The kit includes:

- Three dozen fresh Louisiana raw oysters in frozen packs
- 1 pint Drago's Charbroiling Sauce
- $\frac{1}{2}$ pint Drago's Charbroiling Cheese
- 36 aluminum cooking shells (replacing actual oyster shells)
- New Orleans–style French bread
- Drago's Mardi Gras beads

All for only $69.95, offer void where potluck dinners are considered fine dining.

REASON TO GO: To taste and decide if you want to order the Charbroiled Oyster Kit.
WHAT TO GET: The Charbroiled Oysters.

EMERIL'S

800 Tchoupitoulas St. • (504) 528-9393 • $$$
HOURS: 11:30 a.m.–2:00 p.m., 6:00–10:00 p.m. Mon–Fri, 6:00–10:00 p.m. Sat and Sun

Emeril Lagasse, chef, TV star, empire builder, James Beard Award winner

Over the years, Emeril Lagasse has been as popular as any American chef, yet has had to withstand some (largely unjustified) criticism on his way to über-success. At first the foodie mafia of critics attacked him because they didn't like his Food Network superstar status for what they viewed as his "BAM!" and "Kick It Up a Notch" hucksterism. I recall an article in the *New York Times* that complained about the food served on his TV show, prepared between commercial breaks, as though that was representative of what you'd be served in his restaurants. The food mafia wants to present Emeril as akin to Guy Fieri or Paula Deen, ignoring that he is classically trained and has received *two* James Beard Awards.

When he opened Emeril's as his first restaurant in 1990, it was chosen as Best New Restaurant in America by *Esquire*. He has since received a second James Beard Award, been inducted into the IACP Culinary Hall of Fame, and has opened twelve more restaurants nationwide. Then, Emeril took some hits locally when he chose to stay on a committed author tour for his new book rather than rush back to New Orleans after Katrina. He has largely softened his critics by being a tireless philanthropist, contributing his time and resources to the Emeril Lagasse Foundation, raising millions of dollars, turning many troubled youths toward a restaurant career.

I guess I should add, Emeril's food is excellent too. The restaurant does seafood particularly well: sizzling sea scallops, crusted drum, char-grilled salmon, and shrimp and mussel fettuccine. But then, they do great pork chops, glazed chicken, and quail too.

REASON TO GO: The place that started it all: Emeril's first restaurant and one that led to a kicking-it-up-a-notch restaurant revolution, making the Warehouse District the hottest neighborhood for the hottest chefs.

WHAT TO GET: If you can get a reservation, you're already ahead of the game.

HERBSAINT

701 St. Charles St. • (504) 524-4114 • $$$
HOURS: 11:30 a.m.–10:00 p.m. Mon–Fri; 5:30–10:00 p.m. Sat

Born in Crowley, Louisiana, Donald Link is a "real" Cajun. It's not just the name of his book, *Real Cajun*, which *also* won a James Beard Award, along with his restaurant Cochon winning the award and him being named James Beard Best Chef in the South in 2007, and a 2012 nomination for what he called "The Big One," the James Beard Award for Outstanding Chef. He's been cooking since he could barely see over a bush of spotted beebalm (that's a bayou plant and that means he was young). After gaining some experience in local Louisiana restaurants, Link moved to San Francisco. There, he attended the California Culinary Academy and honed his craft in various restaurants. He came back to New Orleans to work with The Genius, Susan Spicer, for whom he was previously sous-chef, and opened Herbsaint.

Herbsaint's menu can lean a little French (Muscovy duck leg confit with dirty rice and citrus gastrique) or lean a little Italian (gnocchi with pancetta and Parmesan), but is always squarely Southern-style (fried catfish with green rice and chilies). The restaurant's setting is part of the appeal. The intimate one-hundred-seat bistro has an outdoor patio and large interior windows through which diners can watch the St. Charles streetcar roll slowly by.

Louisiana Gourmet magazine listed Herbsaint as one of the Top 50 Restaurants in America. It was also inducted into the *Nation's Restaurant News* Hall of Fame and was listed in the *New York Times* as "one of the top 3 restaurants that count."

> REASON TO GO: Great food by a highly honored chef in the great setting of a highly honored restaurant.
> WHAT TO GET: There are many good choices. The Louisiana shrimp and grits with tasso and okra leans toward being the most acclaimed.

HOOF & CLEAVER
1100 Constance St. (inside the Rusty Nail Bar) • (504) 301-2991 • $$

Hoof & Cleaver is a very casual pork-focused pop-up inside the Rusty Nail Bar. It was founded in 2012 by a pair of chefs, Andrew Shuford and Frank Palmisano, who wanted to focus on a time-honored tradition throughout the South but rarely found in New Orleans—whole hog roasts. You can't get a whole hog roast inside the bar. Even New Orleans has *some* laws. You might check to see if one is scheduled or you can contact Clandestine New Orleans (504-301-2991) to set one up for your group.

Inside the bar, even without a whole hog roast, getting their chicken confit sliders or the Viet Dog, which won second place in the 2012 Hogs for a Cause Porkpourri category, is a far cry from "settling" for what's left.

LA BOCA
857 Fulton St. • (504) 525-8205 • $$$
HOURS: 6:00–10:00 p.m. Mon–Thurs; 6:00 p.m.–12:00 a.m. Fri and Sat

In New Orleans's Steak Zone, you can run by the cluster of Morton's, Ruth's Chris, John Besh Steak House, Chophouse, and Dickie Brennan's Steak House all without breaking a sweat . . . okay, I exaggerate. It's New Orleans—you'll sweat. La Boca is located at the epicenter, but is a steak house unlike the others. After success with Rio Mar, Alfonso Garcia and Argentine-born Nick Bazan decided to open a steak house that pays tribute to the carnivore-centric cuisine of Argentina. The Argentine style is more crusty-crackly than what you've ever had elsewhere. One skirt steak is served with the cow's thin skin membrane intact, which becomes like a crackling duck skin or deep-fried chicken skin during cooking. They also serve vacio, a very large and heavily marinated flank steak, a hanger steak called Centro de Entrana, and Milanesa, thin-cut, breaded, fried beef, topped with a fried egg. All steaks come with three distinct chimichurri sauces, tart, sharp, or smooth. La Boca's french fries are presented in a cone and doused with garlic and parsley. They are arguably the best fries in New Orleans.

> REASON TO GO: A very different presentation of what a steak house can be.
> WHAT TO GET: Start with Provoleta, an addictive appetizer of molten cheese, olive oil, and oregano into which you dip bread. Then, steak away.

LE FORET

129 Camp St. • (504) 553-6738 • $$$
HOURS: 5:30–10:00 p.m. Tues–Sun

Surrounded by star chefs Emeril Lagasse, John Besh, and Donald Link, Le Foret is an often-overlooked gem in the Warehouse District. The restaurant is set in an old building that came close to falling down under its own weight. The building was an old cigar factory, then meeting hall and trade mission for Germany, then vacant flophouse for homeless pigeons.

The restaurant came to be because of a chance encounter between a legendarily gregarious maître-d'-turned-general-manager, Danny Millan, then at Brennan's, later at Restaurant August, and his customer, the intensely wealthy Margaret Shexnayder. Even her name sounds like it should be seen below a garden party photo at the back of *The Hamptons* magazine. Shexnayder and her husband Michael loved Danny Millan. Everyone does. The Shexnayders decided Millan needed a restaurant to call his own.

Then, while vacationing at a Palm Springs resort, Miss Margaret and her husband were impressed with the resort's chef, Jimmy Corwell. They learned he was a graduate of the Culinary Institute of America, earning the designation Master Chef, and he had represented the United States in the Culinary Olympics two years in a row. I'd toss in here something about synchronized souffle-ing, but I've abused you enough (and will in future pages).

The Shexnayders undoubtedly thought pairing Chef Jimmy Corwell with Danny Millan would be oodles of fun, and so approached the chef. Miss Shexnayder said, "I'm opening a restaurant in New Orleans. Why don't you join us?" He did.

The beautifully restored building on Camp is now the four-storied Le Foret. The top floor is for private dining and has a rooftop courtyard, the third floor is event space, a spillover dining room is on two, and the main floor is the lushly appointed primary space. The setting is as beautiful as you'll find, with hardwood floors, large windows flanked by shutters, and huge chandeliers that look as though they were bought from a French Quarter antiques dealer, but are new, made in

Mexico to Margaret Shexnayder's specifications, as are her designed and paid-for Italian china and German crystal.

Chef Corwell was unknown in New Orleans circles when he arrived but quickly made a name for himself. He created Le Foret Champignons, a mushroom confit salad with pâté de foie gras and a hazelnut dressing. He did a not-quite Oysters Rockefeller and grilled prosciutto-wrapped Louisiana quail, caramelized red snapper fillet, and grilled fillet of Raceland beef tenderloin. At the end of each meal, you're offered a baked-by-hand, individually wrapped madeleine. Very French.

However, due to the fact that Danny Millan was presented his chef by Miss Shexnayder rather than choosing his own, the story practically writes itself. Danny Millan wanted more Emeril, more John Besh, someone as charming as he was. A young energertic Brandon Felder was promoted to executive chef, having served two years at Commander's Palace. Of the departed Jimmy Corwell, Millan said, "He's a great chef. I will really miss him, but I really need someone to talk to my guests."

REASON TO GO: Maybe you'll bump into the Shexnayders and they'll buy *you* a restaurant.

WHAT TO GET: Doesn't matter; it's all good, *and* you'll get a madeleine on your way out.

♛ LITTLE GEM

4545 Rampart St. • (504) 267-4863 • $$

HOURS: 11:00 a.m.–10:00 p.m. Mon–Thurs; 11:00 a.m.–11:00 p.m. Fri and Sat; 10:00 a.m.–2:00 p.m. Sun

There is no more perfect dessert in all of New Orleans than the 8:00 p.m. set of Meschiya Lake and the Little Big Horns at the Little Gem. Yeah, we'll get to the food in a minute. The Little Gem first opened roughly one hundred years ago. It was an intimate jazz club and restaurant where Louis Armstrong often performed. After it sat vacant for decades, local physician Nicolas Bazan bought the property and quickly completed a stunning renovation in the historic jazz neighborhood, well on its way to a full revitalization. I don't know who sold the idea or books the musical acts for Little Gem, but they've done an amazing job bringing in superstars like Kermit Ruffins and Delfeayo Marsalis and street stars David and Roselyn, the latter singing on Royal Street since 1975 with six recorded albums. But (for me) the showstopper is Meschiya Lake, voted 2012's Best Female Vocalist. She came to New Orleans as part of a traveling circus. She ate lightbulbs and insects and sang while twirling flame-doused nunchucks. People were amazed . . . by her voice.

Whenever I have out-of-town visitors, I try to get them to the Little Gem, or Spotted Cat, Chickie Wah Wah, a festival tent, or wherever Meschiya is singing. Then I watch their out-of-town jaws drop as they take in this great performance, I think the best New Orleans has to offer. Ask Rosemary from Millburn, New Jersey, or Amy from Cincinnati. The band is casual on stage but tight in their playing. Meschiya's hair, makeup, and dress make her look like a 1940s beauty queen, except for her many tattoos. The Little Big Horns perform both old standards, seriously funked up, and their own songs, seriously funked up.

Now the food. The restaurant's first chef, Robert Bruce, built the launch menu around vintage Creole flavors. He'd worked in kitchens all over New Orleans, including Upperline, Commander's Palace, Ruth's Chris, and Emeril's. He's also been at the helm of Smith & Wollensky and the Palace Café. But his menu at the Little Gem drifted from promising to pedestrian. They started serving Caesar salads, grilled salmon, and the frighteningly named Little Gem Burger. Bruce is a fine cook, but it's hard to draw in a stylish nightclub crowd peddling Little Gem Burgers.

Bazan's son Nicolas Jr. is co-owner of RioMar and La Boca and was brought in to run Little Gem. He brought with him Miles Prescott, his chef and partner at RioMar, to take over the kitchen. Prescott, a Georgia native, has given the menu a decidedly Southern identity. You got yer char-marked, crisp-crusted rabbit tenderloin laid on top of a mix of cheese, cauliflower, and a little mo' rabbit, piled with cabbage and apples. You got yer fried frogs' legs with a tomato concoction they call "jam." You got yer sides like Hoppin' John and cane-syrup sweet potatoes. Then, because yer in New Orleans not Georgia, you got yer oysters (served five different ways). For dee-zert, you got yer foie gras mousse slathered in salty caramel sauce.

REASON TO GO: The #1 best place to dine and hear live music (see Appendix A).

WHAT TO GET: A table with a good view of the stage . . . and the foie gras mousse.

LÜKE

333 St. Charles Ave. • (504) 378-2840 • $$$
HOURS: 7:00 a.m.–11:00 p.m. 7 days a week

Lüke is John Besh's homage to the grand old Franco-German brasseries that once reigned in New Orleans or homage to the Hilton Hotel on St. Charles, I forget which. Lately it seems you can't be a premiere hotel in New Orleans unless you have a John Besh restaurant (or Drago's, MiLa, Café Adelaide, or Criollo). Lüke is the most eccentric of Chef John Besh's restaurants. It's patterned on the bistros of France, particularly those in the Alsace region. It also recalls certain restaurants from a century ago in New Orleans, notably the old German restaurant Kolb's. And, as is the case with any Besh restaurant, there will not be hints, but slap-you-in-the-face pronouncements of his Louisiana food heritage. The menu is kind of like asking three girls to the prom and them all saying "yes."

The range is jumbo Louisiana shrimp "en cocotte," assiette de charcuterie (an assortment of pâtés, rilletes, hog's head cheese, sausages, and garnishes, all made in house), plateau de fruits de mer (another assortment, this time a selection of raw oysters and chilled cooked lobster, shrimp, and mussels), or a simple bowl of gumbo or corn and crab bisque, to the even more simple Lüke Burger with Emmentaler cheese.

Since opening in 2007, Lüke has been highly praised in *Condé Nast Traveler*, *Travel + Leisure*, and the *Times-Picayune*.

REASON TO GO: For the German—no, the Alsace French—no, the Louisiana cuisine.

WHAT TO GET: The assiette and the plateau de fruits de mer and let them fight it out. In Vegas, the oysters are two-to-one favorites over the hog's head cheese.

MILA

817 Common St. • (504) 412-2580 • $$$
HOURS: 6:30–11:00 a.m., 11:30 a.m.–2:30 p.m., 5:30–10:00 p.m. Mon–Sat

The husband-and-wife team, of Slade Rushing and Allison Vines-Rushing were born in Mississipp*i* and Louisian*a*. Check the name of the restaurant again. They each grew up in different rural areas around New Orleans and met while working together at Gerard's Downtown, the short-lived bistro run by Gerard Maras in the early 2000s. After stints at Mr. B's and Brennan's, the Rushings left to work in New York City. Allison worked at Picholine and the four-star Alain Ducasse. In 2004, she received the James Beard Award for Rising Star Chef of the Year. She then took her new New York street cred and left New York. Shorty after Katrina, Allison and Slade took over a restaurant in Abita Springs, an hour and several decades outside New Orleans. They discovered maybe they'd become a little too "New York" for Abita Springs as dishes like sweetbreads with black truffle grits went right over the heads of their customers. Not that you can get sweetbreads with black truffle grits *anywhere* in New York. They shut it down in favor of a deal with the Renaissance Pere Marquette Hotel. In 2007 they took over the former Rene Bistrot and renamed it MiLa.

At MiLa the couple blends their Southern roots with New York training to create a next-step New Orleans cuisine. It's not heavily seasoned Cajun. It's not

MiLa interior

Creole with heavy creams and sauces. Slade notes, "New Orleans food traditionally has an overindulgence of rich items—crab, oysters, filet, and hollandaise on one plate—but our food is about purification. We want you to taste the vegetable just picked yesterday."

Their ever-evolving menu has been called "the most innovative cuisine in New Orleans." They'll serve creative dishes like sweet-potato pappardelle with shiitakes and Georgia cheese on one day, and sweet-potato veloute with seared sea scallop and white truffle oil on another. On any given day, you might find New Orleans–style barbecue lobster; "deconstructed" Oysters Rockefeller; flounder with Jerusalem artichokes, corn, and green beans; and, yes, sweetbreads with black truffle grits.

REASON TO GO: Sometimes you need to get out of your comfort-food zone.

WHAT TO GET: Well, after all this, don't you think you at least need to try the sweetbreads with black truffle grits?

MOTHER'S

401 Poydras St. • (504) 523-9656 • $$

HOURS: 7:00 a.m.–10:00 p.m. 7 days a week

Cabdrivers will all tell you Mother's is a *must*. The perpetually long lines waiting on Poydras Street to get inside may convince you it's a *must*. There are generalist guides like Fodor's and Frommer's that praise Mother's as a *must*. Let me be at least one voice to say *maybe not*. I sense there *was* a time when Mother's was the perfect response when visitors wanted to find "a hole-in-the-wall serving 'authentic' New Orleans food where the locals go." But it's been a long time since the original owners, Simon and Mary (Mother) Landry, first served po' boys to longshoremen and laborers in 1938.

Mother's of today has evolved into a densely packed (almost exclusively by tourists), cafeteria-style joint with minimal service. Their perhaps

Ubiquitous line outside Mother's

too-broad menu, a smorgasbord of "local" dishes, is no longer made by by chefs, but employees who punch in and out on a time clock. It also has surprisingly high prices. The whole experience feels about as *must* as going to Vegas to hear Wayne Newton sing "Danke Schoen" one more time.

REASON TO GO: If you like lines or have a box to check off on your bucket list.

WHAT TO GET: The Ferdi Special—a po' boy packed with baked ham, roast beef, debris, and gravy.

MULATE'S

201 Julia St. • (504) 522-1492 • $

HOURS: 11:00 a.m.–10:00 p.m. Sun–Thu, 11:00 a.m.–11:00 p.m. Fri and Sat

Mulate's is perfectly located for the brisk business they do. They are directly across the street from the entrance to the convention center and blocks from a number of thousand-room hotels. They're a restaurant where you go for the atmosphere and live Cajun or Zydeco music with a well-worn dance floor more than you go for the food. For the tourist crowd they serve, normally spicy Cajun recipes tend to be milder to better align with tourists' palates.

REASON TO GO: To hear live Cajun or Zydeco music with your meal.

WHAT TO GET: Anything—you're here for the music.

PÊCHE

800 Tchoupitoulas St. • (504) 522-1744 • $$$
HOURS: 11:00 a.m.–10:00 p.m. Mon–Thurs; 11:00 a.m.–11:00 p.m. Fri and Sat

Donald Link and his co-chefs and partners, Stephen Stryjewski and Ryan Prewitt, betray their Cajun roots in this new seafood house. You don't get your fish reduced to a fillet nor rounded into a cake. You get the whole fat fish, fresh onto your plate with head, tail, and all. It's like a redfish or speckled trout boucherie. I can already imagine a hundred reviews saying "Pêche does for seafood what Cochon (another noteworthy Donald Link restaurant) did for pork." If you have any "I don't eat seafood" whiners in your group, they serve a skirt steak and chicken diablo. Yes, I'm trying to lose my readers, one food allergy at a time.

Link and Stryjewski were inspired by a trip to Uruguay, where seemingly every restaurant and roadside stand had a wood-burning *parrilla*. A *parrilla* is a style of grill used for cooking *asado*, a style of barbecue. Pêche, with its large, unvarnished wood beams, bench-style seating, and roaring wood-fired grill, custom built by Link's cousin and used as the restaurant's centerpiece, feels very much like you've entered a *pequeño lugar donde se sirve de comer*. What? I have to translate *everything*?

With the pedigree of Herbsaint and Cochon restaurants, Pêche opened to immediate fanfare as diners fill it each night. *Bon Appétit* chose it, months after opening, as a Top 50 Best New Restaurants in America.

REASON TO GO: "Pêche does for seafood what Cochon (another noteworthy Donald Link restaurant) did for pork."

WHAT TO GET: Whatever is the fish of the day, and then root around in the nooks and crannies of the whole fish for tasty morsels.

♔ RESTAURANT AUGUST

301 Tchoupitoulas St. • (504) 299-9777 • $$$$
HOURS: 11:00 a.m.–2:00 p.m., 5:30 p.m.–10:00 p.m. Mon–Fri; 5:30 p.m.–10:00 p.m. Fri and Sat

Restaurant August did not win the 2013 James Beard Award for Outstanding Restaurant (the culinary equivalent of the Oscar for Best Picture). We'll get over it. Someday. The fact that there were only three restaurants in the entire country nominated helps ease the pain. Blue Hill in New York won the award. I've never eaten there, but I'll still cry foul and allude to a New York City bias for this award, presented each year *in New York City*, at Lincoln Center no less. Highlands Bar & Grill in Birmingham, Alabama, was the third nominated. I have eaten there. Their shrimp & grits may be the best I've ever had, but let someone from the city ingloriously tabbed the "Pittsburgh of the South" write about Highlands in *Eat Dat B'ham*.

Restaurant August is the flagship of John Besh's mini-empire of New Orleans restaurants. That doesn't mean Commander John Besh will be on board. Chef de cuisine Michael Gulotta pretty much now runs the show that was originally written, cast, and directed by Besh. The setting is wood-paneled elegant in a renovated French-Creole building that dates back to the 1800s, with high ceilings, large windows, twinkling chandeliers, and brocade-draped dining rooms. The service is the highest caliber, executed with military precision (silverware changes for every course), as befits Besh's background in the Marines, but friendly, even a little chatty, as befits New Orleans.

The food ranges from deceptively simple, like heirloom beets or gnocchi with crabmeat, to dishes so complex you might feel they're just showin' off. The Amuse-Bouche appetizer is a seafood sabayon, fish fumet, and egg custard with a hint of truffle, topped with bowfin caviar, and served in an eggshell. Not something you could pop in the toaster oven. Dishes like Pâté de Campagne of La Provence, pork with radishes, pickled chanterelle mushrooms, and homemade marmalades and mustards; or ghost pepper caviar atop oysters atop a velvety cauliflower soup; or the dessert strawberries made three ways: fresh, sorbet, and crispy, on top of a pistachio shortbead with a crème fraîche, are all riddled with flavors and are beautifully presented. While all the components are simple, most of them a nod to John Besh's commitment to locally raised ingredients (many from his own farm at La Provence), it requires a don't-try-this-at-home mastery to pull them together. Have you ever looked at a Jackson Pollock painting and thought "I could do that," but when you tried, you just ended up with a splattered mess? Same thing here.

Restaurant August is not cheap—the entrees are all in the mid-to high $30s. There is also a four-course degustation menu that'll run close to $90. But, August does offer a "best value in town" lunch on weekdays. The three-course lunch is only $20.13 as I write this. It'll be $20.14 by the time *Eat Dat* is published. In a hundred years, the lunch will be a dollar more expensive. Best come as soon as you can.

REASON TO GO: To dine at a James Beard also-ran that may be the best meal you've ever had.

WHAT TO GET: You almost must start with their Amuse-Bouche. Then, their culinary world is your oyster (topped with ghost pepper caviar).

Rollin' Down the Bayou
OR The Food Truck Wars

New Orleans had a love/hate relationship with food trucks. The residents loved them, but city council seemed to hate them. At a time when food-truck vendors had blown off the stigma of roach coaches, had evolved into mobile mini-huts for inventive chefs serving gourmet food, and were flourishing all over the country and even in Paris, France, where Cantine California, an artisanal taco truck, and Le Camion Qui Fume ("the smoking truck") can be seen parked along the Champs-Élysées, they were conspicuously absent from New Orleans streets.

Perhaps backed by the powerful Louisiana Restaurant Association and jittery brick-and-mortar business owners, New Orleans placed unreasonable restrictions on food-truck operators. City regulations grouped food trucks with sno-ball trucks, Mr. Okra's fruit-and-vegetable truck, even souvenir carts. Only one hundred permits were available for all these disparate operations citywide. The $300 permits had to be renewed every year. Food trucks were not allowed to sit in one spot for more than thirty minutes, and could not return more than once every twenty-four hours. They had to be six hundred feet from a school cafeteria or restaurant. Operators had to carry $500,000 liability insurance, had to be approved by the state Department of Health, could not have trucks more than twenty-six feet long or eight feet wide, and had to clean up after themselves. They couldn't sell alcohol nor be open for business after 7:00 p.m. And they couldn't sell seafood . . . in New Orleans. No seafood. You could stumble down our streets while drinking a half gallon of Everclear, but you'd be arrested for eating a fish taco at 7:15.

This came to a head with the formation of the New Orleans Food Truck Coalition and what might be termed a "No Justice, No Grease" movement. Coalition spokesperson and Taceaux Loceaux food-truck operator Alex del Castillo complained, "It's embarrassing to hear people brag about the food-truck scenes in places like Austin and Portland, while New Orleans is still a hostile environment." He added, "If we're at odds with anybody, it's people who run crappy restaurants and survive by being in the CBD [Central Business District] and not having any competition."

During the summer of 2013 a long and concerted effort by the coalition with the backing of community support resulted in a complete victory as city council voted 6–0 to approve an ordinance authorizing a great many more licenses and greatly reducing the restrictions placed on how and where the food trucks could operate. Now they can hug a curb for four hours and even longer if they buy a franchise agreement for a specific spot.

Now there are food-truck festivals and "Rolling Through" parties where groups of trucks gather in one spot at the same time and, shockingly, at one event the Boston Brewing Co. served beer. The vendors even have their own website, Nolafoodtrucks. com.

Listed below are some, but not all, of the top food trucks in New Orleans. Probably three new ones have opened up

since I began writing this side dish. You can find out when and where they're open for business on the site Roaminghunger.com/nol.

Big Cheesy has nine varieties of grilled-cheese sandwiches, like cheddar, onion, garlic, and leek on sourdough or strawberries, Nutella, and cream cheese on brioche.

Brazilian BBQ specializes in grilled kabobs, garlic bread, and a Brazilian po' boy.

Brigade Coffee serves first-rate coffee from a cool retro truck that looks like a WWII armored vehicle.

Drago's restaurant has a truck selling their famous charbroiled oysters.

Empanada Intifada has savory hand pies (aka empanadas). Their specialty is the Mestizo—a combination of a traditional empanada and a Louisiana meat pie.

Fat Falafel has Middle Eastern sandwiches with many vegetarian options.

Fork in the Road serves a changing menu of salads, soups, and sandwiches from Cubans to barbecue chicken.

Frencheeze is easy to spot with the large French bulldog painted on the side of the truck. The "about us" page on their website is not even one sentence long and says it all: "Lover of bread, cheese, and butter."

Fry Bar bundles herb-covered french fries with sauces like Calabrese chili aioli or Green Goddess dressing.

Geaux Plates combines Vietnamese food with Cajun and Creole flavors in their po' boys.

La Cocinita ("Little Kitchen") serves up Latin American street food: customized tacos or arepas (stuffed corn cakes) or rice bowls with your choice of meats, cheeses, beans, and other fillings.

Meltdown has ice-cream bars in inventive flavors like saffron rose, pineapple chili, wheatgrass pineapple, Vietnamese coffee, and the ever-popular salted caramel.

Que Crawl *may* still be around. Its purple truck was an early and exceptional NOLA food truck where Chef Nathanial Zimet showcased his barbecue and inventive Southern cooking. Now that he's won *Chopped* and has opened the restaurant Boucherie, the truck's been less visible.

Slider Shak offers up Creole malted milk shakes, pommes frites, a variety of dipping sauces, and meat and veggie sliders.

Taceaux Loceaux has specialty tacos like Cartinal Knowledge (brisket) and Messin with Texas pork taco. It was featured on Anthony Bourdain's *Layover.*

The Yakamein Lady is a venerable food truck serving Yakamein (meat, eggs, green onions, and noodles in a spicy, salty broth with soy sauce). It's a dish with some history, created in the Korean War and brought back to New Orleans by returning soldiers. Its nickname is "Old Sober" for its power to rid pain and hangovers. Chef Linda Green has been selling her nourishing hot soup along parade routes for more than twenty years. She's been featured on Anthony Bourdain's *No Reservations* and she won her segment on *Chopped.*

I am most intrigued by a food truck seen on Magazine Street by the zoo, where I have never eaten, where I will never eat, but I smile each time I pass the Deep-Fried Oreos truck.

RIO MAR

800 S. Peters St. • (504) 525-3474 • $$

HOURS: 11:30 a.m.–2:00 p.m. Mon–Fri; 6:00–10:00 p.m. Mon–Sat

Adolfo Garcia, New Orleans born with Panamanian roots and trained in Spain, started Rio Mar in 2000. Named for a beautiful town in Panama, where the river meets the sea, the restaurant blends traditional Latin American and Spanish seafood. It is best known for its four-styles-of-ceviche sampler, and has more than forty rare Spanish wines.

In the summer of 2012, Garcia left Rio Mar to focus on his other new restaurants. Miles Prescott stepped in almost seamlessly. He'd previously been the chef de cuisine under Garcia for two years, as well as working at Delachaise and Bayona. "Every time I changed jobs, I would check in with Rio Mar to see if they had a spot for me," Prescott said. "I always respected their singular place in New Orleans. Where else do you get this food?"

Of his transition into Rio Mar, Prescott said, "I tweaked some dishes, enshrined others that would break my heart to delete." Rio Mar still serves small-plate Portuguese octopus, *empanadas ropas viejas*, and large plates of *lechon* (pork), *escabeche* (poached fish), and Louisiana black drum. You can still get the signature four-ceviche sampler. You'd be a fool not to.

> REASON TO GO: "Where else do you get this food?"
> WHAT TO GET: The ceviche sampler.

♛ ROOT

200 Julia St. • (504) 252-9480 • **$$**
HOURS: 11:00 a.m.–2:00 p.m., 5:00–11:00 p.m. Mon–Thurs; 11:00 a.m.–2:00 p.m., 5:00 p.m.–2:00 a.m. Fri; 5:00 p.m.–2:00 a.m. Sat; 11:00 a.m.–2:00 p.m. Sun

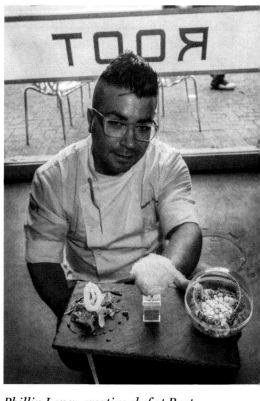

Phillip Lopez, creative chef at Root

Root opened at the tail end of 2011 and has been racking up awards and accolades ever since. The restaurant was named one of *Bon Appétit's* 50 Best New Restaurants; was awarded Best New Restaurant 2012 by *New Orleans* magazine; received the "So Hot Right Now" Eater Award for New Orleans; and earned a rare four-bean review by the *Times-Picayune*. Root has been featured in *Southern Living*, *Fodor's Travel Intelligence*, and *Forbes* magazine. Owner and executuve chef Phillip Lopez has been honored as the 2012 Eater Awards for New Orleans "Chef of the Year," Star Chefs named him one of its "Rising Star Chefs" in 2012, and *Louisiana Cookin'* magazine named him a "Chef to Watch."

Chef Lopez has said, "To me, cooking is a form of communication, and I want to talk to my guests through each bite they take." For some diners, Root is the most inventive and outstanding restaurant in New Orleans. For others, each bite will communicate, "WTF?" Root is most definitely not like any other restaurant in New Orleans (except their new location, Square Root in the Lower Garden District). They famously serve scallops in cigar boxes. You can order marrow baked in the bone and served with toast points infused with squid ink. My "WTF?" moment came with my Ménage à Foie appetizer. I love foie gras. But I was less enthused when one of the three varieties started snapping in my mouth as though it had been stuffed with Pop Rocks candy. The mere listing of the last three dishes should resolve the question of whether Root's culinary creativity is spot-on perfect for you or meant for more adventurous eaters.

REASON TO GO: Playfully creative (and award-winning) dishes.
WHAT TO GET: Whether you end up savoring it or spitting it out, you've gotta try the Ménage à Foie.

RUBY SLIPPER

200 Magazine St. • (504) 525-9355 • $$
HOURS: 7:00 a.m.–2:00 p.m. Mon–Fri; 8:00 a.m.–2:00 p.m. Sat; 8:00 a.m.–3:00 p.m. Sun

The original Ruby Slipper is in Mid-City (139 S. Cortez Street). There's a third location at 2001 Burgundy Street in the Marigny. I choose to use their Warehouse District location to profile because it is more convenient for most visitors. There is most often a line waiting to grab a table or counter stool at Ruby Slipper, but not as long a line as nearby Mother's and the wait is so much more worth it. Their offerings lean toward the eclectic with signature dishes like Bananas Foster Pain Perdu (French-bread-based French toast topped with rum-flambéed bananas and raisins, served with applewood-smoked bacon), Eggs Cochon (poached eggs over apple-braised pork debris and an open-faced buttermilk biscuit, finished with hollandaise), and their most popular BBQ shrimp and grits (sautéed Gulf shrimp with an amber beer and rosemary reduction, over Falls Mill creamy stone-ground grits, served with a buttermilk biscuit). The A-list judges of Appendix A in this book chose Ruby Slipper as the #1 Best Breakfast Spot in New Orleans.

REASON TO GO: Unusual (and delicious) breakfast options.
WHAT TO GET: Something not offered at thirty other breakfast spots.

RUTH'S CHRIS STEAKHOUSE

525 Fulton St. • (504) 587-7900 • $$$$
HOURS: 11:30 a.m.–10:00 p.m. Mon–Thurs; 11:30 a.m.–11:00 p.m. Fri and Sat; 11:30 a.m.–9:30 p.m. Sun

In a city where the stories and the soul of a restaurant are a big part of why you'd eat there, Ruth's Chris offers a bit of a quandary. As a chain based in Winter Park, Florida (they abandoned New Orleans and relocated there a week after Katrina), with 135 locations nationwide, their New Orleans restaurant located inside Harrah's Hotel, they seem easy to dismiss. But, historically, Ruth's Chris is as much a part of the city's food fabric as any restaurant.

Chris Steak House was founded in February 1927 by entrepreneur Chris Matulich. It was located at 11 Broad Street near the New Orleans Fairgrounds Racetrack. During Matulich's thirty-eight years running the business, he sold it six times, then six times the restaurant failed, allowing him to buy it back at a better price. Maybe it's fitting the new location is in Harrah's; Chris had found a run of six pigeons. In 1965 Ruth Fertel became the seventh owner. Ignoring the advice of her friends, lawyer, and banker, Ruth bought the restaurant, a business about which she knew nothing, for $18,000—then realized she hadn't budgeted any additional money she'd need to buy food. Fertel had a hand in every aspect of her new business. She had to teach herself how to butcher steak, and would saw thirty-pound short loins by hand until she could afford an electric band saw. She staffed her restaurant with single mothers, like herself. For many years, Chris Steak House was the only upscale restaurant in New Orleans with an all-female wait staff.

Ruth Fertel, the Empress of Steak

In 1976 the restaurant was destroyed by a fire. Within seven days, the tough little entrepreneur had relocated the restaurant to a new spot a few blocks away at 711 Broad Street. The sales agreement with Matulich prevented her from using the original name at any other address, so she named the new restaurant Ruth's Chris Steak House in order to keep continuity. She admitted later, "I've always hated the name, but we've always managed to work around it."

In addition to hiring single mothers, Ruth created the first, and then only, fine dining establishment where blacks felt comfortable. A white oilman from the West Bank once approached Ruth Fertel and announced loudly enough to fill the room, "If that boy stays, I'll never eat here again." "There's the door," she replied.

Thereafter, the Ruth's Chris story starts to lose its romance. They began franchising in 1977, sold to the investment company Madison Dearborn Partners of Chicago in '99, went public in 2005 following a successful IPO valuing the company at $235 million and an increase of 15 percent in first-day trading. Blah blah blah. Even before relocation to Florida, you knew the soul of Ruth's Chris had been shown the door when the chain cultivated paid endorsements from Rush Limbaugh and Sean Hannity.

REASON TO GO: Memories of Ruth Fertel, dubbed "The First Lady of American Restaurants" and "The Empress of Steak."

WHAT TO GET: The USDA prime steaks, seared at 1,800 degrees and topped with an ounce of butter, added just before the plates leave the kitchen in order to create the signature sizzle. Ruth firmly believed that the success of her steaks was due to the sound and smell of the sizzle.

TOMMY'S

746 Tchoupitoulas St. • (504) 581-1103 • $$
HOURS: 5:30–10:00 p.m. Sun–Thurs; 5:30–11:00 p.m. Fri and Sat

Tommy's Cuisine opened in 2004 as a result of the divorce of the (former) husband-and-wife owners of Irene's Cuisine. Tommy's is a near clone of Irene's but is in a bigger space that takes (and honors) reservations. Above all else, the biggest difference is it has Milton Prudence as executive chef. Milton is a story unto himself.

Heading back home to New England to pursue a career in teaching, he meant to stop off in New Orleans for a short family visit. His mother, grandmother, uncle, and cousins all worked for Galatoire's. Milton agreed to help out "for a few days" as Galatoire's dishwasher. Twenty years later, Mr. Milton became Galatoire's first African American executive chef. He continues to cook many of Galatoire's specialties at Tommy's. Galatoire's-inspired crabmeat au gratin, stuffed eggplant, and Oysters Rockefeller share the table with Irene's-inspired veal Marsala, soft-shell crab linguine, and Italian rosemary chicken. Mr. Milton takes pride in preserving both culinary traditions, saying, "It's not something I take lightly. . . . I have teachers that taught me this and for me to pass it on and—or even for me to do it, and do it to the point where people like it and can say nothing changed with it—that's very important to me."

His specialty appetizer, Oysters Trio, is Mr. Milton's playful interpretation of others' menus: Oysters Tommy (baked with Romano cheese, pancetta and, roasted red pepper), Oysters Rockefeller (cooked with spinach, fresh herbs, and herbsaint), and Oysters Bienville (prepared with crawfish, shrimp, and fresh herbs).

Tommy's restaurant and private rooms are capable of accommodating three hundred guests. They have a piano player on weeknights and bands on weekends.

REASON TO GO: So you can fit in Irene's and Galatoire's in one visit.

WHAT TO GET: A little Oysters Rockefeller, a little soft-shell crab linguine, and you've got the best of both worlds.

WINDSOR COURT GRILL ROOM

300 Gravier St. • (504) 522-1994 • $$$$

HOURS: 11:30 a.m.–2:30 p.m., 5:30–10:00 p.m. 7 days a week

The Windsor Court is usually the highest- or second-highest-rated hotel in America, according to *Travel + Leisure* magazine's annual poll. The halls and rooms are appointed with real antiques and real oil paintings. I've stayed there twice, but on someone else's expense account. The hotel's restaurant, the Grill Room, has also racked up the awards. *Zagat* has awarded it "Top Décor" and "Top Bar Service" in 2009, and "Best Restaurant Décor" 2007. *Forbes Travel Guide* (formerly *Mobil Travel Guide*) gave it four stars in 2001, 2002, 2003, 2005, 2006, 2007, 2008, 2009, 2010, 2011, and 2012. I guess 2004 was an off year. According to *Forbes*, the rating signifies the restaurant to be "of the finest establishments in the world, delivering guests an experience beyond expectations." The Grill Room is one of only two Louisiana restaurants to receive four stars.

The restaurant first came to prominence in the late '80s and early '90s with Chef Kevin Graham in charge. Since then the hotel has run through Grill Room chefs like Jerry Jones does head football coaches. Greg Sonnier, whose restaurant, Gabrielle, was regarded as one of the city's best, was the first. General manager Bruno Brunner insisted, "This was purely a budgetary decision." Then Brunner became a budgetary decision and was replaced by general manager David Teich, formerly from Charleston Place, a hotel with a well-regarded food program in Charleston, South Carolina. Teich was joined by Drew Dzejak, formerly the chef at Charleston Place. Drew was replaced by Kristin Butterworth. She'd been the chef at Lautrec, the fine-dining arm of the Nemacolin Woodlands Resort in Pennsylvania. Unbeknownst to her, the Windsor Court's general manager and a few other hotel principals came in for dinner. They were so impressed with her tasting menu that they invited her down to New Orleans to interview. "The rest is history," Butterworth said at the time. She apparently hadn't checked their history. A year later, she left "to be closer to her family."

This is sounding more like a Hoover's Report than a restaurant profile.

The current chef, Vlad Ahmadyarov, is a native Azerbaijani who lived in Russia. As a boy he worked in his uncle's restaurant. Vlad the fish scaler became introduced to our cuisine when a Louisiana native came to Southern Russia along the Caspian Sea to open Cajun and TexMex restaurants. It was love at first bite. He started working the Russian Cajun restaurant. "Some ingredients were hard to find in Russia," Vlad the roast quailer recalls. When the owner opened a new restaurant in Folsom, Louisiana, Vlad migrated to America to run it. Whether Vlad the braised kaler will be the Grill Room's long-term answer remains to be seen. Their website is hedging its bets, saying simply, "Join our highly acclaimed Executive Chef," listed without name.

CHAPTER 7

Garden District

I love New Orleans. . . . I love the way it looks. I love the way it feels.

—**Sandra Bullock, Garden District resident**

New Orleans food is as delicious as the less criminal forms of sin.

—**Mark Twain, Garden District wannabe**

(he always intended to buy the house next to what would become the Anne Rice house)

The Garden District is where the Americans settled into New Orleans after Napoleon's everything-must-go sale of 1803. They used the opportunity to show off to the French and the Spanish residents how much money they had. The houses in the Garden District are huge. One on Jackson Street at Coliseum is 28,800 square feet. Today two people live in it. I guess they like to go weeks without having to see each other. One "practical" reason the houses are so big was the practice by which boys, upon reaching thirteen years of age, had to move out of the main part of the house and live out back until they married. Families didn't want raging hormones racing around the house, doing whatever destruction thirteen-year-old boys did in the days prior to skateboards or M-80s.

Every house in the Garden District seems to have a layered and eclectic history. There's the Anne Rice house, Archie Manning's house, John Goodman's house (previously owned by Trent Reznor), Sandra Bullock's house, the house where Jefferson Davis died, and the one with my favorite story, the Musson-Bell House at 1331 Third Street. It was the 1800s home of Michel Musson, one of the few French Creoles then living in the predominantly white Garden District. Musson was the uncle of artist Edgar Degas. A noted artisan himself, Musson designed intricate metal grillwork on both the upstairs balcony and street-level porch. The neighboring house shows identical ironwork on just one side of the house. The story goes that Michel woke up one day to see "his" design on the neighbor's house and became so enraged he rushed out to the foundry to destroy all his molds. The other three sides of the neighboring house had to use a different design.

Now, when you come to the Garden District, don't expect Beverly Hills or West Hampton. It *is* the ritziest neighborhood . . . in New Orleans, meaning there's still

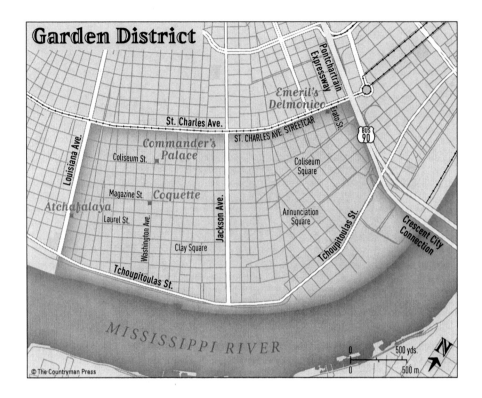

a lot of funk. In the late 1800s, plantationlike estates were chopped up, leaving stunning antebellum mansions now next to flophouses built where expansive yards used to be. The sidewalks and streets are as funky, with potholes and bricks out of place, as the rest of New Orleans.

The restaurants are a similar mix of elegant (Lilette) and historic-stately (Commander's Palace) alongside breakfast spots (Slim Goodies), burger joints (Smashburger), and bar food (the Bulldog).

ATCHAFALAYA

901 Louisiana Ave. • (504) 891-9626 • $$$
HOURS: 11:00 a.m.–10:00 p.m. Tues–Fri, 10:00 a.m.–10:00 p.m. Sat and Sun; 5:30–10:00 p.m. Mon

Atchafalaya is a Choctaw word meaning "long river" and is also the name of the Louisiana-situated largest swamp in America. The restaurant has had a swampy succession of owners, with each having a different idea of what the restaurant should be. Starting in the 1920s, most of the years the building housed Petrossi's, a casual seafood house. In the early 1990s it became a contemporary

Creole bistro called Café Atchafalaya. The café had a series of owners, some trying to be down-home Southern, others trying to go upscale, all rushing toward being out of business, until it was acquired by Tony Tocco and Rachel Jaffe in 2009. Tony might be the last person you'd see as the savior of Atchafalaya. He started the Oak Street diviest of dive bars, Snake & Jake's. The bar has a specialty cocktail called the Possum, named after the time a possum fell through Snake & Jake's waterlogged ceiling and into a man's drink. But Tony and Rachel pulled off a Restaurant Impossible–type makeover, and then went out to market it.

They knocked on doors, asking neighbors to give the place another chance. They set up a food booth at the Wednesday concert series in Lafayette Square. They started hosting wine dinners to bring back a skeptical fine dining crowd. Atchafalaya brought in musicians for live music at Sunday brunch and at dinner on Sundays and Mondays. Weekend brunches include a make-your-own Bloody Mary buffet.

Above all, they improved the food. Atchafalaya does great versions of New Orleans classics like fried green tomatoes with crab rémoulade, BBQ shrimp, and the New Orleans by way of Carrboro, North Carolina, shrimp and grits. They also serve their own bacon-wrapped, boudin-stuffed quail, and fried oysters in tasso cream. The waiters ride with the theme and serve you with energy (sometimes raucous) and a little banter.

REASON TO GO: A sometimes raucous Sunday brunch that is funkier than the more renowned Blue Room, Crystal Room, or Commander's Palace.
WHAT TO GET: Bacon-wrapped, boudin-stuffed quail with a self-serve Bloody Mary will do it for me.

♛ COMMANDER'S PALACE

1403 Washington Ave. • (504) 899-8221 • $$$
HOURS: 11:30 a.m.–2:30 p.m., 6:30–10:30 p.m. Mon–Sat; 10:30 a.m.–1:30 p.m., 6:30–10:30 p.m. Sun

Chef Tory McPhail won the 2013 James Beard Award, joining Emeril Lagasse, Frank Brigtsen, Paul Prudhomme, and other legendary chefs who have passed through the kitchen of this stately Garden District mansion. Winning a James Beard is almost expected at Commander's the way national football championships are expected at Alabama, or snagging a rich husband is expected at Williams. Yes, I'm trying to lose my readers, one college at a time.

Commander's Palace is actually named after a guy named Commander. Emile Commander set up a small saloon in 1880 and within a few years expanded it to a fine restaurant patronized by the wealthy families of the Garden District. Frank Giarratano became the second owner in the 1920s. He lived upstairs with his wife

Commander's Palace

Rose and two sons. Rumor has it that the Giarratanos shared the upstairs with small rented rooms where riverboat captains would take a wench and bottles of illegal libations (this was during Prohibition) while New Orleans's most upstanding citizens ate directly below. When the Brennans bought Commander's in the 1960s, which had since passed through ownership by Frank and Elinor Moran, the upstairs had ceased being basically a bordello but downstairs the restaurant had lost some of its heat as well.

After the Brennan family tiff in 1973, when Ella and Dickie lost control over the original restaurant in the Quarter, they finally focused more intently on their acquisition of Commander's Palace. They redesigned the interior, large windows replaced walls, and they added on custom-built trellises and commissioned paintings to dress up the walls. The biggest change came when they hired seriously innovative chefs like Paul Prudhomme, Gerard Maras, and Emeril Lagasse. Decades ahead of the curve, these chefs introduced the idea of an ever-changing menu based on seasonality of local, farm-to-table foodstuffs. This was nothing shy of a revolution in the New Orleans restaurant scene.

The height of Commander's national and international acclaim came during Chef Jamie Shannon's tenure. He had replaced Emeril Lagasse as executive chef. In 1995, *Food & Wine* named Commander's the No. 1 restaurant in America. The following year, the restaurant won the coveted James Beard Foundation

Outstanding Restaurant Award. In 1999, the James Beard foundation named Shannon the Best Chef in the Southeast while the *Robb Report* claimed him as the number two chef in the entire world. A cloud overtook the restaurant in 2003 when Chef Shannon contracted cancer and died a year later. He was forty years old.

The hiring of Tory McPhail and the need to put the restaurant back together after Katrina (it took over a year) refocused the spirit of Commander's. The restaurant today still serves long-term classics like its third-generation sherry-spiked turtle soup, shrimp rémoulade, and the command-performance bread pudding soufflé. But the menu is intertwined with new dishes like a dome-shaped pastry filled with oysters poached in absinthe, artichokes, bacon, and cream; their foie gras "du Monde" (seared duck liver, foie-gras–infused café au lait, blackberry beignets); and anything from the Chef's Playground, a new menu every night where the chefs experiment with new ideas.

Commander's offers weekend brunches with live music and on weekdays (lunch only), you make your own music with their 25-cent martinis. Limit six, though two would put me under the table. You will never have better service. Anywhere. And a final bonus is calling for a reservation. Jimmy Boudreaux, the effervescent voice on the other end of the line, has his own fan club.

REASON TO GO: To not go would be like going to Green Bay and skipping Lambeau Field or Amarillo and not seeing Cadillac Ranch.

WHAT TO GET: Start with a reservation with Jimmy; end with the bread pudding soufflé.

COPELAND'S CHEESECAKE BISTRO

2001 St. Charles Ave. • (504) 593-9955 • $$

HOURS: 11:00 a.m.–10:00 p.m. Sun–Thurs; 11:00 a.m.–11:00 p.m. Fri and Sat

As a chain with at one time over forty locations in twelve states, now cut back to about half that number, I have a hard time including Copeland's in this book. That Al Copeland Investments also owns a few Best Western Hotels and comedy clubs makes it even harder. Their food is likewise rather un-noteworthy. But Al Copeland's story overcomes any shortcomings. He's sort of the Wayne Newton meets Donald Trump meets Liberace meets Phil Spector of the New Orleans restaurant scene. What a horrifying image.

He began as a rather unremarkable donut prince ("king" is too elevated). Then he had the idea to compete with Colonel Sanders's KFC chain, launching Chicken on the Run. His trademark phrase was, "So fast, you get your chicken before you get your change." After six months, he realized he was getting crushed by the Colonel, so reinvented his chain with a spicier Louisiana Cajun–style chicken and renamed it Popeye's Mighty Good Fried Chicken. Now renamed Popeye's Louisiana Kitchen, there are today over 1,600 locations.

When he tried to go "upscale" with non-fast-food restaurants, Al famously got into a bitter feud with New Orleans's famed vampire novelist, Anne Rice. They each had the money and notoriety to exchange very public body blows. She took out a full-page ad in the *Times-Picayune* to bash his just-opened Straya. She wrote of his art deco, neon-embellished restaurant, "Let me express my personal humiliation, regret and sorrow for the absolutely hideous Straya's restaurant which has opened its doors. This monstrosity in no way represents the ambiance, the romance or the charm that we seek to offer you and strive to maintain in our city. Flop houses have more dignity than Straya."

Copeland snapped back that he wouldn't recognize Rice if she were one of the waitresses in his restaurant, then slapped her with a four-page lawsuit and took out his own two-page ad, stating he "planned to add a little extra garlic in the food at Straya" to keep her away.

Even in death, Al Copeland flamboyantly sought controversy. Plans to raze his opulent home in Metairie and create a memorial park with a performance stage and large statue of Al holding a box of stone-carved chicken have met with horrified/outraged neighbors. So far Copelandia (it's not really called that) remains unrealized architectural sketches.

REASON TO GO: A drive-by will do.

WHAT TO GET: An art deco, neon image of what all the fuss was about.

♛ COQUETTE

2800 Magazine St. • (504) 265-0421 • $$$

HOURS: 11:30 a.m.–3:00 p.m., 5:00–10:00 p.m. Tues–Sun; 5:00–10:00 p.m. Mon

On my first visit to Coquette, I had a very simple red and green tomato sandwich with garlic mayonnaise on house-made toast. That no-frills sandwich made me a lifelong fan of Coquette. It was practically perfect.

In 2008, Chef Michael Stoltzfus and Lillian Hubbard opened the restaurant on a busy (for New Orleans) corner of Magazine and Washington where there'd previously been a grocery store, an auto parts store, and a chef's graveyard as a stream of restaurants opened and closed. With great reviews six feet deep, a growing entourage of regular patrons, and now a 2013 James Beard nomination for Chef Michael, Coquette seems destined to buck the trend.

Two weeks before he was to go to college, Michael's mother decided to open a bakery/breakfast spot in Maryland and enlisted his help. Previously, he knew little more than how to scramble an egg, but working at his mom's place, he discovered his passion. Michael devoured cookbooks, was constantly experimenting in the kitchen, and landed a few jobs in neighborhood restaurants. Then, he got his break, being hired by Restaurant August in New Orleans, where he was promoted to sous-chef within the first half year.

Since opening his own place, Chef Michael still enjoys experimenting and playing around with personalized tasting menus and five-course blind tastings. He's served grilled beef heart at least two ways: with chanterelle mushrooms and pickled peaches, or with giardiniera horseradish and satsuma. But if grilled beef heart doesn't cause yours to flutter, he's working on a first smoked and then fried chicken.

REASON TO GO: A rising star chef, clearly having fun.

WHAT TO GET: A tomato sammitch or grilled beef heart with giardiniera horseradish—you have a range of options.

EMERIL'S DELMONICO

1300 St. Charles Ave. • (504) 525-4937 • $$$
HOURS: 6:00–9:00 p.m. Sun–Thur; 6:00–10:00 p.m. Fri and Sat

In 1998, Emeril refurbished and reopened Delmonico, a classic century-old icon of traditional Creole dining since 1895. The original menu is framed and displayed near the front door. For my personal taste, the new interior is too expansively ecru, but it's a clean look, the staff is inviting, and the food is excellent.

Anthony Scanio was named chef de cuisine in 2012 and has revamped the modern Creole menu, including house-made charcuterie, dry-aged steaks, and updated Creole classics. Here you can order a wealth of dishes with which you may not be familiar. Soppressata Calabrese is hand-cut Southern Italian–style dry-cured salami with chile and anise. Capocollo is cured pork shoulder, aged three months. And the perfect (for some) lingua is a red-wine-cured beef tongue salumi. You can also have the Bacalao Beignets, which aren't even a distant cousin of what you get at Café Du Monde. It's house-cured salt cod, pickled okra, and rémoulade sauce . . . in a fry bread.

Even the drinks at Delmonico sound like a meal. Creole 75 is gin, fresh basil, mango puree, and prosecco. The Matador is Absolut, jalapeño, fresh cilantro and lime, and ginger beer. Delmonico has been rated a top ten craft cocktail bar in America, as well as a top ten steak house.

REASON TO GO: Very contemporary Creole in a very classic hundred-plus-year-old setting.

WHAT TO GET: You know that lingua is calling to you.

IGNATIUS EATERY

3121 Magazine St. • (504) 899-0242 • $$

HOURS: 11:00 a.m.–10:00 p.m. Sun–Thur; 11:00 a.m.–11:00 p.m. Fri and Sat

The original Ignatius Eatery opened in a shoe box masquerading as an old corner grocery a few blocks down Magazine Street. When a liquor license was approved for the location on Magazine where stood the coffee shop Rue de la Course, both owned by Jerry Roppolo, he used the opportunity to bring Ignatius to the larger space where the restaurant could serve alcohol. Some coffee addicts and would-be novelists tried to stage an Occupy Ignatius sit-in to keep their free-Wi-Fi coffeehouse. But with little coverage (I think my last sentence doubled their press), the "movement" fizzled.

Now resituated, Ignatius has a menu that's largely the same as before. They do New Orleans standards like roast beef po' boys, gumbo, and shrimp Creole mixed in with the slightly less prevalent boudin meat loaf or shrimp rémoulade po' boys.

REASON TO GO: Join the anti-anti-Ignatius movement.

WHAT TO GET: *What do we want? Meat loaf! When do we want it? Now!*

IRISH HOUSE

1432 St. Charles Ave. • (504) 595-6755 • $$

HOURS: 11:00 a.m.–10:00 p.m. Sun–Thur; 8:00 a.m.–10:00 p.m. Fri and Sat

They call themselves an Irish gastropub, meaning they serve high-quality food, not that you'll be farting up a storm after the fifth Guinness. This is not a pint-and-potatoes kind of place. Well, you can get potatoes here, but they'll be prepared by an actual chef, Matt Murphy (no relation).

As a teen, Dublin-born Murphy worked double shifts between his grandfather's restaurant and his father's pastry shop. Matt went on to study culinary arts at the prestigious Cathal Brugha College, then worked in top restaurants, such as the Restaurant in London and the Tea Room in Ireland. He went east as a young man, went east. In China, Thailand, and Hong Kong, he learned new flavors and cooking styles. In Hawaii, he developed a mastery of preparing and cooking fish. "Looking back, I can see that all of my travels, all of those techniques I learned across the globe, were preparing me for my career in New Orleans. Someone once told me that New Orleans cuisine is more than a fusion of different cooking styles, it's a fusion of cultures." Here in New Orleans, Chef Matt worked as sous-chef at Commander's Palace before becoming the chef de cuisine then executive chef at the Ritz-Carlton's restaurant, which the hotel renamed M Bistro in his honor. M Bistro was ranked as one of the top four farm-to-table hotel restaurants by *Travel + Leisure*. Chef Matt has been named Best Chef in the Southwest by La Chaîne des

Rôtisseurs, as well as winner of the New Orleans Wine & Food Experience's Grand Tasting for six years in a row, and he was a 2012 season champion on *Chopped*.

At Irish House, you can get the more typical shepherd's pie, bangers and mash, corned beef, and beer-battered fish-and-chips, but also Chef Matt's New Orleans fusion dishes like boudin cake with colcannon and smoked tomato sauce.

REASON TO GO: New Orleans's best Irish fare.

WHAT TO GET: You can get some pints of Gat at the bar, but by Jaysus, don't get all ossified before you sample Chef's excellent food.

JOEY K'S

3001 Magazine St. • (504) 891-0997 • $

HOURS: 11:00 a.m.–9:00 p.m. Mon–Sat

Joey K's has been a classic neighborhood joint since 1992. They've been voted Best Lunch and Best Red Beans & Rice by readers of *Gambit Weekly*. Their menu is all the local jambalaya and oyster po' boys, plus what could be described as Southern Casual: fried pork chops and white beans, turkey with stuffing, yams and green beans, lima beans simmered with a ham hock. The portions are massive; they have an all-you-can-eat catfish deal every day. The prices are minimal. The wait staff is amusing.

LA DIVINA

3005 Magazine St. • (504) 342-2634 • $

HOURS: 11:00 a.m.–9:00 p.m. Sun–Thur; 11:00 a.m.–10:00 p.m. Fri and Sat

While living in Florence, Italy, Katrina and Carmelo Turillo fell in love with the leisurely Italian way of life. Often, an evening stroll included a scoop or two of Italian ice cream, gelato. The couple traveled across Italy and studied the artisanal method of making gelato and sorbetto from scratch. La Divina Gelateria opened in 2007, after two yearlong delays because of Hurricane Katrina. La Divina is the only place in the state of Louisiana to make gelato from scratch without using any pastes, powders, or bases. The results are captured in the following endorsements:

"Amazing."
—Alton Brown

"The best Italian ice cream and sorbet I've ever tasted."
—Chef John Besh

"Some of the best gelato artisans in the United States."
—*New York Post*

Slim Goodies' irregular regulars

SLIM GOODIES

3322 Magazine St. • (504) 891-3447 • $
HOURS: 6:00 a.m.–3:00 p.m. 7 days a week

Slim Goodies serves breakfast food all day, or at least until they close at 3:00 p.m. Slim Goodies opens very early, 6:00 a.m., so is the breakfast joint of choice for any Uptowners who can't wait for the laggards at Camellia Grill (8:00 a.m.) or Refuel (7:00 a.m.). Their best egg dishes are smothered in anything from chili, black beans, or bacon to hash browns or cheese. There are many vegetarian options, including a tofu omelet covered in vegan chili or smoked tempeh (a fermented soybean cake). Burgers are also available for lunch and have cool names like the Low Carbonator and a bacon and blue cheeseburger named after Fluxus artist Robert Johnson for reasons no one seems to know. The waitstaff has been elsewhere called disinterested or apathetic. I disagree and find them sheepishly engaging. The walls are covered in cool woodblock and retro-type posters surrounded by hundreds of taped-up Polaroids, many pictures of pug dogs. Having had six pug dogs in my life, I feel right at home.

> **REASON TO GO:** Breakfast food all day.
> **WHAT TO GET:** Definitely try the St. Louie Slammer (hash browns, eggs, and bacon, all smothered with house-made crawfish étouffée).

Tom Fitzmorris

When you first move to New Orleans, or come for an extended stay, radio station WWOZ (90.7 FM) becomes your soundtrack to the city. They play twenty-four-hour New Orleans music, both historic and contemporary. But the Voice of New Orleans, as far as food goes, is Tom Fitzmorris. Monday through Friday, 3:00 till 6:00 p.m., he hosts *The Food Show*, a call-in radio show (1350 AM). And he's been doing it since 1975.

The show is similar in format and feel to the ubiquitous sports call-in shows, where both regular and new callers fill the air with questions, opinions, and the occasional argument. Only instead of the talk being about who's better, LeBron James or Kobe Bryant, or reminiscing about Mickey Mantle, Tom and his callers debate where to get the best gumbo (Tom's is Mr. B's gumbo ya-ya; callers split the vote among the Gumbo Shop, Galatoire's, Li'l Dizzy's, and Dooky Chase's; I favor Casamento's) or the host and callers fondly remember the no-longer-open great restaurants of yesteryear like Mandich and Uglesich's. Tom also provides cooking tips, informs listeners where to get difficult-to-find dishes to eat or ingredients to cook, offers his strongly held opinions, and, like a Facebook friend you've never met, shares the intimate details of his life. Knowing he was born on Mardi Gras Day or that his dog's name is Popcorn seems okay. But should I be privy to his weight (a claimed 232 pounds), or that he has an arthritic big toe, or what he and his wife did on the night of their wedding anniversary (watched *Jackass*)?

Tom and his show have their detractors. Many feel he's too old and conservative for the contemporary New Orleans food scene. Some just don't like *him*, as he can be curt with some callers while talking long-windedly over others. Websites debate if he's a "relevant foodie commentator or pompous arse?" I had my own moment with Tom as he initially agreed to be a judge for Appendix A but then withdrew his commitment when he grasped that his opinions would be joined by others, claiming such a list was "useless." I guess the Oscars, Grammys, James Beard Awards, and Nobel Peace Prize are all useless because they're chosen by committee. But like the famed sportscaster Howard Cosell, love him or hate him, you can't dismiss him. Tom is a part of the conversation here in New Orleans. And you can't argue Tom's encyclopedic knowledge of our food culture.

At this risk of utter hyperbole (a risk I'm always willing to take), I'll offer the opinion that Tom Fitzmorris is representative of New Orleans itself. A little out of step, provincially self-loving, at times fussy, and while Tom is never without a jacket and tie, he manages to look like the Napoleon House, dressed up but ready to collapse into a heap at any moment.

The mere existence of *The Food Show* makes me love New Orleans even more. What other city would dare break up ESPN's slick twenty-four-hour sports coverage for three hours of rambling conversation about local restaurants and recipes?

STEIN'S DELI

2207 Magazine St. • (504) 527-0771 • $
HOURS: 7:00 a.m.–7:00 p.m. Tues–Fri; 9:00 a.m.–5:00 p.m. Sat and Sun

Stein's has no competition as the best Jewish (and Italian) deli in New Orleans. Literally. Kosher Cajun is outside the city limits. To the good, the shelves are lined with hard-to-find food items. They have a treasure trove of drinks: sodas, teas, mash, and egg creams, plus more than 450 beers that you can buy there, but, until Stein's gets a license, you cannot drink on premises. To the less good, without competition, their corned beef, pastrami, brisket, or chicken liver are all "fine" but will not be impressive if you're visiting from New York, Chicago, or a city that has a more evolved deli tradition. To the much less than good, the matzo ball soup tastes like dishwater (I've given it three tries).

> REASON TO GO: Best Jewish deli in New Orleans, if you must have Jewish deli food while in the Holy Land of seafood, Cajun, and Creole cuisine.
> WHAT TO GET: Something off the well-stocked shelves.

SUCRÉ

3025 Magazine St. • (504) 520-8311 • $
HOURS: 8:00 a.m.–10:00 p.m. Sun–Thurs; 8:00 a.m.–12:00 a.m. Fri and Sat

Sucré is an emporium of everything sugar—gelato, chocolate, and what they do absolutely best, macaroons. The confection shop also has their ultimate and gloriously excessive treat: the All Things NOLA Sundae. It starts with a base of classic bread pudding made with yesterday's croissants and brioche and topped with butter-pecan gelato. Then on goes Bananas Foster sauce, with crystallized pecans and a drizzle of Steen's as the finishing touches.

The website claim "We are *the* dessert place in New Orleans!" is easily dismissed by two words: Angelo and Brocato's.

> REASON TO GO: It's *one of* the better dessert places in New Orleans.
> WHAT TO GET: The macaroons.

SURREY'S

1418 Magazine St. • (504) 524-3828 • $$
4807 Magazine St. • (504) 895-5757 • $$
HOURS: 8:00 a.m.–3:00 p.m. 7 days a week

Surrey's has two locations, both on Magazine Street. Owner Greg Surrey was actually hoping to siphon off some of his customers from 1418 Magazine when he opened the second Surrey's three miles down the road. He felt he was frustrating and possibly losing customers because the wait lines were too long.

As much as any dish, Surrey's is known for its extensive list of fresh-squeezed juices. They have numerous vegetarian options. Their tofu breakfast platter, which features blocks of ginger-tinged tofu and sautéed vegetables over brown rice, swings both ways, equally appealing to vegetarians and serious carnivores. The meat-on-meat-on-meat corned beef hash with crumbled andouille and bits of boudin is strictly and passionately carni-only. Most dishes have a little flair. French toast is stuffed with caramelized apples, eggs Benedict was sauce on eggs on sheets of hog's head cheese on a scone drizzled with bacon. The bagels are homemade.

> REASON TO GO: Not no waiting, but now less waiting for a great breakfast.
> WHAT TO GET: Their juice is better than even the dollar-an-ounce gourmet juice you buy at Whole Foods. Their shrimp and grits are right up there with New Orleans's best.

TRACEY'S

2604 Magazine St. • (504) 897-5413 • $$
HOURS: 11:00 a.m.–10:00 p.m. Sun–Thurs; 11:00 a.m.–12:00 a.m. Fri and Sat

Tracey's is payback. Owner Jeff Carreras had been running Parasol's, a bar and po' boy shack, for twelve years when the owners chose to sell it. Jeff was outbid by John and Thea Hogan, an absentee couple living in Florida. Carreras responded by reopening Tracey's just around the corner, and bringing Parasol's famous roast beef po' boy recipe with him.

Tracey's takes its name from the original and oldest Irish Channel bar. The new Tracey's has become *the* place to see a football or basketball game with a lively crowd watching one of the twenty TVs or eating the advertised "Best Roast Beef Po' Boy on Earth!"

> REASON TO GO: Catch the game.
> WHAT TO GET: Roast beef po' boy.

Zapp's Potato Chips

Ron Zappe graduated from Texas A&M University with a degree in industrial engineering and became a distributor of pumps and other oil-field equipment. But his four companies went bankrupt during the 1980s oil bust. As he was sitting around, trying to figure out "what's next?," his wife came home from the grocery store with a bag of kettle chips. He'd never before tasted the thicker, sturdier, caramelized flavor of kettle chips and fell so immediately in love, he chose to dedicate the rest of his professional life to making them.

"My wife, Anne, thought I'd gone nuts," Mr. Zappe once said. The banks shared Anne's initial reaction and the first ten lenders "all laughed me out of the office," he recounted. "The eleventh finally gave me my start. I never gave up. That's the secret."

Zappe bought the former Faucheux Chevrolet dealership in Gramercy, just outside New Orleans, where he began making his own thicker-cut, kettle-fried potato chip cooked in peanut oil. Appearing on *Oprah* in '97, he retold Zapp's Chips' inauspicious beginnings: "We made chips on the showroom floor and teenagers would park outside, watch us like a movie, and do a lot of kissing."

Zappe's first creation, the Spicy Cajun Crawtator, was introduced in 1985 as the nation's first spicy Cajun chip. Zapp's markets itself using its Cajun heritage, with other flavors such as Voodoo, Sour Cream and Creole Onion, and Cajun Dill Gator-tators, in addition to their regular flavors, Hot N' Hotter Jalapeño, Salt & Vinegar, Mesquite BBQ, and their newest, Baby Back Rib. They have also marketed limited-edition chips such as Mardi Gras, Who Dat (in honor of the Saints), and Tiger Tators (Crawtators packaged in an LSU-designed bag). Other flavors didn't catch on. "We did a Key Lime flavor. That was one of our *most* limited editions." Twice they've tried pizza flavors that just didn't take.

Today Zapp's uses 120,000 pounds of potatoes each day and fries them in nearly 8,000 pounds of peanut oil.

Former industrial engineer turned entrepreneur Ron Zappe also turned into a tireless promoter. Early on, he would stand in the middle of busy intersections, handing out bags of his chips. His business card was a coupon for a free bag of chips. He received national attention in '88, using Vice President Dan Quayle's spelling bee gaff to develop a job-creation campaign co-created by his potato*e*-chip company and Quayle.

One of the chips' slogans was, "It'll make ya want to kiss your horse . . . or spouse . . . or both." Not sure what that means, but I get the spirit of the comment. Tru dat.

CHAPTER 8

Central City

We must have a pie. Stress cannot exist in the presence of a pie.

—David Mamet

I came down here originally in 1972 with some drunken fraternity guys and had never seen anything like it—the climate, the smells. It's the cradle of music: it just flipped me. Someone suggested that there's an incomplete part of our chromosomes that gets repaired or found when we hit New Orleans. Some of us just belong here.

—John Goodman, actor and New Orleans resident

Not to be confused with Central Business District, Central City has been an on-again, off-again neighborhood for a few decades, and currently is evolving to become . . . well, it's not exactly clear what it's becoming. The formerly depressed neighborhood still has feral houses, where overgrown ivy seems to be the only thing holding them upright. There remain many vacant buildings, but they're mixed in with new condo developments. Hip art galleries and art spaces like the Zeitgeist Arts Center and the Three Ring Circus Gallery seem to feed off the edgy quality of the current neighborhood. The future is looking up as the Southern Museum of Food & Beverage has chosen a spot in Central City as its new home. They were formerly located in the Riverwalk Marketplace, a mall that looked like an airline concourse and featured stores like Foot Locker, the Gap, and Brookstone. I called it a piece of Akron, Ohio, dropped upon New Orleans. Yes, I'm trying to lose readers, one city at a time. There will also be a culinary library at a separate address associated with the museum. Freret Street, which may or may not be considered part of Central City (it's hard to tell in this area), is thriving with new restaurants, including our best burger and hot dog joints. Cool restaurants such as Casa Boregga, our most funky-beautiful setting, are spouting up along O. C. Haley Boulevard. It's a bit off the beaten path and may seem scary for tourists, but (a) the neighborhood is more tired than dangerous—I call it Blight-Lite; and (b) you're a traveler, not a tourist.

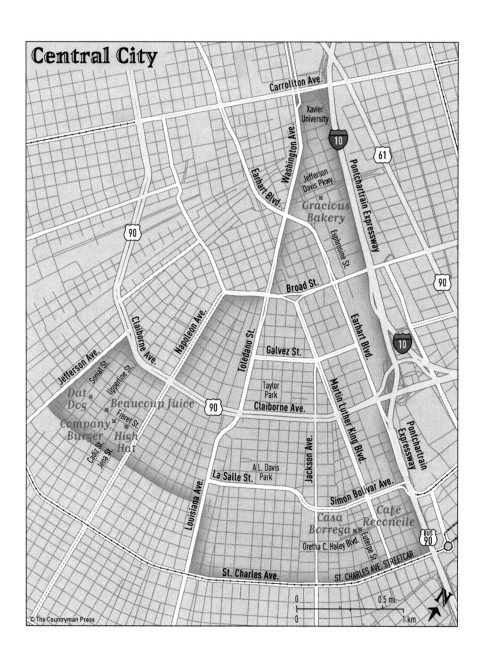

Central City

Carrollton Ave.

Xavier University

Jefferson Davis Pkwy.

Gracious Bakery

Broad St.

Euphrosine St.

Galvez St.

Washington Ave.

Earhart Blvd.

Pontchartrain Expressway

Claiborne Ave.

Napoleon Ave.

Toledano St.

Taylor Park

Claiborne Ave.

Earhart Blvd.

Martin Luther King Blvd.

Jefferson Ave.

Soniat St.

Upperline St.

Dat Dog

Beaucoup Juice

Freret St.

Company Burger

High Hat

Cadiz St.

Jena St.

Louisiana Ave.

La Salle St.

A.L. Davis Park

Jackson Ave.

Pontchartrain Expressway

Simon Bolivar Ave.

Casa Borrega

Cafe Reconcile

Oretha C. Haley Blvd.

Euterpe St.

St. Charles Ave.

ST. CHARLES AVE. STREETCAR

| 0 | 0.5 mi. |
| 0 | 1 km |

© The Countryman Press

BEAUCOUP JUICE

4719 Freret St. • (504) 430-5508 • $
HOURS: 11:00 a.m.–7:00 p.m. Mon–Sat

Dylan Williams had a run-of-the-mill career going in phone and Internet sales until trips to Central America introduced him to fresh fruit smoothie stands on every corner and inspired him to create a New Orleans sno-ball stand with fresh fruit blends. A New Orleans sno-ball is what elsewhere might be called a snow cone, or flavored ice. But just as there's pizza and there's New York pizza, the New Orleans version is a different food group, with gourmet homemade syrups poured over finely shaved ice and topped with can cream or sweetened condensed milk.

Williams sources from local providers, especially Edible Schoolyard, a nearby elementary school with a food-centric curriculum. Dylan names his sno-balls after local legends like a psychedelic-colored blend of orange and beet with ginger he calls the Night Tripper after musician-icon Dr. John. On site he has no liquor license, but if hired for weddings or off-site events, he can whip up his piña colada or fresh juice mojito sno-balls.

CASA BORREGA

1719 Oretha Castle Haley Blvd. • (504) 427-0654 • $$
HOURS: 11:00 a.m.–3:00 p.m., 5:00 p.m.–12:00 a.m. Wed–Sat; 11:00 a.m.–3:00 p.m. Sun

Hugo Montero, a local artist and first-time restaurateur, and his wife Linda Stone, co-founder of the Green Project and director of the New Orleans office of Global Green, have totally refurbished a nineteenth-century house into a dreamland. For Linda's green dream, everything in the interior is salvaged, recycled, and repurposed including the handmade tables, the stained glass, iron chandeliers from Mexico, LP album covers decorating the walls, plenty of ceramic skulls, and the most beautiful ceiling fan I have ever seen. Hugo told me he spotted the fan in a hotel lobby in Cuba. For Hugo's dream, he said the restaurant is his art installation, a labor of love on which he worked for four years. It is, in my mind, the most beautiful restaurant setting in New Orleans. You could spend the entire meal just taking in the rotary phones used as decorative accents, the fanged two-headed piñata riding in an antique child's car, and the little altars everywhere.

The menu springs from what Hugo remembers of his mother's kitchen and street food in Mexico City, his hometown before he moved here twenty-five years ago. He received his US citizenship the day we ate at the restaurant. Linda showed us her cell-phone picture of Hugo holding his citizenship papers standing in front of the flag. No extra charge.

Hugo Montero inside his art installation/restaurant

The food is "real" Mexican food, very unlike what you may be used to. Sounding like Leah Chase and her dismissal of sticky gumbo as not "real Creole," Hugo states, "I adore Tex-Mex, but it's not Mexican." Don't ask for burritos. "No one ever ate burritos where I'm from," notes Hugo. Casa Borrega's menu, prepared by a young chef, Fernando Gutierrez, features antijitos, Mexican appetizers such as tostadas, gorditos, panuchos, and griddled masa cakes called sopes. The traditional entrees include the namesake Borrega, slow-braised lamb with a slight buzz, cooked in tequila and mescal, and for God's sake get anything with the not-too-sweet mole sauce. Side bowls made from (recycled) hollowed-out gourds are filled with black beans and guacamole several continents better than anything served at Don Pablo's or Chi-Chi's.

But the showstopper was the first thing served, the Coctel de Camarones, a shrimp cocktail appetizer served in a large rococo blue Mexican margarita glass. With at least six or seven large shrimp served with avocado, cilantro, onions, celery, garlic, and crushed tomatoes in what could pass for the best tomato soup ever, it tempted me to skip the meal and tell the waitress, "Bring me another and leave the bottle on the table."

Latin jazz or Afro-Caribbean bands perform on Friday and Saturday nights, completing what Hugo and Linda call their *peña* rather than merely a restaurant. *Peña* is a Mexican word meaning a community meeting place where artistic expressions, accompanied by food and drink, are showcased. The only English word of caution is "price." Be prepared to pay for "real" Mexican food rather than Taco Bell. It's not expensive compared with most Creole restaurants, and not expensive for what you'll be served. Hugo bemoans having to charge over $20 for top entrees ($7 to $9 for appetizers), but many of his authentic Mexican ingredients can't be locally sourced. He told us, "My mother would *kill* me if she saw what I was charging!"

REASON TO GO: Just sitting and looking around should come with a bill, but you also get great, as in *the best*, Mexican food this city has.

WHAT TO GET: I recommend anything with mole sauce. I demand you order a Coctel de Camarones.

CAFÉ RECONCILE
1631 Oretha Castle Haley Blvd. • (504) 568-1157
HOURS: 11:00 a.m.–2:30 p.m., 5:30–10:30 p.m. 7 days a week

Café Reconcile is a good restaurant and a better cause. Initiated by Reverend Harry Thompson in 1996, in addition to the street-level restaurant, the five-story building houses a twelve-week training program for at-risk youth between the ages of sixteen and twenty-two.

Formerly homeless or addicted or troubled in any number of ways, young people are taught life skills, interpersonal skills, and work skills, enabling and empowering them to successfully enter the workforce. Reconcile has graduated more than six hundred students, placing them in restaurants all over New Orleans, including Acme, Arnaud's, and Emeril's. But you come for the very affordable food as much as the cause. They're known for their meat loaf and garlic mashed potatoes, white beans and shrimp, desserts, and cornbread. Jan and Michael Stern's respected *Roadfood* wrote of the restaurant, "Café Reconcile is a worthy *Roadfood* beacon simply because it is a great place to eat, home of Creole soul food."

REASON TO GO: For the cause.
WHAT TO GET: The Blue Plate Special.

COMPANY BURGER

4600 Freret St. • (504) 267-0320 • $
HOURS: 11:00 a.m.–3:00 p.m., 5:00–10:00 p.m. Wed–Mon; closed Tues

Why Company Burger is different from any other burger joint I've ever been to starts with the fact that it has an actual chef. Adam Biderman is obsessive about producing the perfect burger. All of the meats—the lamb, the turkey, and brisket mixed with chuck—he uses for his burgers are bought locally and ground in house. All are antibiotic-free and hormone-free. They make their own pickles. They resource locally made buns, baked the same day you'll eat them. Don't ask for tomato slices if out of season; Company Burger won't serve them. Hand-cut and twice-baked fries, onion rings, tater tots, and sweet-potato fries are regular sides, and there are seasonal offerings like fried okra fingers served with sharp vinegar. But the showstopper is Adam's self-serve condiment bar. In addition to ketchup and Creole mustard, it offers a half dozen house-made mayos, including bacon mayo, roasted garlic mayo, and basil mayo. All of them (yes we tried all of them in one sitting) enhance the flavor of the burger or fries without overwhelming them. Unlike McDonald's or Burger King, Company Burger has a liquor license, so you can have $7 drinks like the old-fashioned Rum & Coke (house-made Mexican Coca-Cola reduction with Old New Orleans Amber Rum, Angostura bitters, Peychaud's bitters, and orange). But we preferred the subtly sweet Mae-Mae's Iced Tea Punch, which may be more addictive than any of the hard stuff.

While waiting for your burger or devouring the burgers, you can choose to read a book from the first-rate cookbook library on the counter. We chose Gabrielle Hamilton's *Blood, Bones, & Butter*, which Anthony Bourdain called "simply the best memoir by a chef ever. Ever." They, amazingly, also display and invite mayo-covered fingers to flip through pages of *Modernist Gourmet*, called "a masterpiece . . . the most important cookbook of the 21st century," which retails for a mere $625.

> REASON TO GO: Best burgers in this or any other town.
> WHAT TO GET: You get to choose a single or a double, both with American cheese, and you can add a fried egg (+$1) or bacon (+$2), but you *must* have the mayo.

DAT DOG

5030 Freret St. • (504) 899-6883 • $
3336 Magazine St. • (504) 324-2226 • $
HOURS: 10:30 a.m.–10:00 p.m. 7 days a week

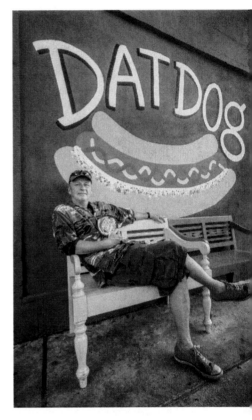

Skip Murray, the Hot Dog King

Skip Murray returned to New Orleans after Katrina, having been on a twenty-seven-year hiatus in London. Across the pond, he ran the Real American Hot Dog Company and was the unofficial and self-appointed Hot Dog King of the UK. Back in New Orleans, he reconnected with high-school friends Constantine Georges and Laurence Turk to create a gourmet hot dog stand. Their first location was a shed on Freret Street, where they were an early pioneer in the renewal of a once-vibrant retail area fallen on sedimentary and igneous hard times. The shed has evolved into a hot dog parlor on two sides of the street, and they've opened a second location on Magazine Street.

You'll pay, on average, $7 for a single dog, which may seem like a lot unless you've ordered a limp, luke-cool tube on a two-month-old bun at any major sports stadium. But these are no ordinary dogs. They're purebred beef, pork, bratwurst, or kielbasa, plus alligator sausage, crawfish, a tempura cod Sea Dog, and the beloved Turducken—duck, turkey, and chicken in an unholy alliance on a steamed and toasted bun. They also do a vegetarian chipotle dog. "The biggest complaint about it is that it tastes like meat," Murray says. Toppings include crumbled bacon, guacamole, pico de gallo, hummus, and a green sauce of diced pickled jalapeños, chopped green onions, and chopped white onions, mixed by hand. Yes, there's ketchup and mustard for more tedious taste buds.

Dat Dog has as many varieties of fries as they do dogs. Chili, cheese, bacon, ranch, sour cream, andouille sauce fries, diced tomatoes, guacamole, crawfish étouffée fries, Anna's White Trash Fries in honor of all things white-trashish, and golden brown fries named after "one of their biggest fans," Poppy Tooker Fries.

REASON TO GO: To do it Dat Doggy style.
WHAT TO GET: Well . . . a hot dog. But don't forget their fries.

GRACIOUS BAKERY

1000 S. Jefferson Davis Pkwy. • (504) 301-3709 • $
HOURS: 6:30 a.m.–3:00 p.m. Mon–Fri; 8:00 a.m.–2:00 p.m. Sat

Gracious Bakery is kind of in No Man's Land. There are currently no other restaurants, nor other retail stores, in an area of industrial offices, storage centers, and warehouses. I wasn't even sure whether to place them in the Carrollton chapter or the Mid-City chapter or the Central City chapter, where I've put them with serious reservation, but I knew they had to be included.

Megan Roen Forman, a New Orleans native, cut her cupcake-making teeth in New York. She spent a number of years working in restaurants and patisseries, among them Park Avenue Café and Payard. She then returned home to New Orleans to take a position as pastry chef at Bayona, later joining the pre-opening team of Sucré.

In the fall of 2012, she opened her own spot, Gracious Bakery, what Ian McNulty called "the corner bakery everyone says they want in their neighborhood" except this one has no neighborhood. They are easily overlooked on the ground floor of the new clean and chic (very un–New Orleans–like) headquarters for a local construction company. But, once inside, you are greeted by the bakery case filled with elegant palm-sized Black Forest cakes, slices of peanut butter opera cake, gourmet moon pies, the Doberge of the day (Doberge is a New Orleans–style layer cake), and croissant dough rolled in hazelnut and chocolate and molded into cupcake-sized "cruffins," sometimes called "Kermit Cruffins."

For any reader not yet immersed in New Orleans culture, Kermit Ruffins is royalty here, a local trumpet player some view as the heir apparent to Louis Armstrong. He also had my all-time favorite line in the HBO series *Treme*. In the episode, the Steve Zahn character is trying to convince Kermit to go speak with Elvis Costello to help boost his career. When Kermit seems uninterested, Zahn's character implores, "Don't you want to be famous? Are you standing there telling me that all you want to do is get high, play some trumpet, and barbecue in New Orleans your whole damned life?" Kermit's answer: "That'll work."

Gracious Bakery also functions as a (boutique) lunchtime sandwich shop, serving rosemary-crusted roast beef with horseradish cream cheese and caramelized onion on kaiser roll, meat loaf with tomato jam and cheddar on ciabatta, and ham with pecan cheddar spread, pepper jelly, and apple slices on a baguette. As a baker, Megan's bread absolutely makes the sandwich. The artisan bread also multitasks as the perfect thing to dip into her soups. I've had her eggplant-and-chickpea soup and pumpkin soup. Both were great.

Megan has appeared in the *New York Daily News*, *Pastry Art and Design*, *Modern Bride*, *Chocolatier*, and *Art Culinaire*, and has been selected as a Rising Star Pastry Chef by Starchefs.com. More than being among the best pastry chefs in New Orleans, she is easily the hardest working. I watched one day in amazement as she single-handedly banged out beautifully presented and undoubtedly delicious lunch plates for the twenty-six customers in the small shop (yes, I counted them).

REASON TO GO: To support the up-and-coming, hardest-working pastry chef in New Orleans.

WHAT TO GET: Great pastries, great sandwiches, or a simple baguette (also great).

HIGH HAT CAFÉ

4500 Freret St. • (504) 754-1336 • $$

HOURS: 11:00 a.m.–9:00 p.m. Sun–Thurs, 11:00 a.m.–10:00 p.m. Fri and Sat

New Orleans chef and restaurateur Adolfo Garcia (of La Boca, Rio Mar, and A Mano) teamed up with (or rather harassed) Memphis restaurateur Chip Apperson to open High Hat on the revitalized Freret Street. Apperson had come to New Orleans to retire and renovate a gracious home. "He [Garcia] kept ribbing me, saying, 'Hey, what's this retirement thing?' And truly, I was thinking about the restaurant business every day. I knew that if I went back in a restaurant, it would not be fine dining. I'd seen the success of Soul Fish (in Memphis) and said I'd do something like that, if we could find the right place."

The right place combines Garcia's New Orleans roots and Apperson's Memphis-style soul food. Perhaps it was Garcia's involvement that gave me unrealistic expectations. I thought the meal served was hit and miss and then hit again . . . sometimes on the same plate. Fabulous slow-roasted pork was served with just okay eggs on top and grainy and tasteless grits. Others, like the reviewer for the *Times-Picayune*, have written, "the stone-ground grits are some of the best in the city." So maybe I caught them on a bad day. Sides like collard greens, coleslaw, and okra and tomatoes were all excellent. Their creamy pimiento mac 'n' cheese is the best in New Orleans. But the cornbread was dry and tasteless and the homemade ginger ale is a definite *must not*. They also make a homemade satsuma lemonade that may be worlds better. Others have praised the gumbo ya-ya. We found the dark roux a bit runny and the excess of shallots seemed to be more about presentation than taste.

Our biggest departure came over the oyster rémoulade po' boy. We'd heard

Po' Boys Do Not Live BY Bread Alone

When comparing po' boys, the difference between the best and also-rans is minute. The bread in most every Parkway, Mahony's, or Johnny's sacred spot is zackly the same, coming from zackly the same bakery. Most po' boys in New Orleans, except the gas-station variety, are served on bread baked by Leidenheimer's. George Leidenheimer came to New Orleans from Germany and set up shop in 1896. At first he baked the dense, dark breads of his native land and would have gone out of business before the twentieth century had he not adapted to the tastes of the predominantly French city. More than adapted, he perfected the crispy crust and airy interior of the best French breads and has dominated the New Orleans market for well over one hundred years. Leidenheimer Bread has been baked in the same brick building on Simon Bolivar Avenue since 1904. Their signature trucks with *Vic & Nat'ly* cartoons painted on the side can be seen dropping off bread at nearly every po' boy shop in town.

Vic & Nat'ly is the cartoon strip of New Orleans personality Bunny Matthews.

Bunny is now or has been an artist, a writer, musician, album-cover designer, T-shirt designer, vinyl-record delivery boy, dancer on the John Pela Saturday morning TV show, commissioned mural painter, founding member of Galerie Jules Lafourge, a visionary imagist, the self-taught world's leading anthropologist of Yat culture, and an award-winning talk show host who has interviewed Cab Calloway, Marilyn Chambers, a voodoo priestess, and a couple of dog groomers. His cartoon strip depicting *Vic & Nat'ly*, the Nint' Ward's mos' famous couple, started appearing in the Sunday section of the *Times-Picayune* in 1982. His reputation was born from an earlier strip, *F'Sure—Actual Dialogue Heard on the Streets of New Orleans*, which ran in an independent weekly. His seminal work, sure to live on for generations, is *A Roach's History of New Orleans Hurricane Katrina*. You can buy *Roach's History of New Orleans Hurricane Katrina* designer sneakers for $90 at Bunny Matthews's website.

But I digress . . .

Some will say the term "po' boy" is

High Hat's oyster po' boy was the best in the city. I was initially disappointed. The too-fat bread overwhelmed the contents. By the time my wife finished it off, the gravy and rémoulade had soaked into the bread, making it all work together in a way that had her agreeing it was among the best oyster po' boys in New Orleans.

REASON TO GO: Bluff City meets the Big Easy.
WHAT TO GET: The oyster po' boy . . . then wait a few minutes.

Leidenheimer man delivering the goods

derived from the French word *pourboire*, referring to a tip given to a waiter. But, the by far more popular theory claims that "po' boy" was coined by restaurant owners Benny and Clovis Martin. In 1929, during

a four-month strike against the streetcar company, the Martin brothers, former train conductors, served their past co-workers free sandwiches, often no more than gravy on bread. The Martins referred to the strikers as "poor boys." The sandwiches served to them took on the name.

Typically, the French bread comes in two-foot-long "sticks." Standard sandwich sizes might be a half po' boy, about six inches long (called a "Shorty"), and a full po' boy, at about a foot long. The traditional versions are served hot and include fried shrimp and oysters, soft-shell crab, catfish, crawfish, Louisiana hot sausage, fried chicken breast, and roast beef. Parkway Bakery has perhaps the longest menu and includes meatballs in marinara, corned beef, potato, sweet potato, barbecue, turkey breast, grilled cheese, a Reuben, a surf and turf, and alligator sausage.

Unless you specify otherwise, your po' boy will come "dressed." A dressed po' boy has lettuce, tomato, pickles, and mayonnaise. Having now read this section, I don't want you to ever again say, or even think, "Oh. It's like a grinder or a sub."

Poppy Tooker

To call Poppy Tooker the head cheerleader for New Orleans food culture is sexist and demeaning. To call her ambassador is too formal and stuffy. Advocate, champion, emissary, enthusiast, aficionado don't quite do. Maybe we'll call her Pope Poppy of New Orleans, chief pastor to what is our holy devotion to all things food.

To list all of her accomplishments will exceed the word count in my contract for this book. As a writer, her book *Crescent City Farmers Market Cookbook* was awarded the Eula Mae Dore Tabasco Cookbook Award for its historic content and named Cookbook of the Year by *New Orleans* magazine. *Mme. Begue's Recipes of Old New Orleans Creole Cookery*, first published in 1900, was reissued 112 years later with a new foreword and revised recipes by Poppy Tooker. Her newest book, *Louisiana Eats!*, came out in fall 2013. She's an associate editor of *Louisiana Kitchen & Culture* magazine and also a contributing editor for *Hallmark* magazine. Online, Poppy is a regular contributor to *Zester Daily*. On the airwaves, Poppy's shared the screen with food celebrities such as *Extreme Cuisine*'s Jeff Corwin and *Foodography*'s Mo Rocca and bested Bobby Flay in a seafood gumbo throwdown on the Food Network. On Super Bowl Sunday, Poppy appeared on *CBS Sunday Morning*, making gumbo with New Orleans jazz legend Wynton Marsalis. She has done documentary projects such as *Savouring the World* and *Taste of New Zealand*. The History Channel cast her for the "Holiday Foods" episode of *America Eats*. Poppy was a featured guest on *Dining After Hours* with Chef Daniel Boulud. My guess is, you've seen her.

Locally, Poppy is best known for her twice-weekly radio show on the NPR affiliate, *Louisiana Eats*. As host and producer, she's our Marlin Perkins of *Wild Kingdom* (for any of you old enough) or

Dark Roux Photography LLC

Crocodile Hunter's Steve Irwin (for the rest) as she takes listeners into the fields, the waters, the markets, and kitchens to hear directly from the people who maintain our storied food traditions and create new dishes as a part of Louisiana's rich (irreplaceable) food culture. She also contributes colorful commentary on the WYES weekly arts and entertainment show, *Steppin' Out.*

Foremost, Poppy Tooker is a teacher and historian. She didn't intend to be a professional chef, cookbook author, or radio talk show host. She wanted to be an actress. But while attending the California Institute of the Arts in Los Angeles, she took a detour. "I needed work study so I took a job running the café for the students," Tooker said. "I discovered that food gave me the same thrill as the theater." Thereafter she was classically trained by Madeleine Kamman and awarded both a chef's and cooking teacher's diploma from Kamman's renowned professional course.

For over twenty-five years, Poppy's cooking classes have centered on history and tradition as well as the food science behind her preparation. She has been a mainstay on the Food Heritage stage at the New Orleans Jazz and Heritage Festival. Her teaching has been showcased across the world at the Salone del Gusto in Turin, Italy, and Books for Cooks in London as well as in classes and cooking demonstrations across the United States. She is an integral part of the New Orleans Cooking Experience, weekly classes where visitors can learn from Poppy, Frank Brigtsen, Boo Macomber, Gerard Maras, and other noted local chefs. *Food & Wine* magazine described Poppy: "She may wear ceramic red beans in her ears and make finger puppets out of crawfish, but her class is certainly no joke. Rather, it compels you to take reams of notes so as not to forget a single nugget of her fascinating culinary wisdom."

In '99 Poppy brought the international Slow Food movement to New Orleans by founding the local chapter, one of the first in the United States. She served as an international governor and chair of the US Slow Food Ark and Presidia committee. In 2006 Poppy was the only person ever awarded the Carlo Petrini Slow Food Leadership Award.

Following Hurricane Katrina, Poppy was recognized by the *Times-Picayune* as a "Hero of the Storm." She organized fund-raisers to get traditional food markets, like the Crescent City Farmer's Market, and restaurants, like Dooky Chase's, back on their feet. In 2012, *Southern Living* magazine named Poppy a "Hero of the New South." The International Association of Cooking Professionals recognized Poppy's rebuilding efforts at their annual conference in April 2008, with their first-ever Community Service Award.

In spite of national and international recognition, Poppy Tooker is essentially New Orleans. "I was born and raised here," she said. "This is my place. I love New Orleans like people love their mothers. It's everything to me. I've been all over the world—London, Paris, Rome, San Francisco, Los Angeles, New York. I can't understand why anybody would want to live anywhere else but New Orleans."

CHAPTER 9

Uptown

New Orleans is the one place in America where cooking is considered an art.

—Count Hermann Alexander Graf von Keyserling

Food is symbolic of love when words are inadequate.

—Alan D. Wolfelt

Uptown is becoming our Chevy Chase, Oyster Bay, or San Marino, where there are the best schools, the most chi chi shops, and the highest median income. There's a bumper sticker seen on cars in Bywater and the Marigny that states, "Uptown is becoming a problem." Not that they didn't come from all over town to pay tribute to Uptowner Drew Brees after the Super Bowl win. Drew lives not far from Audubon Park. After the Saints victory, his front gate looked like a Buddhist shrine. Fans left offerings of notes tied to the front fence, flowers, and baked goods. Uptown also has some superstar chefs. Justin Devillier of La Petit Grocery was nominated for 2013's James Beard Award for Best Chef. Gautreau's Sue Zemanick received her fifth nomination!

To the naked eye, where the Garden District ends and Uptown begins is hard to tell. Massive mansions line St. Charles Avenue all the way out past Audubon Park and Tulane. But directions here are always challenging. New Orleans is built at the double crescent of the Mississippi River. All our main thoroughfares double-snake as well. The West Bank is on the east side of the river, unless you are standing in Uptown, which is downtown from the French Quarter, in which case the West Bank is south. Lasalle, who first laid claim for the French king in 1699, couldn't find New Orleans on his return trip. After wandering around lost in the swamp for a year, Lasalle's men killed him. At least once a month I will be driving down a street at sunset and think, "What is the sun doing over there?" and I live here. About the only place where you can always rely on your sense of direction is Lee Circle when you look up at Robert E. Lee's statue. The general is always looking north, vigilantly standing watch to ensure that while New Orleans continues to absorb other cultures, we will never be a Yankee city. The South is a place. East, west, and north are mere directions.

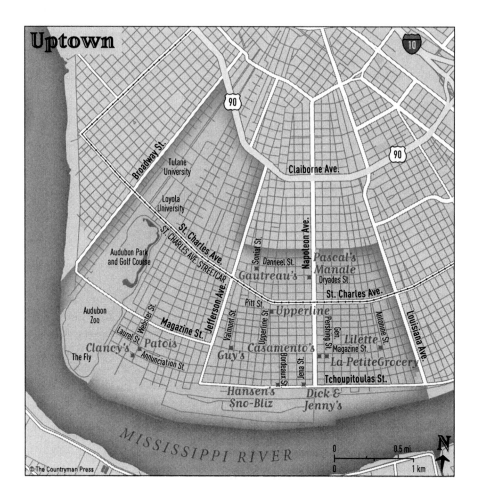

Uptown

Tulane University
Loyola University
Audubon Park and Golf Course
Audubon Zoo
Claiborne Ave.
St. Charles Ave.
Broadway St.
ST. CHARLES AVE. STREETCAR
Magazine St.
Napoleon Ave.
Soniat St.
Danneel St.
Dryades St.
St. Charles Ave.
Jefferson Ave.
Pitt St.
Valmont St.
Upperline St.
Gen. Pershing St.
Antonine St.
Louisiana Ave.
Webster St.
Laurel St.
Annunciation St.
Bordeaux St.
Jena St.
Magazine St.
Tchoupitoulas St.
Pascal's Manale
Gautreau's
Upperline
Lilette
Patois
Clancy's
The Fly
Guy's
Casamento's
La Petite Grocery
Hansen's Sno-Bliz
Dick & Jenny's

MISSISSIPPI RIVER

0   0.5 mi.
0   1 km
N

© The Countryman Press

ALBERTINE'S TEA ROOM

3811 St. Charles Ave. (inside the Columns Hotel) • (504) 899-9308 • $$
HOURS: 7:00–10:00 a.m., 3:00 p.m.–12:00 a.m. (till 2:00 a.m. Fri and Sat)

Just being inside the Columns Hotel makes everything taste better. The Italianate house was commissioned by Simon Hernsheim, owner of the largest cigar manufacturer in the United States at the turn of the twentieth century, and designed by one of New Orleans's great architects, Thomas Sully. The interior is considered the grandest in any nineteenth-century Louisiana residence. It's easily my favorite hotel in New Orleans. The controversial movie *Pretty Baby* (it featured a nekkid twelve-year-old Brooke Shields playing a nekkid twelve-year-old prostitute) was filmed here. You might think *Barton Fink* was as well. The hotel has more personality than Sybil on a double date. Ghosts on the third floor. Wack-a-doodle receptionists on the first.

The cozy Albertine's Tea Room, just off the lobby, is a beautiful room and perfect place to have a leisurely meal. The food is basic "two eggs any style" but that doesn't matter. The setting, with overhead fans, concave mirrors, French stained glass, brass sconces, and whatever you call those round couches that used to be in movie-theater lobbies (love those round couches), takes over.

They have a Sunday Jazz Brunch but an even better daily set-a-spell. In the late afternoon and evening, sitting out on the front veranda with a cigar in one hand, a whiskey in the other, and watching the streetcars slowly roll by is a quintessential New Orleans experience.

REASON TO GO: Beautiful setting.
WHAT TO GET: In sync with the pace of New Orleans.

BISTRO DAISY

5831 Magazine St. • (504) 899-6987 • $$$
HOURS: 6:00–11:30 p.m. Tues–Sat

It is easy to drive or walk by this small, unassuming yellow cottage nestled between private residences and an art supply store. Inside, three rooms have been beautifully converted into dining areas with richly painted walls, hardwood floors, and trompe l'oeil ceilings. Chef Anton Schulte and his wife, Diane, who works the front of the house, are transplants from Anne Kearney's late, great Peristyle restaurant, which she closed when she took her talents to the Dayton, Ohio, area. Chef Anton adds personal tastes and flair to sophisticated dishes like braised lamb leg over goat cheese polenta; grilled red onion, arugula, and pine nuts with a tomato-rosemary ragout; or crispy seared leg of duck confit topped with breast slices over spinach, olive, and almond risotto with clementine marmalade and brandy reduction.

REASON TO GO: To dine on food that rivals any restaurant in New Orleans with 99 percent local residents, many of them regulars, in an intimate and beautiful setting.
WHAT TO GET: Whatever Diane suggests.

♛ CASAMENTO'S

4300 Magazine St. • (504) 895-9761 • $$
HOURS: 11:00 a.m.–2:00 p.m. Tues–Sat; 5:30–9:00 p.m. Thurs–Sat

In a town where we will argue (intensely) about where to get the best gumbo or po' boy, Casamento's is routinely considered the best oyster house. Period. Acme, with its location in the French Quarter, is more popular, particularly with tourists, but Acme can't touch the ambience or the food of Casamento's with a ten-foot shucking knife.

Started in 1919 by Italian immigrant Joseph Casamento and then run for fifty years by his son, also Joseph, the restaurant is now in the hands of great-nephew C. J. Gerdes and his wife Linda. A sleeveless C. J. is always cooking in the kitchen, which you get to walk through if you use their toilets. Linda is always waiting on tables or working the cash register.

Casamento's may be the least romantic restaurant in the city. The decor is floor-to-ceiling white tile (with green accents). The stark floor and walls are shown off in harsh fluorescent lighting. Calvin Trillin described it as "having lunch in a drained swimming pool."

During the hard-to-remember hours they are open, you will undoubtedly have to stand in line before getting a table in one of their two small dining rooms with a total seating capacity of only thirty-three. If you make it to Casamento's after a Saints loss, hold out for the back dining room. Front-room waitress Angela is a passionate Saints fan and will be severely depressed. Be advised to do one of two things while you're waiting for a table: (1) You can practice the art of conversation, and it is an art in New Orleans, with others waiting in line. Or, (2) you can belly up to the oyster bar where the effervescent, gap-toothed Mike Rogers, a five-time city-wide shucking champion, can quickly pop open a dozen raw oysters. He may even make you his "special" dipping sauce with perfectly balanced ketchup, horseradish, Worcestershire, lemon, and hot sauce.

When you do get a table, you'll discover a short menu. Casamento's only offers a few dishes, like oyster loaf, shrimp loaf, and soft-shell crab. But everything they do is simple and excellent (well, maybe the spaghetti is merely passable). Their seafood is fresh, bought locally, and fried immediately before serving. Somehow, even their pan bread is great. Pan bread is nothing more than uncut loaves of Bunny Bread, cut into Texas toast–sized hunks, and sent through the grill. The result of this simple process is perfect for sopping up the last of their exceptional oyster stew or soupy but superb gumbo, a gumbo I'm convinced has healing powers.

If you're in New Orleans during the summer, be forewarned that Casamento's subscribes to the credo, "Raw oysters should only be eaten in months with an R." Since 1919, Casamento's has been closed May through August.

REASON TO GO: Oysters and their gumbo.

WHAT TO GET: A dozen, maybe two, and a bowl, maybe two.

CHARLIE'S STEAK HOUSE

4510 Dryades St. • (504) 895-9705 • $$

HOURS: 5:00–9:30 p.m. Tues–Thurs; 5:00–10:00 p.m. Fri–Sat

To enter Charlie's Steak House, a storied backstreet icon, you first got to get yourself into a New Orleans groove or this place will drive you crazy. As rich as our food and music are, as friendly and resilient as our people are, we admit New Orleans is kind of Third World as a functional city (and that's kind of why we love it). You get your mail . . . or not. Offices and shops are open when they're open. The streetcars come . . . well, that's *if* they come. Charlie's fits right in. The restaurant is a no-rhyme-nor-reason kind of place. There are no menus. There's not much of a staff, usually just one waitress. And many times there's not much food. You order what they have.

Miss Dottye, the spacy but sweet-as-their-spumoni daughter of the steak house's founder, was the one waitress from 1952 until the hurricane in 2005. Though "waitress" may not be the right word. She might ask you how large you wanted your steak and how rare you wanted it cooked. Just as often, she didn't take your order so much as tell you what you were having. If they were out of their famous potatoes au gratin, you were having onion rings. Sometimes your food would show up before you ordered anything because . . . well, that's what they had. Every customer, regulars and first timers, would be blessed with a wave of Miss Dottye's "Sweeties." Then they'd be sprayed with sputtering-hot butter when she brought steaks to the table. First-time diners would often leave the restaurant with a "What just happened?" look.

The steak house remained closed for three years following Katrina. Neighbor Matt Dwyer finally bought Charlie's because he couldn't stand the thought of it not being open. Matt had been their part-time, out of necessity, bartender. Charlie's didn't really have a bar, but did have a liquor license. In crunch times, they'd simply knock on Matt's door and he'd rush over to make and serve drinks. Under his direction, the menu has remained basically unchanged. When they have it, the restaurant still serves chunky blue cheese dressing on wedges of iceberg salad, the same thin and flaky onion rings, and the creamy potatoes au gratin.

The one change: Charlie's now has a wine list, whereas it was a few choices (sometimes) from the boxed wine of the old days.

REASON TO GO: Without Dottye it's not quite as compelling, but their prices are still quite a bit cheaper than other steak houses.

WHAT TO GET: I'm not going there.

Mike Rogers

In the Old West, John Wesley Hardin was often said to be the legendary fastest gun. In the 'hoods of New York, Pee Wee Kirkland is the legendary greatest street basketball player of all time. And in New Orleans, where food is king, Mike Rogers, the five-time oyster-shucking champion, is our local legend. Well . . . I might be overstating that, as nine out of ten natives probably wouldn't know him. But, they have probably eaten from his artistry.

For nearly forty years, Mike Rogers has been shucking oysters, or "heaven on the half-shell," as he calls them, at Uglesich's, Felix's, and Drago's, and now is a fixture at Casamento's. As a thirteen-year-old, he left his spot on the street outside Preservation Hall, shining other people's shoes and dancing with bottle caps affixed to his own, to take up sweeping the floors at one of the city's greatest joints, Uglesich's, or "Ugly's" as it was often called. He was captivated watching Anthony Uglesich and his uncles shuck. When he finally earned the right to open oysters himself, he said it took four months to get the hang of it. At that point, he said, "I had been watching for a year or two."

Shucking, is an art, or at least a skill, by which a closed, seemingly cemented, oyster is prepared for eating. With a sharp knife and a quick, precise hand the hard shell is cracked open, the meat quickly separated from the shell and cleaned, all without damaging the meat. "It's a real skill," said Drago's owner Tommy Cvitanovich. "It's not like you can train somebody and the next week he's a shucker. To open an oyster, to know where the sweet spot on the oyster is, there's nothing but experience that's going to tell you where that spot is. It's not going to take a month or two. It takes years."

The best shuckers, like Mike, do more than open oysters. Lined up front and center behind their counters, the shuckers are also both the knife-wielding maître d' and the night's entertainment. They greet customers and prepare an eat-at-the-counter dozen while regaling diners with stories as they wait for a table. Mike can also prepare you a small cup of what he sells as his "special sauce," made from the exact same ingredients (hot sauce, lemons, ketchup, horseradish) resting on every table in the restaurant.

While not as famous as the chefs, shuckers here have names and reputations. There's Thomas "Uptown T" Stewart at Pascal's Manale and Storm'n Norman at Acme. They were in high demand after Katrina. The biggest hurdle facing restaurants was not getting raw oysters, but finding people to pry them open. Drago's Cvitanovich tracked down Mike Rogers and flew him from San Antonio back to New Orleans. He was only half kidding when he talked about picking Rogers up at the airport in a limousine: "That's how important oyster shuckers are right now."

Mike has his own Katrina tale of wading through neck-deep water filled with oil, snakes, and sewage after his home was flooded. Mike slept under a bridge and then caught a bus to San Antonio. As he tells it, the story is one of inspiration, not despair. "I have a good life," he says, "The only difference between a good day and a bad day is your attitude." And then he might go all lounge singer on you, and break into his favorite song: "Ain't no need to worry what tonight is gonna bring . . . It'll be all over in the morning . . ."

CLANCY'S

6100 Annunciation St. • (504) 895-1111 • $$$

HOURS: 5:30–10:00 p.m. Mon–Sat; 11:30 a.m.–2:00 p.m. Thurs and Fri

When it opened in the 1940s, Clancy's was one of many neighborhood bars serving po' boys. In 1983, with no heirs, Ed and Betty Clancy sold the space to a group of Uptown businessmen who converted it into a white-tablecloth Creole bistro. The menu is not adventurous but is reliably consistent and good with a variety of Creole pork, veal, chicken, lamb, oyster, and crabmeat standards. Brad Hollingsworth, who now owns Clancy's and was earlier a waiter at Galatoire's and LeRuth's, has a sense of how to keep a popular neighborhood spot filled with satisfied regulars and sometimes draw out tourists from the Quarter and Warehouse District. With his passion for wine, he's built up one of the better cellars in the city.

> REASON TO GO: If you're feeling between highbrow establishments like Galatoire's and middlebrow neighborhood joints like Liuzza's, Clancy's is it.

COULIS

3625 Prytania St. • (504) 304-4265 • $

HOURS: 7:00 a.m.–2:00 p.m. 7 days a week

For many years the Bluebird Café was an "insiders'" best breakfast spot. A few years after it closed and in the exact same location, Coulis opened and for many reclaimed the best-breakfast mantle. The original chef and owner, James Lenning, passed away in 2011. He had an impressive resume of having worked in some of the best kitchens in the city: Brigtsen's, Dickie Brennan's, Palace Café, Commander's Palace, and, just prior to opening Coulis, Chef James had been the executive chef at Dick & Jenny's. Having never eaten at Coulis when Chef James executed their meals, I have the unjustifiable opinion that his passing cost Coulis a spot on the Appendix A list of Best Breakfast Spots.

You can still get a good huevos rancheros, grillades and grits, the Ultimate French Toast (stuffed with cream cheese, then topped with caramelized apples, smoked sausage, pecans, maple syrup, and whipped cream), or eggs Benicio, a Cuban version of eggs Benedict (jalapeño cheddar corn cakes topped with pulled pork, two poached eggs, and hollandaise sauce). At lunch, the signature item is the very good Coulis Crispy Cuban Sandwich (pulled pork, smoked ham, pickles, Gruyere, mustard, and chipotle mayonnaise on sourdough bread).

> REASON TO GO: Hallowed ground for great breakfasts.

> WHAT TO GET: The lunchtime Coulis Crispy Cuban.

DICK & JENNY'S

4501 Tchoupitoulas St. • (504) 894-9880

HOURS: 11:00 a.m.–2:00 p.m. Mon–Fri; 5:30–10:00 p.m. Tues–Sat

I hope when you come to New Orleans Dick & Jenny's remains the same restaurant that won my heart as a personal favorite. Dick & Jenny's was recently bought by Cristiano Raffignone and Kelly Barker, owners of Martinque Bistro. They keep issuing scary statements like, "Dick & Jenny's has been there for so long, we don't want customers to think we're coming in and taking it away. We want to get through the summer and get to know everybody." I've been through mergers and acquisitions. "Get to know everybody" is never a comforting statement. Even scarier, Cristiano's executive chef Lindsay Mason will start working with Stacy Hall, the restaurant's current and brilliant and I consider irreplaceable chef. I once asked former owner Will Peters why Stacy hadn't won any awards. He said she simply didn't want to work the James Beard or IACP scene the way actors are required to work for their Oscars and Golden Globes. Scariest of all, by early fall 2013, Dick & Jenny's will start introducing a few of Cristiano's dishes. As a lover of the old version, I am preemptively heartbroken.

Dick & Jenny's is housed in a mustard-yellow mid-nineteenth-century cottage. The outside is strung with cheap Christmas lights and a hand-painted sign. All of this belies the casual elegance, exceptional waiters, and exquisite cuisine on the inside. Dinner plates line the walls and bear the names of Dick & Jenny's founding customers. I've convinced visitors to go there by simply reading their elegantly written menu . . . which the new owners have removed from the website! But, thanks to *Zagat's*:

Men's room at Dick & Jenny's

Seared Duck Breast & Chorizo Sausage with Sweet Potato,
Apple & Brie Gratin, Southern Greens and Cranberry
Demi Glace

Pecan-Crusted Gulf Fish with a Lump Crab & Micro Green
Salad, Creamy Cheese Grits, Smoked Mushrooms & Creole
Meuniere

Warm Shrimp & Chorizo Cheesecake with Black Bean Coulis
& Seared Smoked Shrimp

REASON TO GO: It was my favorite. I feel I now need to "get to know" the
new people.

DOMILISE'S PO-BOY & BAR

5240 Annunciation St. • (504) 899-9126 • $
HOURS: 10:00 a.m.–7:00 p.m. Mon–Wed, Fri, and Sat

Babe Ruth is generally considered the greatest Yankee. There's a strong argument to be made for Lou Gehrig, Joe DiMaggio, or Mickey Mantle. Parkway
Bakery is most often considered the best po' boy in New Orleans. I personally think
it's Killer PoBoys. Domilise's also has a devoted and sizable following that will
never-ever-never consider any other place as serving the best. Sometimes hard to
find (the corner of Annunciation & Bellecastle in a residential area), it has been the
epitome of a neighborhood joint for over seventy years, forever run by the Domilise
family. Since Sam Domilise died in 1981, his wife, Miss Dot, had left her next-door
apartment five days a week to be the longtime friendly face of the restaurant. She
passed away in the summer of 2013. Aside from different family members running
the place, very little has changed since it opened in the 1930s. They did discontinue
their unique pepper wiener when the supplier stopped making them. Otherwise
Domilise has perpetually served the same gravy-drenched roast beef, fried shrimp,
or fried oyster po' boys, and their best-known hot sausage po' boy, embellished with
a secret sauce. The restaurant is often jammed, especially on Saturdays, with regular
customers, politicians seeking a vote, and local celebs. You can see on their walls
faded Polaroids of Peyton and Eli Manning as preteen kids.

REASON TO GO: To eat where Peyton and Eli Manning hung out as kids.
WHAT TO GET: Hot sausage po' boy (or a drenched roast beef).

DOMINIQUE ON MAGAZINE

4213 Magazine St. • (504) 891-9282 • $$$

HOURS: 5:30–9:30 p.m. Mon–Thurs; 5:30–10:30 p.m. Fri and Sat

Dominique's well-traveled chef, Dominique Macquet, was born on an island in the Indian Ocean, grew up with Creole, Asian, African, and Indian home-cooked dishes, and was educated as a chef in South Africa, London, Southeast Asia, and Beverly Hills. He's cooked aboard the *Queen Elizabeth II*, at the James Beard Foundation, and at the US embassy in Paris.

The restaurant was a popular and critical success, getting the DiRoNa (Distinguished Restaurants of North America) award; *New Orleans* magazine named Macquet its Chef of the Year in 1997, and *Esquire* magazine named Dominique's among the Top 20 Best New Restaurants. A year later, *Bon Appétit* included it as one of the nation's seven best.

Much of what appears on the plate has been grown within arm's reach of the tables, in Macquet's home garden or by men such as Philip Soulet, a farmer with whom Macquet has developed a mutually beneficial relationship. The chef estimates that he procures about 85 percent of his ingredients locally, including the crab and shrimp.

REASON TO GO: A change-of-pace setting. If you've had enough of our rustic places, Dominique, with clean, white, hard-edge surroundings, feels rather midtown Manhattan.

WHAT TO GET: The Wagyu beef, however he's serving it—sometimes grilled with Creole cream cheese, other times as meatballs with spaghetti.

FAT HEN GROCERY

7457 St. Charles Ave. • (504) 266-2921 • $$

HOURS: 8:00 a.m.–9:00 p.m. Wed and Thurs; 7:00 a.m.–10:00 p.m. Fri–Mon; closed Tues

One of then problems with writing a restaurant guide for an entire city is that between signing a book contract and having to deliver a manuscript three months later, I've had to jam in quite a few restaurants at which I'd not previously dined. In addition to my gaining twelve pounds, some restaurants suffer by being sandwiched in between two better restaurants. Fat Hen Grocery is such a victim. Had I come here under "normal" circumstances, Fat Hen may have fared better. However, being in the middle of a two-day Ba Chi Canteen and Booty's binge, it felt very much like a just-miss also-ran.

The pimiento cheese had too much mayonnaise, replacing bite with unwanted creaminess. The baked beans, chili, pulled pork, sour cream, and cheddar toppings on the Honkey Tonk Nachos were all fine, but the nachos themselves were too thick and overcooked. The grilled veggie sandwich had way too much onion, which overwhelmed the too little eggplant. So, why I am including Fat Hen in this book? Because I ate from their lunch/dinner menu. Fat Hen Grocery is also known for great breakfast items, including the signature "Womelette," a waffle-omelet hybrid. Chef Shane Pritchett also does a breakfast oyster-and-Brie Benedict and billionaire's bacon, Fat Hen's take on praline bacon. Chef Shane is a certified barbecue judge with the Kansas City Barbeque Society and is a member of several other barbecue societies. His awards, largely from Hogs for the Cause, decorate a front table.

REASON TO GO: The breakfast I didn't have.
WHAT TO GET: The Womelette I've not tried.

FLAMING TORCH

737 Octavia St. • (504) 895-0900 • $$$
HOURS: 11:30 a.m.–2:00 p.m., 5:30–10:00 p.m. 7 days a week

The restaurant gets its name from the French-Moroccan chef, Pouri, cooking his meals with a blowtorch. This was back in Metairie, when the restaurant was first called Scheherezade. Chef Pouri left the business and sold it to his manager, Hassan Khaleghi, who moved to Magazine Street, where fire codes were more stringent than the suburbs and permitted the new location to be Flaming Torch in name only. Even without Chef Pouri's peculiar style/gimmick, the Flaming Torch's new chef, Nick Gile, has been dishing out noteworthy traditional French-Creole dishes, rack of lamb, mussels, scallops, and bouillabaisse, along with personal flairs, but not flames, Sazerac shrimp with peppers, herbs, saffron, reduction of beer and rye whiskey, and the rumored best coq au vin (boneless chicken braised in red wine and root vegetables) in New Orleans.

The Flaming Torch was chosen one of the city's top twenty restaurants by *Gambit Weekly* and French Restaurant of the Year by *New Orleans* magazine.

REASON TO GO: A top French, not Creole, restaurant.
WHAT TO GET: Others will tell you the coq au vin. I'd nudge you more toward the crabmeat beignets.

GAUTREAU'S

1728 Soniat St. • (504) 899-7397
HOURS: 6:00–10:00 p.m. Mon–Sat

Sue Zemanick is going to win one of them James Beard Awards someday, hopefully soon. She's been nominated for Best Chef five times. She did win *Food & Wine*'s Best New Chef in 2008. The thirty-year-old Gautreau's restaurant has been a breeding ground for talented young chefs including John Harris, Mat Wolf, and Larkin Selman. Each chef has faithfully produced the signature dishes: the duck confit, the scallops, the filet, and Gautreau's best known, a simple but perfectly done roast chicken, served with natural jus, green beans, and garlic mashed potatoes, which owner Patrick Singley insists remains exactly the same no matter who the chef is. But each chef has been allowed to scratch his or her creative itches with other dishes in a constantly turning menu. Chef Sue has introduced modern dishes like pierogi stuffed with wild mushrooms and potato, topped with caramelized Vidalia onion–spiked crème fraîche.

Finding the restaurant the first time isn't easy. It's in a residential Uptown block, and is well camouflaged. The small main dining room, in a century-old building, was once an antique pharmacy, from which some relics remain.

REASON TO GO: To eat Zemanick's meals before she finally wins a James Beard so you can say, "I knew her when."

WHAT TO GET: Better get the roast chicken, or Patrick Singley will hunt you down.

GUY'S

5259 Magazine St. • (504) 891-5025 • $$
HOURS: 11:00 a.m.–4:00 p.m. Mon–Sat

Guy's was and is basically one guy—originally the guy was Guy Barcia; then when he sold it nearly twenty years ago, the guy became Marvin Matherne, who vowed not to change a thing. He hasn't; he's still making all the sandwiches, one at a time, while engaging in clever banter and witty repartee with the customers, most of whom are regulars. The restaurant has built up a tremendously loyal following. I'll bet even money any day you go, there'll be one or two UPS deliverymen at a table. The UPS men seem to eat lunch at Guy's every day of the week. Larry Savoie dines at Guy's three times a week, and each time he orders the grilled shrimp dressed with extra pickles. One of the loyal customers shocked Marvin one day when the owner-chef bumped into a contractor sizing up his tired, what Marvin called "bus-soot gray," building for a plaster-and-paint job. Marvin said, "You got the wrong building. I didn't hire anyone." That's when he learned one of his cus-

**Marvin "the Man" Matherne, makin'
po' boys**

tomers, who asked not to be identified, had paid for the job.

I find their fried shrimp po' boy exceptional. Guy's uses peanut oil, which is worse for your heart but so much better for taste. Though, if you're worried about your health, what are you doing in a po' boy joint? For the roast beef po' boys, Marvin cooks the meat and makes the gravy himself. There are also off-the-menu specials, many of them thought up by regulars. The Bomb, for instance, is the brainchild of New Orleans's incredible band Galactic (sort of our Talking Heads, infusing a broad band of music styles, from jazz to bounce). It's a grilled catfish, shrimp, and onion po' boy topped with melted cheddar and Swiss. "We make a chicken Parmesan," Matherne revealed. "It's not on the menu, but people who know about it know it's about the best thing you'll ever eat. But you gotta be in the know." You are now in the know.

REASON TO GO: To be in a po' boy version of *Cheers* or *Mr. Rogers' Dressed and Deep-Fried Neighborhood.*
WHAT TO GET: The on-menu shrimp or off-menu chicken Parmesan.

♛ HANSEN'S SNO-BLIZ

4801 Tchoupitoulas St. • (504) 891-9788 • $
HOURS: 1:00–7:00 p.m. Tues–Sun

Tourists go to Café Du Monde and Acme. Travelers go to Hansen's Sno-Bliz. Hansen's is (for me and many many others) one of the most sacred spots in New Orleans. In a town where sno-ball shops are as common as nail salons, there is really only one that is *the* sno-ball place. Each year since Ernest and Mary Hansen first opened the doors in 1939, they repaint the number of years they've been in business on the side of the building. Hansen's has reached deep into her seventies through three generations. The diminutive and sweet-as-her-syrups Ashley Hansen

Third-generation owner Ashley Hansen working the circa-1934 machine

currently runs the shop, most often with her friend since childhood, Sharon, at her side. Their ice-shaving machine was custom built by Ernest in 1934, before they had their sno-ball shrine. Ernest, a machinist by trade and absentminded-professor-like tinkerer, built the machine just for family use. Mary started dragging the ice-shaving apparatus to the street, where she'd sell flavored syrups for two cents. That was twice the price elsewhere, but the Hansen ice was more of a fine powder than any other sno-ball stop in the city.

Their homemade gourmet syrups are both richer and more complex than the jarringly sweet store-bought flavors of most other stands. I recommend the limeade and ginger, topped with sweetened condensed milk . . . but I also really like root beer with can cream . . . and am nuts for satsuma orange with vanilla bean . . . and . . . heck, I like 'em all. My daughter is strictly a wild cherry girl, the wilder the better. If you go to Hansen's you have to be prepared to stand in line. Whether there are thirty people waiting to be served or just three, you'll probably be there a good thirty to forty minutes. And that's kind of the point. Hansen's interior has signs stating "Quality cannot be rushed," mixed in with yellowed Polaroids of people ravishing their Sno-Bliz cups and old newspaper clippings with forgotten reporters raving about the place. In addition to the best sno-balls in New Orleans, non-rushed quality also refers to the quality of conversations and the sharing of baby pictures you're likely to experience while waiting in line.

REASON TO GO: Their sno-balls are the nectar (cream) of the gods. The stand is a holy shrine to both sno-balls and the Big Easy spirit of New Orleans.

WHAT TO GET: Get right with the food gods and leave any impatience outside their old screen door.

LA BOULANGERIE

4600 Magazine St. • (504) 269-3777 • $
HOURS: 6:00 a.m.–6:00 p.m. Wed–Mon; closed Tues

Less restaurant and more artisan French bakery, La Boulangerie serves croissants and pastries made by real French bakers and rung up by real French clerks working the cash register. You can't get that kind of authenticity at Au Bon Pain nor Panera Bread. I like their savory spinach or ham-and-cheese croissants, am less a fan of their sweet items, and think their bags of crunchy crostinis for salads are about the best I've had.

LA CRÊPE NANOU

1410 Robert St. • (504) 899-2670 • $$
HOURS: 6:00–10:00 p.m. Mon–Thurs and Sat; 11:00 a.m.–3:00 p.m., 6:00 p.m.–10:00 p.m. Fri and Sun

La Crêpe Nanou definitely has the look and the feel of a "real" Paris bistro with their beautiful wine-red art nouveau exterior. The food is likewise classic "authentic" bistro fare: Crêpe Lorraine, Crêpe aux Crevettes (sauteed shrimp in lobster sauce), Omelette au Crabe, Le Gigot d' Agneau (roast leg of lamb with cognac sauce), Croque Monsieur and Madame.

Mariano de Racznyski, aka Nanou, a "real" Frenchman, moved to Louisiana with the intention of working as an airline pilot. However, on a visit to New Orleans he met a local and fell in love. In 1983, de Raczynski began his crepe shop with modest expectations, serving only crepes, both sweet and savory. But the crepe concept did not catch on in New Orleans as de Raczynski thought it would. When his choices were to expand or go out of business, he expanded and widened the menu to include a great variety of French dishes from his childhood. The restaurant flourished, eventually taking over the neighboring space as well. Like other "real"

Paris bistros, La Crêpe Nanou even has, or had, a house cat, an orange cat named Little Man who died in April 2013. There will undoubtedly be a new Little Man.

REASON TO GO: A very intimate and romantic setting.
WHAT TO GET: Crepes, both savory and sweet.

LANGENSTEIN'S

1330 Arabella St. • (504) 897-0869
HOURS: 8:00 a.m.–8:00 p.m. 7 days a week

Langenstein's was New Orleans's first supermarket. Michael Langenstein and his boys, George and Richard, opened a corner grocery in 1922. Today, catty-cornered from a Jewish cemetery, Langenstein's shelves contain many unusual and gourmet brand items plus a large spread of prepared foods like stuffed artichoke, red beans and rice, oyster stew, and the more unusual baked Brie with praline sauce and mirleton casserole, all made in their kitchen across the street. They stock certain items based solely on a single regular customer's request. In certain sandwich shops, there may be a sandwich named after a regular. Here, the reason you'll find a certain brand of peanut butter with oil on top is because a certain customer, Mary Price Robinson, likes it. Langenstein's is sort of New Orleans's Zabar's or Balducci's.

Unlike Zabar's or Balducci's, the cashiers are delightful and chat filled, and offer above-and-beyond service. As she was ringing up a ninety-year-old, mostly deaf, and probably absentminded customer, I heard one cashier yelling, "Mrs. A, you don't need these cigarettes. You bought a carton yesterday!" Now, that's service.

LA PETITE GROCERY

4238 Magazine St. • (504) 891-3377 • $$$
HOURS: 11:30 a.m.–2:30 p.m. Tues–Sun; 5:30–9:30 p.m. Tues–Thurs; 5:30–10:30 p.m. Fri and Sat

In 2013, there were four chefs nominated for the James Beard Award as Best Chef in the South, all four less than two miles from one another. Commander's Palace's Tory McPhail won the award. Sue Zemanick at Gautreau's deserves to win one soon—she's been nominated five times. Coquette's Michael Stoltzfus is a beloved dark horse because he never went to culinary school (but his food is fantastic). Rising star Justin Devillier of La Petite Grocery may be the top of the class. He's certainly a chef to watch, as he was named "Chef to Watch" by both the *Times-Picayune* and *Louisiana Cookin'* magazine. In addition to the James Beard nomination, Chef Justin is the current reigning Hogs for the Cause Grand Champion. In an Iron Chef–style local competition he beat out Galatoire's esteemed chef Bryan Landry to win the top spot.

The California native came here by an odd route, Disneyland. The Happiest Place on Earth undertook a big entertainment development in downtown Anaheim. A new restaurant, Ralph Brennan's Jazz Kitchen, was part of the project and hired Justin. Through this association, he got a job at Bacco, another Brennan restaurant, but this one actually in New Orleans. Once here, Justin's "favorite city in the country," he was like a kid in a candy store. He took a series of jobs with many of our best chefs. From Bacco, he first went to work with Anne Kearney as her morning prep cook at Peristyle. After a year there, which he described as "the best restaurant experience I've ever had," Kearney sold the restaurant. Anton Schulte, Kearney's chef de cuisine at Peristyle, was opening La Petite Grocery and invited Devillier to join him. Over the next year, Devillier worked every station, prepared every kind of dish, yet he couldn't resist when acclaimed owner-chef Scott Boswell offered him the sous-chef position at Stella! This was April 2005. Four months later Katrina hit. Justin returned to New Orleans in September and worked furiously to serve meals with Boswell from an open-air grill in the parking lot. In mid-October, La Petite Grocery reopened and asked Devillier to return. Eight years having since passed, he seems to have found a home.

You can get your pork cheeks or octopus here. They make their own pasta— "We don't roll it out until 5 p.m. on the day we serve it," he said. "It's not the same if you allow it to dry out." The fresh pasta is used for dishes like handmade ravioli with butternut squash, toasted hazelnuts, and brown butter or their potato gnocchi with in-house cured smoked bacon, Parmesan, crème fraîche, and chives. If you have an obnoxiously picky eater, they also do a really good cheeseburger.

REASON TO GO: A chef already risen but still worth watching.

WHAT TO GET: Anything with pasta made at 5:00 p.m. the same day you eat it.

Chef-owner John Harris.

LILETTE

3637 Magazine St. • (504) 895-1636

HOURS: 11:30 a.m.–2:00 p.m. Tues–Sat, 5:30–9:30 p.m. Tues–Thur, 5:30–10:30 p.m. Fri and Sat

Lilette was featured in Gwyneth Paltrow's favorite things website, Goop, noted especially for the "weird" wallpaper on the bathroom walls. If that doesn't get you running there, perhaps awards will. Chef-owner John Harris has been a James Beard finalist for Best Chef in the South in 2009, 2010, and 2011. He was a cover boy on *Food & Wine*'s issue of America's Best New Chefs and was named Best Chef New Orleans by *New Orleans* magazine. Lilette has been named a Top Ten Best Restaurant six of the last eight years by the New Orleans *Times-Picayune*. *Travel + Leisure* wrote they have "the sexiest dining room in New Orleans."

Chef John's cuisine is French-Italian and includes his great-grandmother's labor-intensive spinach gnocchi, bathed in Parmigiano cream and sage brown butter. All of his dishes have little flourishes, such as feathery quenelles; goat cheese and crème fraîche glazed with lavender honey; his boudin noir, or blood sausage, served with spicy mustard and cornichons; or his near-signature white-truffle Parmesan on toast with mushrooms, marrow, and veal glacé.

Save room for dessert. Pastry chef Beth Biundo gilds the lily as skillfully as Chef John. They serve house-made sorbets in flavors like grapefruit Campari or Nutella custard, topped with a quenelle of caramel cream, nuggets of chocolate hazelnut brittle, and a dusting of fleur de sel.

REASON TO GO: Gwyneth told you to.
WHAT TO GET: Eat light-ish so you have room for the Nutella custard dessert.

MAHONY'S

3454 Magazine St. • (504) 899-3474 • $$
HOURS: 11:00 a.m.–10:00 p.m. Mon–Sat

Mahony's website makes them seem like a po' boy stand on a mission: "Soon after Hurricane Katrina, Chef Ben became frustrated with the declining number of neighborhood restaurants and quality po-boys. . . . Despite their long history, many of New Orleans's famous po-boy shops have begun to disappear. Mahony's Po-Boy Shop is a tribute/throw-back to the old neighborhood restaurants of New Orleans. It was founded to bring the po-boy back into fashion." Declining? Disappear? Back into fashion? I guess Chef Ben didn't own a car or he might have passed by the long-standing and still-standing Guy's or Domilise or Parasol's or Johnny's or Serio's or Parkway Bakery. No matter the silliness of their website, Mahony's does make a good po' boy. Their "Peacemaker" (fried oysters, bacon, and cheddar cheese) won an award at the 2008 Po' Boy Festival. The next year, a Po' Boy Festival winner was their chicken liver with Creole slaw. They also have interesting sides such as crab fingers with rémoulade and three types of fries: homemade, dirty with gravy, and dirty with gravy and cheese.

REASON TO GO: To save the po' boy from extinction.
WHAT TO GET: A fried shrimp or oyster po' boy before they're gone.

MARTINIQUE BISTRO

5908 Magazine St. • (504) 891-8495 • $$$
HOURS: 5:30–9:30 p.m. Tues–Thurs; 11:00 a.m.–2:30 p.m., 5:30–10:45 p.m. Fri–Sun

Chef Hubert Sandot, a French chef who was born on the island of Martinique, opened the restaurant in 1994 with a menu centered on French Caribbean food. In 2003, it was bought by a New York couple, Cristiano Raffignone and Kelly Barker, who had fallen in love with the restaurant during a visit five years earlier. Then they started behaving like the husband in Nathaniel Hawthorne's "The Birth Mark."

Eric LaBouchere has replaced Hubert Sandot as chef. They remodeled the place, where now an outdoor patio takes up more than half the dining space. And they changed the menu, phasing out Chef Hubert's island flavors. In other words, they've changed everything about what they loved.

I have eaten there and it was . . . good. I did not have the mussels, which they are known for, nor the duck, which gets high marks. I guess I'm just wary and weary because the New York couple has now gone and bought Dick & Jenny's, one of my favorite restaurants in New Orleans. They've already started doing their "Birth- Mark" dance there too, bringing in a chef from their Houma restaurant to work with Dick & Jenny's brilliant chef, Stacy Hall, and to commit Houma-cide by inflicting Northern Italian stab wounds to a previously perfect menu.

REASON TO GO: To sit outside on the large patio; unless it's raining, or too hot, or humid, or the pollen count is high, or it's Formosan termite season.

WHAT TO GO: Ask for pelau, callaloo, or Crepes Saintoise (all French Caribbean dishes). They won't have them, but ask.

McCLURE'S BARBECUE

4800 Magazine St. • (504) 301-2367 • $

HOURS: 6:00–9:00 p.m. Tues; 11:30 a.m.–2:30 p.m., 6:00–9:00 p.m. Wed–Fri; 11:30 a.m.–9:00 p.m. Sat and Sun

After a time as a pop-up inside Dante's Kitchen, Neil McClure opened his restaurant in a former Uptown veterinary clinic just prior to my manuscript being due in to the publisher. I had time for just one visit. Inside, the small dining area is surrounded by prints by my favorite contemporary New Orleans artist, Scott Guidon, and a sidebar table housing plastic squeeze bottles of five barbecue sauces: Memphis, a vinegary North Carolina, a mustardy South Carolina, a sweet New Orleans East, and a spicy mayonnaise-based sauce called Alabama. On my night, McClure's was sold out of chicken and ribs, making me think back to the Joint being out of chicken and pulled pork and wondering if this was some kind of New Orleans BBQ "thing."

Neil McClure, ever present and always welcoming, learned to barbecue using a redneck rig consisting of a washing machine motor and a car axle. His words (below) sell his restaurant better than I could ever do:

"I wanted to do traditional, authentic barbecue, but without those canned sides that every one of them has. I've been in gourmet food my whole life, so I wasn't going to do things half-assed, so to speak. My macaroni and cheese is from scratch, the baked beans take six hours to put together, we shred all of our slaw by hand because preshredded cabbage tastes terrible. I shred my own cheese, because preshredded cheese has all that cellulose fiber in there to keep it from caking. I mean . . . no thanks."

REASON TO GO: Good BBQ made by a really nice owner-chef, who really cares what you think.

WHAT TO GET: Reviews and online comments all rave about the ribs (sold out the night I was there).

PASCAL'S MANALE

1838 Napoleon Ave. • (504) 895-4877 • $$
HOURS: 11:30 a.m.–9:00 p.m. Mon–Fri; 5:00–9:00 p.m. Sat

Frank Manale opened the restaurant in 1913 as a neighborhood Italian café. His nephew Pascal Radosta bought it some years later (thus the weird possessive name). But it became an institution in 1954 when a customer described (poorly) a dish he'd had in Chicago. Pascal tried to re-create it and came up with one of New Orleans's now signature dishes, barbecued shrimp. Of course, in New Orleans playing with the facts is an art form. Our oldest restaurant in America is not as old as one in Boston. One of our great architects, James Gallier, was really an Irishman named Gallagher, but he was advised to have a French name if he wanted to get any work in New Orleans. And our barbecue shrimp has no BBQ sauce and is not smoked nor put on the grill. The shrimp are cooked in a sauce with a little garlic, Worcestershire, paprika, and then, as described by Richard Collin, aka the Underground Gourmet, "all the butter in the world, and half the pepper."

Pascal's is more than barbecued shrimp, and is, in fact, one of the pillars of Creole cuisine. They serve excellent Oysters Bienville and Rockefeller and Spaghetti Collins with green onions and herbs. Their front room has one of the most beautiful oyster bars in the city. Sadly, the main dining room may be seen as a Katrina victim. The complete renovation has it now looking like a clubhouse in the whitest of white Republican country clubs. Yes, I'm trying to lose my readers one political party and one ethnic race at a time.

REASON TO GO: Barbecued shrimp.
WHAT TO GET: Barbecued shrimp.

PATOIS

6078 Laurel St. • (504) 895-9441 • $$$

HOURS: 5:30–10:00 p.m. Wed–Sat; 11:00 a.m.–2:00 p.m. Fri; 10:30 a.m.–2:00 p.m. Sun

A year ago, Patois was probably best known as the filming location of Desautel's, the fictional restaurant in *Treme* run by the fictional chef Jeanette Desautel (played by Kim Dickens). Now that the HBO series has ended, it can go back to being a real and highly regarded restaurant run by the real and oft-honored chef Aaron Burgau.

Before he opened Patois in 2007, New Orleans–born Aaron Burgau had worked with a dream team of the city's best chefs, including Susan Spicer of Bayona and local legend Gerard Maras, then at Gerard's Downtown. Chef Aaron was was named one of the top five "Chefs to Watch" by *Louisiana Cookin'* magazine. He has been nominated for the James Beard Best Chef Award three years running.

The menu is his personal interpretation of Creole food, most often using fresh, locally sourced ingredients, but not at all resistant to importing Spanish, Italian, Mediterranean, and even Asian flavors, from piquillo peppers to yuzu. He can play French, with steak served with a red wine and marrow reduction and skinny fries, or he can play South American, with a bright chimichurri and a corn, poblano, and tomato salad. *GQ* magazine characterized Chef Aaron's work as "well-thought-out food that's distinctively French but wholly Southern."

> REASON TO GO: Superstar chefs Tom Colicchio, Eric Ripert, Wyle Dufresne, and David Chang have raved about the place. No wait, that was the fictional Desautel's.
>
> WHAT TO GET: You can build a meal around moules frites in a smoky tomato broth.

ST. JAMES CHEESE COMPANY

5004 Prytania St. • (504) 899-4737 • $$

HOURS: 11:00 a.m.–6:00 p.m. Mon–Wed; 11:00 a.m.–8:00 p.m. Thurs–Sat; 11:00 a.m.–4:00 p.m. Sun

If you're a student of New Orleans, you might have thought the St. James of St. James Cheese Company stands for the blues song made famous by Louis Armstrong and covered by everyone from the Animals to the White Stripes. But you'd be wrong. Husband-and-wife proprietors and cheese enthusiasts Richard and Danielle Sutton began their careers at Paxton & Whitfield, a cheese shop established in 1797 in the St. James neighborhood of London. Since 2006 they have relentlessly put forth effort to bring artisanal cheeses to New Orleans. As their website states, "We

Roman Candy Carts

I have never in my life tried Roman Candy, a taffy stick, but it is an integral part of the New Orleans food story. The taffy treat was made by Angelina Napoli Cortese for special events like Christmas and St. Joseph's Day. Her son, Sam,

was a street vendor from the age of twelve and would sometimes sell his mother's leftover candy with his fruits and vegetables. Seeing the reaction of customers to his mother's treats, Sam concocted a design for a special horse-drawn candy cart with a wheelwright named Tom Brinker and the two launched the new company during World War I. For years the cost was 5 cents a stick, and never more than 5 cents from the company's inception in 1915 until 1970. While the price for a stick of Roman Candy has risen, they are still sold off the back of a horse-drawn carriage with the distinctive red-spoked wheels. You can usually find the horse half asleep and the cart parked in a shady spot along St. Charles Avenue. They also sell the taffy from a jar at Angelo Brocato's, but that's not the same.

✦ SNACKS ✦ SNACKS ✦ SNACKS ✦ SNACKS ✦ SNACKS ✦ SNACKS ✦

know people who know people who know people. We figured out that the best way to get the farmhouse cheeses we go crazy for was to find the individuals as enthusiastic about making them as we are about selling them. We've built an international network of cheese makers and affineurs who hook us up with the artisan and farmhouse cheeses not found in other shops."

Their website states they operate on the premise that "cheese should be fun." Definitely—Ubriaco Prosecco always cracks me up.

While daily inventory varies, you can find blue cheeses from distant places like Roquefort, France, or the more local Sweet Grass Dairy in Thomasville, Georgia.

Their cheese is used not just on a cutting board, but in many sandwiches like their Hooks Cheddar, which is Wisconsin cheese with house-smoked turkey, and avocado that souffles as the cheese melts when panini-pressed. Their Eat a Peach sandwich is Asiago cheese with prosciutto and fresh-picked peaches.

In 2013 they won the Cheesemongers' Invitational in New York. I'm sure it's a perfectly wonderful award but, I'm sorry, the word "cheesemonger" sounds like someone who's a hoarder and a bully and won't let anyone else have any cheese. The definition is actually the less interesting "someone who sells cheese."

REASON TO GO: The cheese.

WHAT TO GET: As a joke, ask them for something non-dairy and see how fun cheese can be.

TARTINE

7217 Perrier St. • (504) 866-4860 • $

HOURS: 8:00 a.m.–3:00 p.m. Mon–Sat; 8:00 a.m.–2:00 p.m. Sun

For visitors, Tartine is a small, kind of hard to find, but exceptional bakery that also serves sandwiches at lunchtime. For residents, Tartine also has Plat du Jour, a gourmet to-go option when the idea of making dinner after a long, hard day feels as nauseating as the loudmouth, egg-throwing Atlanta Falcons fans. In general, Saints fans graciously welcome fans for other teams—except those Dirty Birds. Takeout dinners, five courses for $18, are available Tuesday and Thursday. They must be ordered in advance and picked up between 5:00 and 6:30 p.m.

Owner and chef Cara Benson went to New York to attend the pastry program at the French Culinary Institute, collared a husband, Evan, as well as a culinary degree, and headed back to New Orleans. She worked at Muriel's for nearly four years before setting up her own bakery. Tartine is a French word for buttered bread. The bakery sells a lot more than that. Her lunch includes a two-steps-better-than-normal ham sandwich with Brie or a salad Niçoise with the added kick of fierce sardines. Her house-made pâté combined with crushed pistachio and bits of dates garnished with sweet onion jam and Dijon mustard is a staircase better than normal.

Normally I feel about social media sites like Urbanspoon and Yelp similarly to how I feel about those Falcon fans. But Nina M. on Foursquare.com got it succinctly just right when she wrote, "The quiche will make you cry."

REASON TO GO: To cry over simple food.

WHAT TO GET: I'm all over pâté with pistachio and dates; you may opt for a more basic, but not basic, ham and Brie.

UPPERLINE

1413 Upperline Rd. • (504) 891-9822 • $$$
HOURS: 5:30–9:00 p.m. Wed–Sun

Upperline has two attractions. One is, of course, the food, which explodes with flavor, starting with the jalapeño cornbread. The second is the owner, JoAnn Clevenger, who explodes with personality. She's just two steps away from the circus and she'll regale you with stories as she works the room. With her trademark hair-do, called "a sinuous approximation of a meringue knotted into a bun the size of a beignet," she elevates the role of hostess to theater. Ask her about the Rebecca Wells

JoAnne Clevenger caught in rare moment not regaling diners with a story

Reception. JoAnn Clevenger also has a philosophy of what makes a good restaurant: "Restaurants were originally more than just a place to find a meal; restaurants existed to soothe and bolster the weary soul with comfort and indulgence. Like the earliest restaurants, my goal for the Upperline is to be a haven for our guests, restoring their serenity after the daily hassles of the world with great Louisiana food, serious wine, and Creole hospitality."

The menu is a murderer's row of signature dishes like duck and andouille étouffée with corn cakes, drum piquant with hot-and-hot shrimp, and a legendary deep brown gumbo. Upperline invented one of New Orleans's best appetizers (I think *the* best), which you can now get all over town, shrimp rémoulade over fried green tomato.

Southern Living wrote, "If you can eat at only one fine restaurant in New Orleans, make it the Upperline."

When JoAnn lost her great chef Ken Smith to the priesthood (not your usual career path), two replacement chefs came and left within a year. There were rumblings of Upperline "slipping." However, her hiring of Chef David Bridges has returned the food to its former high standing.

REASON TO GO: Great Creole food, interesting artwork on the walls, the incomparable JoAnn Clevenger working the floor.

WHAT TO GET: Start with the jalapeño cornbread and the shrimp rémoulade over fried green tomato, and you're off and running.

Marvin Day, one of Camellia Grill's stylin' waiters

CHAPTER 10

Riverbend
and
Carrollton

Canned food is a perversion. I suspect that it is ultimately very damaging to the soul.

—**Ignatius P. Reilly, A Confederacy of Dunces**

After a good dinner one can forgive anybody, even one's own relations.

—**Oscar Wilde**

Carrollton and Riverbend are sort of the Alaska and Hawaii of New Orleans, the last to be annexed, becoming the city's sixteenth and seventeenth wards. The area is adjacent to Tulane and Loyola University, whose students frequent the shops, dive bars, and music clubs, and continually stroll the Black Pearl section, trying to identify the "real" House of the Rising Sun. Student tastes also influence the area's restaurants, making it the hub of (affordable) international cuisine. Within blocks of one another are Babylon Café (Middle Eastern), Lebanon Café (another Middle Eastern), Mona's Café (part of a Middle Eastern chain), Café Granada (Spanish tapas), Jazmine Café (excellent Thai), 5 Happiness (New Orleans's best but a little bit expensive Chinese restaurant), Chinese Kitchen (a surprisingly good dive that looks like a thousand lesser order-by-number Chinese places), Panchita's (Mexican), and Basil Leaf Thai & Sushi Bar. I'm not going to profile any of these restaurants because few visitors come to New Orleans for our Middle Eastern or Chinese food, and most likely you have as good or better Mexican and Thai restaurants back home. The area also has a James Beard Award–winning chef, Frank Brigtsen, iconic places like Camellia Grill, and several restaurants as good as any in New Orleans.

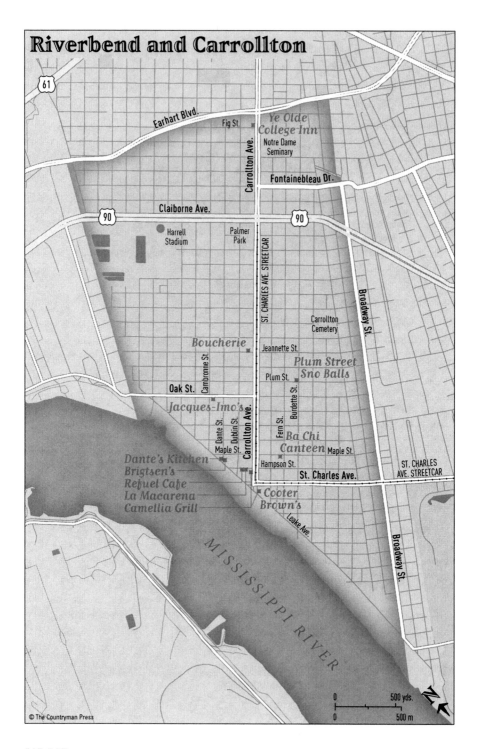

Riverbend and Carrollton

61

Earhart Blvd.

Fig St.

Ye Olde College Inn

Notre Dame Seminary

Carrollton Ave.

Fontainebleau Dr.

90 Claiborne Ave.

90

Harrell Stadium

Palmer Park

ST. CHARLES AVE. STREETCAR

Broadway St.

Carrollton Cemetery

Boucherie

Jeannette St.

Plum Street Sno Balls

Plum St.

Cambronne St.

Oak St.

Burdette St.

Jacques-Imo's

Carrollton Ave.

Fern St.

Ba Chi Canteen

Maple St.

Dante St.

Dublin St.

Maple St.

Hampson St.

St. Charles Ave.

ST. CHARLES AVE. STREETCAR

Dante's Kitchen
Brigtsen's
Refuel Cafe
La Macarena
Camellia Grill

Cooter Brown's

Leake Ave.

Broadway St.

MISSISSIPPI RIVER

0   500 yds.
0   500 m

N

© The Countryman Press

BA CHI CANTEEN

7900 Maple St. • (504) 373-5628 • $$
HOURS: 11:00 a.m.–2:30 p.m. Mon–Sat; 5:30–9:00 p.m. Mon–Sat

Tan Dinh won the judges' pick for best Vietnamese in Appendix A, and it was far ahead of their #2 choice. Located on the West Bank, Tan Dinh has not been profiled in this book. Fortunately the same owners recently opened Ba Chi Canteen on Maple Street, a block from Carrollton, so I can write how good it is. The menu is broader and wildly more creative than any of the many new Vietnamese restaurants cropping up in New Orleans. Their bacos are brilliant . . . all of them, from their coconut curry shrimp to their BBQ roast pork to their honey ponzu catfish. The menu describes baco as a Vietnamese taco. I'd say they are closer to the famous-to-tourists baseball-shaped dough filled with BBQ pork served at the White Swan Hotel in Guangzhou, but that may translate to only one or two of you. The Vietnamese crepe is a sensational starter. Then you mix your carbs (jasmine rice, sticky rice, or vermicelli noodles) with your meats (including the three pork fecta, Saigon shrimp, or lemongrass chicken) to create small-plate masterpieces. My one word of warning is to beware the bottle of "House Sauce" left on the table next to soy sauce and chili garlic sauce. It is so good you'll be tempted to soak everything in it, thus obliterating the subtleties and differences of each dish.

REASON TO GO: Probably the best Vietnamese in striking distance.
WHAT TO GET: Some meats, some carbs, and definitely some bacos.

BOUCHERIE

8115 Jeannette St. • (504) 862-5514 • $$
HOURS: 11:00 a.m.–3:00 p.m., 5:30–9:30 p.m. Tues–Sat

In 2006, Chef Nathanial Zimet launched Que Crawl, his increasingly sought-after purple food truck. He was usually parked outside Tipitina's, where he prepared his word-of-mouth-famous fried boudin balls and duck gumbo. Zimet always said his intention with Que Crawl was to earn enough money to open his own restaurant. His vision was to have a steeped-in-meat restaurant where the food was as good as Commander's Palace and Stella! where he had apprenticed, but the atmosphere would be much more casual.

Boucherie is a full-blown realization of that vision. He serves creative dishes like mussels cooked with collard greens in rendered bacon fat, blackened shrimp with bacon vinaigrette, and a "where's the bacon?" smoked Wagyu beef brisket. Zimet has a reputation for combining Southern comfort food, Asian vegetables, and French technique. His prices are remarkably reasonable, rarely exceeding $15, making Boucherie one of the best values in the city. The service, though, is slow even by New Orleans standards. Boucherie didn't even change out the sign for Iris, the prior restaurant that occupied the space, for a good six months.

Chef Zimet's vision was almost obliterated when he was shot three times during a robbery. He spent nearly a year recovering. Resulting financial difficulties were greatly alleviated by his staff, who kept the restaurant open without him, plus his friends and loyal customers who staged benefits with names like Beers Not Bullets.

REASON TO GO: Support Chef Zimet by more than satisfying your stomach.
WHAT TO GET: Something with bacon.

BRIGTSEN'S

723 Dante St. • (504) 861-7610 • $$$
HOURS: 11:00 a.m.–9:00 p.m. Mon–Sat

Gene Bourg, restaurant critic for the *Times-Picayune*, described Brigtsen's as "the place against which all other restaurants serving South Louisiana cuisine have to be measured." Chef Frank Brigtsen has won the James Beard Award, plus he was featured as a Top Ten New Chef in America by *Food & Wine* magazine, Chef of the Year by *New Orleans* magazine, the Lauriers Du Terroir Award, the DiRoNa Award as a Distinguished Restaurant of North America, the Gault Millau, an IVY Award, and is in the Fine Dining Hall of Fame.

Chef Brigtsen got here, a small house just past where St. Charles Street becomes Carrollton, by way of Commander's Palace. Paul Prudhomme hired him there, took him under his wing, and then took him to his own restaurant, K-Paul's, when he opened in 1979.

The menu at Brigtsen's changes every day. This is the best place in town to eat rabbit. Chef Brigtsen, an avid fisherman, is felt by many to be New Orleans's most skilled chef with fish.

REASON TO GO: The Aretha Franklin (most Grammys) or Katharine Hepburn (most Oscars) of New Orleans restaurants.
WHAT TO GET: Rabbit? Fish? I don't think he does a turducken type of rabbit stuffed inside a fish, but get that if offered.

CAMELLIA GRILL

626 S. Carrollton Ave. • (504) 309-2679 • $

HOURS: 8:00 a.m.–12:00 a.m. Mon–Thurs and Sun; 8:00 a.m.–2:00 a.m.
Fri and Sat

After Katrina, Camellia Grill took longer to reopen than many other nearby restaurants and businesses. The reason wasn't as much damage from the storm, which was minimal, as it was getting back their staff, which had been scattered to Houston, Atlanta, and other distant cities. The waiters at Camellia are as much a reason to go as their burgers and breakfast-anytime menu. In their white shirts with black bow ties, they greet diners with quick wit and easy familiarity. And their skills presenting drinking straws rival anything Michael Jordan ever did with a basketball. Many of the waiters are long-standing fixtures, none more so than Harry Tervalon Sr., who was the first waiter hired in 1946, and who, even after his retirement in '96, remained a part of the restaurant (including cutting the ribbon when Camellia Grill finally reopened after Katrina), until his death in August 2007.

During the months the restaurant remained closed, loyal patrons began posting notes on the locked front door. Said a note signed "Ashleigh," "I came here for law school just so I could have my Camellia Grill fix regularly. Please come back." Eventually there were hundreds of notes with messages such as, "I miss coming here after every baseball game," or "We came from Florida. I'm hungry. I need a handshake. And a milk shake," and another, "I can't bear the thought of you not being here. My parents dated here. I dated here or came with friends in the late '60s and early '70s. . . . Now I've been bringing my kids here," signed "Janet."

The iconic Riverbend diner was opened in December 1946 by the Schwartz family. Son Michael Schwartz ran it for the last twenty years up to Katrina. In 2007, he sold the restaurant to Hicham Khodr, a prominent restaurateur and partner of Emeril Lagasse. "The feel of the Camellia Grill is not going to change," says Khodr. "I know it's a New Orleans landmark that people love."

A second Camellia Grill location opened in the French Quarter (540 Chartres St.) in December 2010 with the same serpentine Formica counter, where all patrons "belly up." A sign outside the new establishment says, "Since 1946." It's two years old.

REASON TO GO: The waiters.
WHAT TO GET: Burgers, huge omelets, homemade pies, and any drink to be presented with a straw (we most recommend the chocolate freeze, a not-quite-milk shake).

A mural outside; the good stuff's inside

COOTER BROWN'S

509 S. Carrollton Ave. • (504) 866-9104 • $

The name says it all. Cooter Brown was a historical figure who decided to get drunk and stay drunk the entire Civil War so that he'd be seen as unfit for military service and wouldn't be drafted. Cooter Brown's, the tavern, is a delightfully demented brew house featuring 400 different kinds of beer, 350 of which are imports and 42 of which are on draft. The joint may be most famous for its mural, depicting famous dead celebrities drinking theme-appropriate beers; among them, John Wayne's holding a Lone Star, Richard Nixon a Tsingtao in honor of his China diplomacy, Mickey Mantle a Michelob (or "Mick"), and a harder-to-decipher W. C. Fields has a Rolling Rock. Rolling Rock is brewed in Philadelphia, thus honoring his "All things considered, I'd rather be in Philadelphia" epitaph.

Cooter Brown's is included here because they serve raw oysters, boiled crawfish, and overstuffed po' boys. They are consistently rated "Best Bar Food" in New Orleans.

REASON TO GO: The mural.

WHAT TO GET: What goes better with raw oysters than a Santa's Butt beer?

DANTE'S KITCHEN
736 Dante St. • (504) 861-3121 • $$
HOURS: 6:00 p.m.–12:00 a.m. Wed–Mon; 10:30 a.m.–2:00 p.m. Sat and Sun

Chef-owner Emanuel "E-man" Loubier opened his place in 2000 after an extended tour at Commander's Palace, where he was the late Chef Jamie Shannon's apprentice. The Commander's master chef was one of the early proponents of the now ubiquitous buy-local, farm-to-table, and in-house-made movements. E-man, using what he learned, has built up a deeply rooted supply network of area farmers. At Dante, he can "push the envelope" with his supplied goods in ways that never would be allowed at the venerable Commander's. Here, ingredients are local but also offbeat. A perfect example is the Amuse-Bouche, a cube of a beet-and-chocolate cake resting in creamy buttermilk dressing, topped with onion jam and a little sliver of chive. Chocolate and beet seems an odd, almost off-putting combination, but it works.

The menu is built around what the kitchen refers to as the "big three": (1) Trois Mignons (meaning "the dainty or darling three"), a small steak with pork debris, Stilton, and marchands du vin, (2) Chicken Under a Brick, a historical dish with roots in either Italy or Russia or both, using a technique of searing a split chicken under a heavy weight (most often a tinfoil-covered brick), and (3) Redfish on the Half Shell, a skin-on fillet covered with crabmeat and a salad of parsley, cilantro, mint, dill, and tarragon. The simple dishes demonstrate how common local ingredients can produce something quite uncommon.

Dante's setting, a converted cottage, is also a part of the story. There's a network of close, small dining rooms on the inside with high ceilings and massive wooden beams, and outside you can dine on a patio under interlocking umbrellas or a narrow porch. The feeling as a whole has a *Big Chill* atmosphere as a lively but casual crowd wanders to their tables or samples from jars of vegetables resting around the bar.

REASON TO GO: The Big Three. Maybe all Big Three.
WHAT TO GET: You've got to at least try beets and chocolate (with buttermilk and onion jam).

☗ JACQUES-IMO'S
8324 Oak St. • (504) 861-0886 • $$
HOURS: 5:00–10:00 p.m. Mon–Thurs; 5:00–11:00 p.m. Fri and Sat

Outside the restaurant hangs a paid-for sign: "Warm Beer. Lousy Food. Poor Service." Like so much about Jacques-Imo's, they're just playing with you. When I visited New Orleans, but did not yet live here, Jacques-Imo's was, with-

The late great Austin Leslie out in front of Jacques-Imo's

out question, my favorite restaurant in the city. But when I visited here and did not yet live here, Austin Leslie manned the kitchen. With his passing Jacques-Imo's is now *among* my favorite restaurants in the city. Jacques Leonardi, the irrepressible owner and chef, is still very visibly on premises as he works the room, generally two but not three sheets to the wind.

Jacques is another in the long and forever ongoing line of expat Yats. Raised on a farm in upstate New York by a French mother and an Italian father, he came to New Orleans as part of his tour of duty with the Coast Guard. Like so many, Jacques fell in love with New Orleans and all it had to offer . . . and stayed. His restaurant career began working for minimum wage in the bowels of Chef Paul Prudhomme's K-Paul's Louisiana Kitchen, this while he was still in the Coast Guard. In 1996, he purchased the building on Oak Street. With considerable help from legendary chef Austin Leslie combined with his own wild creativity, he established one of the most popular New Orleans restaurants. They only take reservations for parties of five or more. Parties of four or fewer wait up to two hours for a table. Or you could, if you choose, be seated and served in the flatbed of the decorated truck parked in the front of the restaurant. My wife, daughter, and I have done this. The food's just as good in the truck and you'll have lively conversations with people waiting to get in or just passing by on the street.

The restaurant does great appetizers, like a fried oyster salad, a small sample of shrimp and grits, oyster Brie soup, duck and andouille gumbo, and something amazing with eggplant. Jacques-Imo's is known for their signature concoction, a shrimp-and-alligator cheesecake.

REASON TO GO: A funky, lively, eccentric, distinctly New Orleans spot with eccentric, delicious, and distinctly New Orleans dishes.

WHAT TO GET: Start with or close with the shrimp-and-alligator cheesecake.

LA MACARENA

8120 Hampson St. • (504) 862-5252 • $
HOURS: 11:30 a.m.–10:00 p.m. Mon–Sat; 10:00 a.m.–9:00 p.m. Sun

I'll let you in on a little secret: La Macarena's address is 8120 Hampson Street. Nowhere on their website will you find that information. When I called, Manny couldn't remember the address and had to call in the back. He is forgiven for not knowing the address; the restaurant has changed locations many times over the years. Manny Ochoa-Galvez is the gregarious front-of-house owner who greets you, then seats you, then gives you a tutorial about the menu, then talks with you throughout your meal. He's kind of a Salvadoran JoAnn Clevenger.

The main dish is the *pupusa*, a flat masa-dough disk filled with sour cheese, beans, and, usually, bits of pork. Manny calls them "Mayan pancakes." They seem to offer a challenge to North American eaters as you'll see a variety of methods being used by fellow diners trying to navigate the too-pliable-to-pick-up pupusa toward their mouths.

Maybe ask Manny for suggestions.

They also serve Salvadoran enchiladas, which have as much in common with Mexican enchiladas as your grandma's bingo hall has with the Bingo! Show here in New Orleans. Sorry, inside joke. They do seared redfish, a tart shrimp ceviche, and a thin-cut carne asada. Do not pass up their blackberry iced tea. It's as non-alcoholically addictive as Company Burger's Mae-Mae's Iced Tea Punch.

> **REASON TO GO:** Food good enough to make you forgive that horrible song used as the restaurant's name.
>
> **WHAT TO GET:** You have to get the pupusa, or what was the point?

MAT & NADDIE'S

937 Leonidas St. • (504) 861-9600 • $$
HOURS: 5:30–9:30 p.m. Mon, Tues, Thur–Sat

Mat & Naddie's looks like a place you'd drop off the kids for preschool day care, right down to the goofy hand-painted "Good Food" front yard sign, mimicked in the goofy neon-lit sign attached to the little house on the corner, accented with a cute knee-high picket fence. The look belies the sophisticated cooking going on inside, with walls painted a bright, canary yellow. The restaurant evolved from a catering business run by Michael and Paula Schramel, whose children are Nat and Maddie, an alteration of the Mat & Naddie's restaurant name. O Lord, more cuteness!

I wanted to dismiss Mat & Naddie's for looking like a place your grandma would take you when you visited, but the Steen's cane syrup–lacquered duck with gizzard-and-heart dirty rice, or the sherry-marinated grilled quail with waffles, set off by the sun-dried tomato and roasted garlic cheesecake, left me unable to do so. Like the sign says, "Good Food."

REASON TO GO: Now *this* is a place where tourists rarely go.
WHAT TO GET: The sensational lunch buffet for only $10.

MAPLE LEAF BAR
8316 Oak St. • (504) 866-9359 • $

The Maple Leaf is a bar, and just a bar. No bar food, no pop-up restaurant. Well, actually it's hardly "just" a bar, it's a great bar with pressed-tin walls and framed photographs of old Mardi Gras queens. It's dark. Your feet stick to the floor. It's a perfect bar in which to join the sweaty, jivin' crowd to hear regulars like Joe Krown, Papa Grows Funk, Jon Cleary, and the not-to-be missed Rebirth Brass Band. Rebirth plays every Tuesday night. The reason they are included in *Eat Dat* is their Sunday night crawfish boil served from fold-up tables in the middle of the bar's dance floor. It's just $10 for a night you won't forget.

ONE
8132 Hampson St. • (504) 301-9061 • $$
HOURS: 11:00 a.m.–2:00 p.m. Tues–Fri; 5:00–10:00 p.m. Mon–Sat

Tucked away on a side street around the corner from the more visited (touristy) Camellia Grill, One remains a somewhat secret place, predominantly patronized by locals. They call themselves a "friendly, if upscale, neighborhood hangout." Chef Scott Snodgrass left Clancy's to open One with his gregarious co-owner, Lee McCullough. Lee infectiously works the front room. This is not to say Chef Scott does not likewise engage patrons from his open kitchen. He calls his style "contemporary comfort food." One's duck-and-okra gumbo with homemade boudin was voted Best in New Orleans. They also received the honor of Best New Restaurant. They do many New Orleans standards with an ever-so-slight twist resulting in an ever-so-slightly better dish. Char-grilled oysters, invented and made popular by Drago's, are now served in many restaurants. At One, butter and Romano cheese are replaced by Roquefort cheese and vinaigrette. Their Louisiana crab cakes are served with mirliton fries.

REASON TO GO: You might be the One and only diner not from New Orleans.
WHAT TO GET: Something ever-so-slightly twisted.

PLUM STREET SNO BALLS

1300 Burdette St. • (504) 866-7996 • $
HOURS: 2:00–10:00 p.m. 7 days a week (in season)

New Orleans does not live by one sno-ball stand alone. There are hundreds. Hansen's is the Holy Spot, but Plum Street is the more ubiquitous. Toni Black, daughter of owners Claude and Donna Black, handles off-site events and she is very good at her job. At practically every festival or street fair you'll find a Plum Street tent. They've been tucked into a residential area, and a bit hard to find, since 1945. In addition to probably the second-best sno-balls in New Orleans, they are known for serving them in Chinese takeout containers.

REFUEL CAFÉ

8124 Hampson St. • (504) 872-0187 • $
HOURS: 7:00 a.m.–2:00 p.m. Tues–Fri; 8:30 a.m.–2:00 p.m. Sat and Sun

Opened in 2006, Refuel Café was not named for the rebirth of New Orleans. Leroy Bautista and his wife Aurora had planned to open their breakfast–lunch spot in September 2005, but Katrina had other plans. They serve great coffee and exceptional huevos rancheros, made with fresh pico de gallo, but the calling card should be their grits. Chef Leroy stirs them for an hour each morning, resulting in the creamiest grits in this or any other town. You can add andouille, cheese, bacon, ham, and/or roasted red peppers to your grits.

> **REASON TO GO:** An alternative to breakfast spots.
> **WHAT TO GET:** The grits.

SARA'S

724 Dublin St. • (504) 861-0565 • $$
HOURS: 11:30 a.m.–2:30 p.m., 5:30–10:30 p.m. Tues–Fri; 5:30–10:30 p.m. Sat

Since opening in 1980, Sara's has pretty much run the gamut of cuisines, passing through a gauntlet of chefs. Mac Rahman initially envisioned a straightforward curry house, rare in New Orleans. In the '90s, he and Chef Ganesh Ayyengar jumped aboard the fusion craze bandwagon. The menu was a crazy mix of French, Indian, Creole, and Southeast Asian. A consulting chef came in and attempted to modernize the place with more current trends of local sourcing and craft cocktails. He left Sara's after a few months. Chef Cristina Trinh then jumped in, taking Sara's on yet another new course.

Her menu had a "sounds like fun, let's try it" attitude and included tofu in a spicy, Thai-style coconut milk curry, or Peking duck two-way, with a confit duck leg and chopped duck meat wrapped in pancakes. She had a crab soup with hobak, a Korean pumpkin.

Bart Thomas, the restaurant's newest manager and consulting chef, is from North Louisiana and is a graduate of the Culinary Institute of America. He previously ran his own private chef business in New York and London. Homesickness brought him back to Louisiana. "I stumbled into Sara's one night because it's near my house and I thought this was a place with a lot of potential that needed some help." Longtime chef Ganesh Ayyengar and original owner Mac Rahman are still involved as Thomas moves toward what he calls "modern New World cuisine." Sara's will go Cajun on a deep-fried Cornish hen, but then add a cranberry sauce and toss bok choy on the plate, to keep diners still guessing, after thirty-plus years, whether they're a few minutes from the Mississippi River or the Mekong.

VINCENT'S

7839 St. Charles Ave. • (504) 866-9313 • $$$
HOURS: 11:30 a.m.–2:30 p.m., 5:00–10:00 p.m. Tues–Fri; 5:00–10:00 p.m. Sat and Sun

Vincent's has been a neighborhood family joint since Vincent Catalanotto and Tony Imbraguglio opened it in '97, a second location to their first in Metairie. The front door is framed by amateurish six-foot-high cement reproductions of Michelangelo statues. Bad statues and fountains are often a sign of really good, family-style Italian food served inside. Seafood, like soft-shell crab in red sauce, is probably what they do best. Breadsticks accompany each table in a charmingly old-fashioned way. Vincent's is noted for serving crab bisque in scooped-out bread bowls. I don't know if the restaurant was always so jammed with tables or if this happened because of demand, but the result is more uncomfortable than intimate. Vincent's wins "Best Italian Restaurant" readers' polls pretty much every year in both *Gambit Weekly* and *New Orleans* magazine. My sense from this is that most *Gambit* and *New Orleans* magazine readers must not venture into Mid-City very often because Venezia has better food, in a less jammed atmosphere, and is considerably less expensive.

YE OLDE COLLEGE INN

3000 S. Carrollton Ave. • (504) 866-3683 • $$
HOURS: 4:00–11:00 p.m. Tues–Sat

At one time, a ye olde long time ago, a Texas-based chain restaurant called the Pig Stand stood where Ye Olde College would take over. When the Pig Stand fell behind on its rent, local lease owner Denis Rufin could stand it no more and took back the space. The fact that Prohibition had just ended might have figured into his action as he immediately converted the Pig Stand into his own restaurant *with a bar*. To run his popular new noon-till-midnight place, Denis brought on his bother Albert and had youngest brother Emil quit the LSU baseball team to slide home to take over the day shift. Ye Olde College Inn, with a very broad menu of affordable, some might say "cheap," comfort foods, became a regular spot for the nearby Tulane and Loyola students. Their fried oyster loaf was famous, or so their sign says.

The restaurant took an abrupt change of direction when Johnny Blancher bought Ye Olde College Inn from the Rufin boys in 2003. Johnny was an entertainment king, owner and walking PR machine for his eccentric Mid-City Rock 'n' Bowl, a bowling alley with a bar, exceptional live music (it'd been a regular home for the very best New Orleans musicians like Beau Jocque, Boozoo Chavis, Geno Delafose, Chris Ardoin, Snooks Eaglin, Wild Magnolias, and Anders Osborne), and a dance floor. On weekends, the country boys would come into the Big City to dance with the pretty ladies. By "boys" I mean seventy-year-old men with more moves than teeth.

Then Johnny's direction for both the restaurant and the Rock 'n' Bowl had to adjust to the aftermath of Katrina. Ultimately, it all turned out to be good news. The storm left a devastated city-block-long acre of land immediately adjacent to the restaurant, where previously stood two large residences. He bought the land on the cheap and initially all he did was cut the grass. Then he started planting things the restaurant could use. Soon it turned it into what Johnny calls his "farm." Ye Olde College Inn now has two farms, a lot on Fig Street in addition to the former home plots on Carrollton Avenue. Every morning the kitchen staff picks cherry tomatoes and tomatillos and eggplants for the restaurant.

Having reinvigorated a restaurant and a bowling alley and set up his "farm," Johnny went to the next logical step—cattle ranching. He's partnering with his uncle's Vermillion Parish ranch with grass-fed cows to use their beef on his customers' plates. Can a brewery or vineyard be far behind?

> **REASON TO GO:** To have a comfortable and affordable meal in one of Drew Brees's favorite spots (he's said "It has a 'Cheers' feel to it"), and then stroll across the parking lot to drink, bowl, or dance at the Rock 'n' Bowl.
>
> **WHAT TO GET:** A steak (from a cow raised on the restaurant's ranch), served with potatoes and heirloom tomatoes (from across the street).

RIVERBEND and CARROLLTON

223

IF YOU CAN'T STAND DA HEAT, *Get Out da Big Easy—The Hot Sauce Wars*

I think it says something about New Orleans, where the *average* temperature is over ninety degrees in July and August (I don't want to print the hottest recorded temperatures or you might cancel your trip), that before eating anything we first reach for the hot sauce. In the shops along Decatur Street and in the French Market, you can choose from literally hundreds of brands. CaJohn, Emeril's, Frank's, Scorned Woman, Cholula, Ring of Fire, Da Bomb, Chile Today–Hot Tamale, Louisiana Gold, Acid Rain, Ass in Hell, Bayou Love, Bayou Passion, Bayou Pecker . . . and I could go on. But there are really only two that have acquired superstar status: Tabasco and Crystal.

Tabasco, created in the late 1860s by Edmund McIlhenny, *may* have been the first hot sauce. After years of that having been a commonly held belief, word of Colonel Maunsel White surfaced, claiming his "Concentrated Essence of Tobasco Pepper" predates McIlhenny by four years. Nasty rumors were circulated that Eddie Mac borrowed, bought, or even stole the recipe from Colonel White. Tabasco created a Myths page on its website to dispel the rumors officially. Though they're now putting qualifying phrases in their copy like, "According to family tradition."

Edmund McIlhenny, food lover and avid gardener, was given seeds of *Capsicum frutescens* peppers that had come from Mexico. He sowed the seeds in his home soil on Avery Island (about two hours from New Orleans). After the Civil War, the cuisine of New Orleans got briefly bland and monotonous, either because during Reconstruction residents couldn't afford better ingredients or because of the stultifying influences of the Puritan Northerners (houses should be white, clothes should be black, food should avoid Satan's beckoning of taste).

This was an ideal time for McIlhenny to introduce his flavor-enhancing spice. He made his sauce by crushing the reddest peppers from his plants, mixing them with Avery Island salt, aging this "mash" for thirty days in jars and barrels, then blending the mash with French white wine vinegar and aging the mixture for another thirty days. He sold his strained concoction in discarded cologne bottles. In 1868 when he started to sell to the public he ordered thousands of new cologne bottles from a New Orleans glassworks. He labeled the bottles "Tabasco," a word of Indian origin meaning "damp earth" and also a region in Southern Mexico. His new sauce became so popular that McIlhenny quit his job as a banker to devote his full time to making and marketing Tabasco Sauce. His first year, he sold 658 bottles at one dollar apiece. Nearly 150 years later, the company ships 3.2 million gallons of hot sauce every year to 165 countries across the world. Tabasco labels are printed in twenty-two languages.

On his death in 1890, McIlhenny was succeeded by his eldest son, John Avery McIlhenny. When John Avery resigned to join Roosevelt's Rough Riders, his brother Edward Avery took over. Upon Edward's death, Walter McIlhenny succeeded, then Edward "Ned" McIlhenny, then Paul McIlhenny, and finally today Tony Simmons. Don't worry, he's a McIlhenny cousin.

Tabasco sauce has been shaken and spritzed nearly everywhere. During the Vietnam War, Brigadier General Walter S. McIlhenny issued *The Charlie Ration Cookbook* featuring the sauce in recipes for Combat Canapés and Breast of Chicken under Bullets. Each cookbook came wrapped with a two-ounce bottle of Tabasco in a camouflaged water-resistant container. Tabasco has been used by NASA, going into orbit on Skylab and the International Space Station. Like Kleenex and Xerox, the name Tabasco has become synonymous with the product. It is easily the most popular hot sauce in the world.

But not in New Orleans.

In 1923 Alvin and Mildred Baumer produced the first bottle of Crystal Hot Sauce at their plant on Tchoupitoulas Street. For many, including me, it is the superior sauce. Most restaurants in New Orleans have a bottle of Tabasco and a bottle of Crystal on the table or they risk being reprimanded by a customer who's fiercely loyal to the brand not represented. Crystal sells to only seventy-five countries, but their 3 million gallons shipped each year come close to Tabasco's 3.2 million. You can buy Crystal Hot Sauce in seven-gram packets (fast-food-ketchup-sized), or six-ounce, twelve-ounce, or thirty-two-ounce bottles, or for people serious about their hot sauce, gallon jugs.

"We believe we sell flavor and not heat," said Al Baumer Jr., son of the creators and current company CEO. Crystal's SHU (Scoville Heat Units) is not revealed. Tabasco's is 2,500 and their kicked-up varieties reach as high as 5,000 SHUs. Theodore Scoville devised a method of calibrating the amount of capsaicin, the chemical compound that stimulates chemoreceptor nerve endings in the skin, particularly the tongue, present in a dry unit of mass. In other words, how hot shit is. There are many brands hotter, a lot hotter, than Tabasco's 5,000 SHU. Endorphin Rush Beyond Hot Sauce is 33,390, Dave's Gourmet "Insanity Sauce" is 95,000, DaBomb is 119,000, and then there's the just-silly Mad Dog (3,000,000), Magma (4,000,000), and Blair's 16 Million Reserve, the hottest hot sauce on the planet. Blair's 16 Million Reserve is an extremely collectible sauce with only 999 bottles ever made and discontinued after 2006. We wonder if they stopped because the thousandth bottle would ruin the song or because of deaths. The SHU of Blair's is 16,000,000. These sauces aren't about flavor. They're about drunk college boys on a dare.

In hot sauce competitions, Tabasco won *Huffington Post*'s Hot Sauce Death Match. Crystal didn't make it out of the first round. But then *Cooks Illustrated* rated Tabasco dead last. Their tasters described it as "flavorless," "vinegary," "out of balance"—even "vile." You're just going to have to jump in, taste each for yourself, choose your personal winner, and then get ready to rumble.

Dessert

(A K A   A F T E R W O R D)

---

*We dance even if there's no radio, we drink at funerals, we talk
too much and laugh too loud and live too large, and, frankly,
we're suspicious of others who don't.*

—**Chris Rose**

Come eat up New Orleans while you can. There is very much a Venice-like quality to the city. While our funk seems up to the task of fighting back Starbucks, Best Buy, and the cancerous corporate homogenization infecting much of America, we cannot fight Mother Nature. The Mississippi River wants to go west, as all rivers want to migrate. If not for the Army Corps of Engineers, we might already be a modern-day Ephesus.

Ephesus was the second-largest city in the Roman Empire, after Rome itself. In its day, Ephesus was really quite the *in* place to be. The city had the premier aqueduct system in the world (then more important than affordable public transportation, pedestrian malls, or a Six Flags Great Adventure), a passion for the arts (it had the largest theater in the world), the top-notch Library of Celsus, and a number of celebrities like the iambic poet Callinus and the satirist Hipponax (his bits about Lucius Verus were hilarious knee-slappers) and the great painter Parrhasius. The city was also a bastion for women's rights; it even had women artists, revolutionary at the time. Ephesus lost its importance as the commercial center of the world as the Cayster River moved on, leaving behind a silted-up dry riverbed. Ephesus no longer had access to the Aegean Sea.

The Army Corps of Engineers is currently keeping the Mississippi River right where it is. In so doing, they have caused the river to not behave like a river. It is not depositing soil at the delta to maintain wetlands. Coupled with the mess aggressive oil companies made of our marshland, we lose the equal of nine football fields of protective wetlands . . . every day. The Gulf of Mexico is currently ninety miles from the city. Someday, experts predict the Gulf will be lapping up against the Aquarium and IMAX Theater. Experts disagree if that someday with be one hundred years from now or next Tuesday.

The city has a long history of almost not being here. On Good Friday 1788, the Great New Orleans Fire destroyed most of the city. We lost 896 buildings.

Another massive fire in 1794 took another 212 buildings. The Crevasse of 1849 was the first recorded great flood of the city, and the Great Mississippi Flood of 1927 was the second. We were more famously and more recently nearly wiped off the map by hurricanes, Betsy in 1965 and the August 29, 2005, Katrina. New Orleans has climbed out of the wreckage each time.

There's a statue of Winston Churchill in the circle in front of the Hilton Riverside. Why Churchill in New Orleans I have no idea. But Churchill uttered a wonderful quotation that typifies New Orleans's spirit:

> **"Success is stumbling from failure to failure without losing your enthusiasm."**

The outside world can toss all manner of hurricanes, fires, outbreaks of yellow fever, BP oil spills, Formosan termites, runaway nutria populations at us. New Orleans has always wiped off the slime, put splints on the broken bones, shoved a Chiclet where our teeth used to be, and we're ready for the next party.

The very first Mardi Gras after I moved here, I bumped into dressed-up people at the St. Ann's parade who were from the New York we'd left behind. Tossing their arms in the air, they exclaimed, "In New York it's just Tuesday. Here it's MARDI GRAS!"

Laisser les étranges temps rouler!

APPENDIX A:
THE BEST OF NEW ORLEANS

I consider Appendix A the highlight of this book. An absolute A-list of New Orleans's food writers and commentators has chosen the top spots in the city. I created twenty-five categories, not wanting to tax their time voting on fifty or more. There could have been, but isn't, a Best Steak House. Would it have been Crescent City, Chophouse, or Dickie Brennan's? There could have been, but isn't, Best Vegetarian. Green Goddess, Carmo, or the veggie options at Root or Maurepas?

For the twenty-five categories that do appear below, each judge was asked to rate his or her top twelve. They did not have to vote for each category if they felt no affinity for Best Vietnamese, Best Sno-Ball stand, or others. They did not need to list twelve if they felt a lesser number more appropriate. Therefore, there are a few categories that list only eight or nine bests.

Where a top choice is listed as "PRO," that means it was a prohibitive favorite, winning its category by more than fifty points ahead of the ≠2 choice. Where "PRO PLUS" shows, the winner received so many points that most judges voted it ≠1 and no judge voted it lower than ≠2 for the category.

THE BEST CAJUN RESTAURANT

1. COCHON
2. K-Paul's
3. Toup's Meatery
4. Crescent Pie & Sausage
5. Brigtsen's

6. Jacques-Imo's
7. Bon Ton
8. Kingfish
9. Mulate's

Pied pense-bête ⚜: Cochon is a great restaurant and deserves its ≠1 ranking. But, I suspect a part of Paul Prudhomme's K-Paul's being ranked ≠2 has to do with the fact that every judge lives in New Orleans. If you live here and eat here every day, the traditional dishes of K-Paul's have less wow factor than the contemporary Cajun dishes being served at Cochon. For the visitor wanting "authentic" or "old school" Cajun food, I'd be tempted to send them to K-Paul's.

⚜ A pretentious way of writing "footnote" in French.

THE BEST CREOLE RESTAURANT

1. GALATOIRE'S
1. DOOKY CHASE'S
3. Arnaud's
4. Upperline
5. Commander's Palace
6. Pelican Club
7. Tujague's
8. Clancy's
9. Olivier's
10. Antoine's
11. Jacques-Imo's
12. Li'l Dizzy's
12. R'evolution

Pied pense-bête: For those more deeply in the know, there are (at least) three types of Creole cuisine: French, Black, and Contemporary. Commander's Palace website refers to their cuisine as a fourth, "Haute Creole." For ease of communication, I've lumped all types together under simply "Best Creole Restaurant." For this reason I'm giving Dooky Chase's (Black Creole) a first-place tie even though Galatoire's (French Creole) did win by a very slight margin.

THE BEST SEAFOOD RESTAURANT

1. G. W. FINS (PRO)
2. Drago's
3. Borgne
4. Pêche
5. Brigtsen's
6. Middendorf
7. Deanie's
8. Rio Mar
9. Clancy's

10. Red Fish Grill
11. Bourbon House
12. Café B

THE BEST OYSTER HOUSE

1. CASAMENTO'S (PRO PLUS)
2. Felix's
3. Bourbon House
3. Pascal's Manale
5. Lüke
6. Drago's
7. Desire
8. Borgne
9. Red Fish Grill
10. Pêche
11. Acme
12. Superior Seafood

THE BEST BREAKFAST RESTAURANT

1. RUBY SLIPPER
2. Elizabeth's
3. Surrey's
4. Croissant D'Or
5. Gracious Bakery
6. Brennan's (currently closed)
7. Camellia Grill
8. Satsuma
9. Somethin' Else Café
9. St. Charles Tavern
11. Lüke
12. Fleur-de-Lis

THE BEST BURGER JOINT

1. COMPANY BURGER (PRO)
2. Port of Call
3. Tru Burger
4. Delachaise

5. Buffa
6. Clover Grill
7. Cowbell
8. Camellia Grill
9. Snug Harbor
10. Lüke
11. Capdeville
12. Beachcorner

THE BEST BUSINESS LUNCH

1. MR. B's
2. Restaurant August
3. Commander's Palace
4. Palace Café
5. Coquette
6. MiLa
7. Ralph's on the Park
7. St. James Cheese
9. Lüke
9. Muriel's
11. Café Adelaide
12. Le Foret

THE MOST ROMANTIC DINNER

1. RESTAURANT AUGUST
2. Café Amelie
3. Café Degas
4. Bayona
5. Irene's
6. Lilette
7. Gautreau's
8. La Petite Grocery
8. Grill Room
10. Vincent's
11. Broussard's
11. Bacchanal

THE BEST ITALIAN RESTAURANT

1. MARIZA
2. Venezia
3. Domenica
4. Vincent's
5. A Mano
6. Tommy's
7. Mosca's
7. Mandina
9. Irene's
10. Italian Barrel
11. Ancora
11. Maximo's
11. Café Giovanni

THE BEST VIETNAMESE RESTAURANT

1. TAN DINH (PRO)
2. Pho Tau Bay
3. Nine Roses
4. Dong Phuong
5. Lilly's
6. Margasin
6. Kim Son
8. Café Minh
9. Ba Mien
10. Eat Well

Pied pense-bête: Ba Chi Canteen, a newish restaurant on Maple Street, I feel did not make the list only because of its newishness. Ba Chi is run by the same owners as our ≠1 Best Vietnamese, Tan Dinh. It's pretty great.

THE BEST BARBECUE JOINT

1. THE JOINT

2. Hillbilly

3. Boo Koo BBQ

4. Shortail's

5. Walker's Southern

6. Ted's Smokehouse

7. VooDoo BBQ

8. Squeal's

9. Saucy's

Pied pense-bête: McClure's wasn't yet open when most of the judges filled out their ballots. My sense is that if *Eat Dat* ever goes to a second edition, the Joint is in jeopardy of losing its top spot to McClure's.

THE BEST SNO-BALL STAND

1. HANSEN'S SNO-BLIZ (PRO PLUS)

2. Plum Street

3. Pandora's

4. SnoWizard

5. Sal's Sno-balls

6. Beaucoup Juice

7. Ro-Bear Snowballs

8. Sno Dome

THE BEST STREET FOOD: Food Trucks, Food Stands, or Horse-Drawn Food Carts

1. LA COCHINITA

2. Roman Candy

3. Taceaux Loceaux

4. Fat Falafel

5. Foodie Call

6. Frencheeze

7. La Coyota

8. Doughboy at French Quarter Fest

9. Empanada Intifada

10. Crawfish Bread at Jazzfest

11. Lucky Dog

Pied pense-bête: Admittedly, this is kind of a crazy catchall category where you have the horse-drawn taffy cart going against a falafel truck and hot dog vendors.

THE BEST LATE-NIGHT DINING SPOT

1. ROOT

2. Camellia Grill

3. Maurepas

4. Snug Harbor

4. Port of Call

6. Bouligny Tavern

6. Booty's

8. St. Lawrence

8. St. Roch Tacos

10. Siberia

11. Delachaise

12. Mimi's in the Marigny

THE BEST JAZZ BRUNCH

1. COMMANDER'S PALACE (PRO PLUS)

2. Arnaud's

3. Blue Room at the Roosevelt

4. Atchafalaya

5. Crystal Room at Le Pavillon

6. Muriel's

7. Antoine's

8. Mr. B's

THE BEST RESTAURANT FOR MUSIC WITH DINNER

1. LITTLE GEM

2. Bacchanal
3. Three Muses
4. Palm Court
5. Café Giovanni
6. Bombay Club
7. Snug Harbor
8. Mojito's

THE BEST SERVICE

1. COMMANDER'S PALACE (PRO)

2. Restaurant August
3. Galatoire's
4. Emeril's
5. Dick & Jenny's
6. Upperline
7. La Petite Grocery
8. Iris
9. Lilette
10. Booty's

WHERE TO GET THE BEST PO' BOY

1. PARKWAY BAKERY (PRO)

2. Crabby Jack's
3. Guy's
4. Mahony's
5. Domilise
6. Killer PoBoy
7. Zimmer's
7. Chicken Sue's
9. Avery's
10. Gene's

10. Johnny's
12. R&O

Pied pense-bête: I have to jump in with my completely unjustifiable opinion that the only reason my personal and enthusiastic favorite, Killer PoBoy, is rated as low as ≠6 is because many of the judges have yet to discover the new pop-up po' boy window located and unadvertised at the back of the Erin Rose Bar. How else to explain it?

WHERE TO GET THE BEST GUMBO

1. GUMBO SHOP

2. Dooky Chase's
3. Mr. B's
4. Casamento's
4. Charlie's Seafood (closed April 2013)
4. Middendorf
4. R'evolution
4. Liuzza's
4. K-Paul's
10. Kingfish
11. Brigtsen's
12. High Hat
12. One Restaurant & Lounge
12. Commander's Palace

Pied pense-bête: The actual ≠1 winner for this category was "My House" as chosen by four judges, proud of their own versions of this New Orleans classic. But since I intuit they may not want a line of readers showing up at "Their House," I list only commercial establishments.

WHERE TO GET THE BEST FRIED CHICKEN

1. DOOKY CHASE'S

2. Willie Mae's Scotch House

3. McHardy's

4. High Hat

5. Li'l Dizzy's

6. Fury's

7. Manchu

8. Fiorella's

WHERE TO GET THE BEST CRAWFISH BOIL

1. PERINO'S

2. Siether's

3. Sal's Seafood

4. Deanie's

5. Cooter Brown

6. Salvo's

7. Galley Seafood

8. Zimmer's

9. Harbor Seafood

WHERE TO GET THE BEST BREAD PUDDING

1. COMMANDER'S PALACE

2. Boucherie

3. Bon Ton

4. Brennan's (currently closed)

5. Li'l Dizzy's

5. Red Fish Grill

7. Ye Olde College Inn

8. Tivoli & Lee

THE BEST USE OF BACON

For this peculiar category, every judge had a completely different choice. So, rather than ranking these 1 through 12, I simply list the 12 cited.

Praline bacon at Elizabeth's

Praline ice cream with bacon at Green Goddess

Buckboard bacon melt at Cochon Butcher

Pork belly and bacon po' boy at Cochon

Quail stuffed with boudin, wrapped in bacon, at Atchafalaya

Bacon, oyster, and blue cheese at Restaurant August

Bacon, duck, and jalapeño poppers at Borgne

Oysters Slessinger, grilled with bacon, shrimp, and Provel cheese, at Katie's

Oysters en brochette at Galatoire's

Maple bacon donut at Blue Dot Donuts

Shrimp wrapped in Italian bacon at Bistro Daisy

Oysters Rockefeller Deconstructed at MiLa

THE MOST "CLEARLY WE'RE NOT IN KANSAS ANYMORE" (DISTINCTLY NEW ORLEANS) RESTAURANT

1. JACQUES-IMO'S

2. Arnaud's

3. Coop's Place

3. LA Bistro

5. Galatoire's

6. Casamento's

7. Antoine's

8. Dante's Kitchen

9. Bacchanal

10. Ye Olde College Inn

11. Elizabeth's

12. Parkway Bakery

THE IF YOU ONLY HAD ONE NIGHT IN NEW ORLEANS GO-TO RESTAURANT

1. **RESTAURANT AUGUST**
2. Cochon
2. Herbsaint
2. Liuzza's by the Track
2. Dick & Jenny's
2. Clancy's
2. Root
8. Mandina's
8. Casamento's
10. Commander's Palace
10. Maurepas
12. Emeril's
13. Stella!
14. Parkway Bakery
15. Upperline

Pied pense-bête: When respected judges are voting for the *one* restaurant to choose if you only have *one* night in New Orleans, I feel compelled to include any restaurant mentioned and so extend this list to all 15 receiving votes.

The Judges

MARCELLE BIENVENU

Bienvenu is a cookbook author, food writer, and chef/instructor at the John Folse Culinary Institute at Nicholls State University. Her books include *Who's Your Mama, Are You Catholic, and Can You Make a Roux?*; *Cajun Cooking for Beginners*; and *No Baloney On My Boat*. She coauthored other cookbooks, including four with Emeril Lagasse and *Cooking Up a Storm* with Judy Walker, which was nominated for a James Beard Award. Marcelle has written a weekly food column, *Creole Cooking*, for the *Times-Picayune* since 1984. Her writing has been featured in *Food & Wine*, *Southern Living*, *Redbook*, the *New York Times*, and other publications. (www.marcellebienvenu.com)

LOLIS ERIC ELIE

From 1995 to 2009, Lolis wrote a column for the *Times-Picayune*. He is the author of *The Treme Cookbook* and *Smokestack Lightning: Adventures in the Heart of Barbecue Country* and co-producer and writer of the documentary based on his barbecue book. Lolis was editor of *Cornbread Nation 2: The Best of Southern Food Writing*. A frequent contributor to the *Oxford American*, his work has also appeared in *Gourmet*, the *Washington Post*, the *New York Times*, *Bon Appétit*, *Downbeat*, and the *San Francisco Chronicle*, among other publications. His writing is included in the anthologies *Best Food Writing: 2008*, *Best African American Essays: 2009*, *Streetlights: Illuminating Tales of the Urban Black Experience*, and *That's What I Like (About the South)*. A former commentator for *CBS News Sunday Morning*, he has also appeared often on National Public Radio programs. Lolis wrote, co-produced, and starred in the PBS documentary *Faubourg Treme: The Untold Story of Black New Orleans*, which won multiple awards as Best Documentary. He was a writer for the HBO series *Treme* and currently writes for the Showtime series *Hell on Wheels*. (www.loliselie.com)

GWENDOLYN KNAPP

Knapp is a sixth-generation Floridian, hailing from New Port Richey. After attending graduate school in North Carolina, she moved to New Orleans in 2007, and has worked as a cheesemonger and a contributor to *St. Charles Avenue*, *New Orleans* magazine, and the *Zagat Survey*. Her writing has appeared in numerous publications including the *Southeast Review*, *Crazyhorse*, the *Best Creative Nonfiction* anthology series, and elsewhere. She is currently the editor of *Eater NOLA*, to which I subscribe and suggest you do as well. (nola.eater.com)

IAN MCNULTY

Ian is an expat Yat, having grown up in Rhode Island, graduated from Rutgers University in Joisey, and only thereafter coming to New Orleans and falling in love with the city. He was previously the restaurant columnist for *Gambit Weekly*, currently does the same for the *New Orleans Advocate*, and is host of his own radio show, *Where Y'Eat* on WWNO. He is the author of two books, *Louisiana Rambles* and *A Season of Night*. Follow him on Twitter @ ianmcnultynola. (www.ianmcnulty.com)

SARA ROAHEN

A Wisconsin girl, Sara is another expat Yat. She the author of the much-acclaimed *Gumbo Tales: Finding My Place at the New Orleans Table* and former restaurant critic for *Gambit Weekly*. She co-edited *The Southern Foodways Alliance Community Cookbook*. Sara has been published in *Food & Wine*, *Oxford American*, *Wine & Spirits*, *Gourmet*, *Tin House*, and *Garden & Gun*. She writes, collects oral histories, and serves as president of the Southern Foodway Alliance's board of directors. (www.southernfoodways.org)

AMY C. SINS

Author of *Ruby Slippers Cookbook*, winner of the Gourmand Award, Amy has guest hosted the *New Orleans Chef Show*, was named a 2013 "Rising Star" by Junior Achievement of New Orleans, and is primarily noted as the owner of Langlois Culinary Crossroads. Her company offers both hands-on cooking instruction as well as culinary tours of New Orleans. *Travel + Leisure* magazine noted it as one of the top cooking schools.

POPPY TOOKER

Her bio reads like she should be considered for sainthood. Following Hurricane Katrina, Poppy was recognized by the *Times-Picayune* as a "Hero of the Storm." *Southern Living* magazine named Poppy a "Hero of the New South." The International Association of Cooking Professionals recognized Poppy's efforts in April 2008 with their first-ever Community Service Award. *Louisiana Eats* is her produced and hosted weekly radio show on the local NPR affiliate. Poppy contributes food commentary on

Steppin' Out, the New Orleans PBS affiliate's arts-and-entertainment show. She has authored *The Crescent City Farmers Market Cookbook*, awarded for historic content and named Cookbook of the Year by *New Orleans* magazine. *Madame Begue's Recipes of Old New Orleans Creole Cookery*, first published in 1900, was reissued 112 years later with a foreword and revised recipes by Poppy Tooker. *Louisiana Eats* is her latest book, published in fall 2013. She is additionally an associate editor of *Louisiana Kitchen & Culture* magazine and was a contributing editor for *Hallmark* magazine. Online, Poppy is a regular contributor to *Zester Daily*. With any time left over from these many activities, Poppy is a walking billboard for the slow-cooking movement and the preservation of time-honored recipes and preparation styles. Poppy has been instrumental in reviving endangered local foods such as Creole cream cheese and rice calas and endangered restaurants like Tujague's. (zesterdaily. com and www.poppytooker.com)

JUDY WALKER

Walker is food editor of the *Times-Picayune* and Nola.com. She is the author and coauthor of six cookbooks, including *Cooking Up a Storm: Recipes Lost and Found from The Times-Picayune* (Chronicle, 2008). Co-edited with Marcelle Bienvenu, it was nominated for a James Beard Award. Every week, she maintains and adds to Nola.com's collection of more than four thousand recipes, and for the past several years has hosted dozens of cooking videos called *In Judy's Kitchen*, yes, in her kitchen. The current series focuses on classic Louisiana recipes. She is a member of the Arizona Culinary Hall of Fame because she spent twenty-one years writing about food for the *Arizona Republic* in Phoenix, and is a past board member of the Association of Food Journalists. (blog.nola.com)

LIZ WILLIAMS

Liz is the founder and director of the Southern Museum of Food & Beverage. I believe it's the only food museum in America outside more focused ones like the Mustard Museum in Wisconsin. SoFAB's mission is to explore the culinary history of the American Southern states and to explain the roots of Southern food and drinks. The museum has been awarded the 2013 Louisiana Heritage Preservation Award for preserving and documenting Louisiana food culture. *Saveur* magazine named SoFAB one of the top five food museums in the world. Liz is a lawyer who writes about the legal aspects of food. Her book, *New Orleans: A Food Biography*, was published in December 2012. She's also coauthored *The A to Z Encyclopedia of Food Controversies and the Law*, is just turning in a book about cocktails, and has published articles in *Gastronomica* and *Southern Culture*. Liz is currently working on a book about obesity lawsuits and other food-related litigation in the United States. (southernfood.org)

RESTAURANTS BY CUISINE OR STYLE

BARBECUE

Bar-B-Q Kings. Gentilly, 2164 Milton St. (504) 949-2210.

Boo Koo BBQ. Mid-City, 3701 Banks St. (Inside Finn McCool's Irish Pub).
(504) 202-4741.

Hickory Prime BBQ. Gentilly, 6001 France Rd. (757) 277-8507.

Hillbilly Barbecue. River Ridge, 2317 Hickory Ave. (504) 738-1508.

McClure's Barbecue. Uptown, 4800 Magazine St. (504) 301-2367.

Mrs. Hyster's Barbeque. Center City, 2000 S. Claiborne Ave. (504) 522-3028.

Squeal Barbecue. Riverbend & Carrollton, 8400 Oak St. (504) 302-7370.

The Joint. Bywater, 701 Mazant. (504) 949-3232.

Ugly Dog Saloon. Warehouse District, 401 Andrew Higgins Blvd. (504) 569-8459.

VooDoo BBQ. Garden District, 1510 St. Charles Ave. (504) 522-4647.

Whole Hog Café. Warehouse District, 639 Loyola Ave. (504) 525-4044.

BREAKFAST

Audubon Club House. Uptown, 6500 Magazine St. (504) 212-5282.

Betsy's Pancake House. Mid-City, 2542 Canal St. (504) 822-0213.

Blue Plate Café. Garden District, 1330 Prytania St. (504) 309-9500.

Café Conti. French Quarter, 830 Conti. (504) 636-1060.

Café Envie. French Quarter, 1241 Decatur St. (504) 524-3689.

Café Soulé. French Quarter, 720 St. Louis St. (504) 304-4636.

Coulis. Uptown, 3625 Prytania St. (504) 304-4265.

Elizabeth's. Bywater, 601 Gallier St. (504) 944-9272.

Fat Hen Grocery. Uptown, 7457 St. Charles Ave. (504) 266-2921.

Fleur-de-Lis Café. French Quarter, 307 Chartres St. (504) 529-9641.

Gracious Bakery & Café. Carrollton, 1000 S. Jefferson Davis Pkwy. (504) 301-3709.

La Madeleine. Riverbend, 601 S. Carrollton Ave. (504) 861-8662.

Milk Bar. Carrollton, 710 S. Carrollton Ave. (504) 309-3310.

Refuel Café. Carrollton, 8124 Hampson St. (504) 872-0187.

Riccobono's Panola Street Café. Carrollton, 7801 Panola St. (504) 314-1810.

Ruby Slipper. Mid-City, 139 S. Cortez St. (504) 309-5531.

Ruby Slipper. Warehouse, 200 Magazine St. (504) 525-9355.

Ruby Slipper. Marigny, 2001 Burgundy St. (504) 525-9355.

Satsuma Café. Bywater, 3218 Dauphine St. (504) 304-5962.

Satsuma Café. Carrollton, 7901 Maple St. (504) 861-3244.

Somethin' Else Café. French Quarter, 620 Conti St. (504) 373-6439.

Stanley. French Quarter, 547 St. Ann St. (504) 587-0093.

Surrey's. Garden District, 1418 Magazine St. (504) 524-3828.

Surrey's. Uptown, 4807 Magazine St. (504) 895-5757.

Tartine. Carrollton, 7217 Perrier St. (504) 866-4860.

CAJUN

Bon Ton. Warehouse District, 401 Magazine St. (504) 524-3386.

Cochon. Warehouse District, 930 Tchoupitoulas. (504) 588-2123.

Cochon Butcher. Warehouse District, 930 Tchoupitoulas. (504) 588-7675.

Crescent Pie & Sausage. 4400 Banks St. (504) 482-2426.

Jacques-Imo's. Carrollton & Broadmoor, 8324 Oak St. (504) 861-0886.

Jax Bistro. French Quarter, 620 Decatur St. (504) 457-8529.

K-Paul's. French Quarter, 416 Chartres St. (504) 524-7394.

Kingfish. French Quarter, 337 Chartres St. (504) 598-5005.

Mulate's. Warehouse District, 201 Julia St. (504) 522-1492.

Roux Bistro. Warehouse, 500 Canal (504) 595-5506.

Toup's Meatery. Mid-City, 845 N. Carrollton Ave. (504) 252-4999.

CHINESE

August Moon. Uptown, 3635 Prytania St. (504) 899-5129.

China Orchid. Carrollton, 704 S. Carrollton Ave. (504) 865-1428.

China Palace. Carrollton, 3415 S. Carrollton Ave. (504) 483-7768.

China Wall. Warehouse District, 1112 Canal St. (504) 522-6802.

Chinese Kitchen. Carrollton, 3327 S. Carrollton Ave. (504) 482-1122.

Chinese Tea Garden. Gentilly, 5226 Elysian Fields Ave. (504) 282-1493.

Dragon King. Carrollton, 6221 S. Claiborne Ave. (504) 865-0222.

Five Happiness. Carrollton, 3605 S. Carrollton Ave. (504) 482-3935.

Gravier Oriental Express. Warehouse District, 1802 Gravier St. (504) 523-1912.

Great Wok. Gentilly, 1554 Mirabeau Ave. (504) 283-2355.

Green Tea. Uptown, 1116 Louisiana Ave. (504) 899-8005.

Jung's Golden Dragon. Garden District, 3009 Magazine St. (504) 891-8280.

Ming Garden. Mid-City, 1151 N. Broad St. (504) 482-2400.

Red Star. Carrollton, 8330 Earhart Blvd. (504) 861-1933.

Yang's Chinese. Mid-City, 2657 Tulane Ave. (504) 821-8899.

Yummy Yummy. Mid-City, 220 N. Carrollton Ave. (504) 483-9122.

CONTEMPORARY CREOLE

5Fifty5. Central Business District, Marriott Hotel, 555 Canal St. (504) 553-5638.

7 On Fulton. Warehouse District, 700 Fulton St. (504) 681-1034.

Allegro. Central Business District, 1100 Poydras St. (504) 582-2350.

Annunciation. Warehouse District, 1016 Annunciation St. (504) 568-0245.

Atchafalaya. Uptown, 901 Louisiana Ave. (504) 891-9626.

Bombay Club. French Quarter, 830 Conti. (504) 586-0972.

Brigtsen's. Uptown, 723 Dante St. (504) 861-7610.

Café Adelaide. Warehouse District, 300 Poydras St. (504) 595-3305.

Café Amelie. French Quarter, 912 Royal St. (504) 412-8965.

Clancy's. Uptown, 6100 Annunciation St. (504) 895-1111.

Commander's Palace. Garden District, 1403 Washington Ave. (504) 899-8221.

Coop's Place. French Quarter, 1109 Decatur St. (504) 525-9053.

Emeril's. Warehouse District, 800 Tchoupitoulas St. (504) 528-9393.

Evangeline. French Quarter, 329 Decatur St. (504) 908-8008.

High Hat Café. Uptown, 4500 Freret St. (504) 754-1366.

Johnny V's Grill by the Hill. Uptown, 6106 Magazine St. (504) 899-4880.

Le Citron Bistro. Center City, 601 Orange St. (504) 566-9051.

Le Meritage. French Quarter, 1001 Toulouse St. (504) 522-8800.

Louisiana Bistro. French Quarter, 337 Dauphine St. (504) 525-3335.

M Bistro. French Quarter, 921 Canal St. (504) 524-1331.

Mia's Balcony. Garden District, 1622 St. Charles Ave. (504) 301-9570.

Mr. B's Bistro. French Quarter, 201 Royal St. (504) 523-2078.

Muriel's. French Quarter, 801 Chartres St. (504) 568-1885.

Neyow's Creole Café. Mid-City, 3340 Bienville St. (504) 822-4529.

Nola. French Quarter, 534 St. Louis St. (504) 522-6652.

One. Carrollton, 8132 Hampson St. (504) 301-9061.

Orleans Grapevine. French Quarter, 720 Orleans St. (504) 523-1930.

Palace Café. French Quarter, 605 Canal St. (504) 523-1661.

Pelican Club. French Quarter, 615 Bienville St. (504) 523-1504.

Ralph's on the Park. Mid-City, 900 City Park Ave. (504) 488-1000.

Redemption. Mid-City, 3835 Iberville St. (504) 309-3570.

Riverfront. French Quarter, 541 Decatur St. (504) 267-0425.

Roux on Orleans. French Quarter, 717 Orleans St. (504) 571-4604.

Rue 127. Mid-City, 127 N. Carrollton Ave. (504) 483-1571.

SoBou. French Quarter, 310 Chartres St. (504) 552-4095.

Tableau. French Quarter, 616 St. Peter St. (504) 934-3463.

The Country Club. Bywater, 634 Louisa St. (504) 945-0742.

The Three Muses. Marigny, 536 Frenchmen St. (504) 298-8746.

Upperline. Uptown, 1413 Upperline St. (504) 891-9822.

Wolfe's. Warehouse District, 859 Convention Center Blvd. (504) 613-2882.

CREOLE

Albertine's Tea Room (Columns Hotel). Uptown, 3811 St. Charles Ave. (504) 899-9308.

Antoine's. French Quarter, 713 St. Louis St. (504) 581-4422.

Arnaud's. French Quarter, 813 Bienville Ave. (504) 523-5433.

Bistreaux. French Quarter, 1001 Toulouse St. (504) 586-8000.

Bistro Daisy. Uptown, 5831 Magazine St. (504) 899-6987.

Café Opera. French Quarter, 541 Bourbon St. (504) 524-7611.

Café Pontalba. French Quarter, 546 St. Peter St. (504) 522-1180.

Copeland's Cheesecake Bistro. Garden District, 2001 St. Charles Ave. (504) 593-9955.

Coquette. Garden District, 2800 Magazine St. (504) 265-0421.

Court of Two Sisters. French Quarter, 613 Royal. (504) 522-7273.

Crystal Room. Central Business District, Le Pavillon Hotel, 901 Poydras St. (504) 581-3111.

Dijon. Warehouse District, 1377 Annunciation St. (504) 522-4712.

Dooky Chase's. Mid-City, 2301 Orleans Ave. (504) 821-0600.

Feelings. Marigny, 2600 Chartres St. (504) 945-2222.

Galatoire's. French Quarter, 209 Bourbon St. (504) 525-2021.

Gazebo Café. French Quarter, 1016 Decatur St. (504) 525-8899.

Gumbo Shop. French Quarter, 630 St. Peter. (504) 525-1486.

Herbsaint. Warehouse District, 701 St. Charles Ave. (504) 524-4114.

House of Blues. French Quarter, 225 Decatur St. (504) 529-2583.

La Bayou. French Quarter, 208 Bourbon St. (504) 525-4755.

La Peniche. Marigny, 1940 Dauphine St. (504) 943-1460.

Little Gem Saloon. Central Business District, 445 S. Rampart St. (504) 267-4863.

Mandina's. Mid-City, 3800 Canal St. (504) 482-9179.

Montrel's Bistro. French Quarter, 1000 N. Peters St. (504) 524-4747.

Old Coffee Pot. French Quarter, 714 St. Peter St. (504) 524-3500.

Olivier's Creole Restaurant. French Quarter, 204 Decatur St. (504) 525-7734.

Palm Court. French Quarter, 1204 Decatur. St. (504) 525-0200.

Patois. Uptown, 6078 Laurel St. (504) 895-9441.

Pere Antoine. French Quarter, 741 Royal St. (504) 581-4478.

Praline Connection. Marigny, 542 Frenchmen St. (504) 943-3934.

R'evolution. French Quarter, 777 Bienville St. (504) 553-2277.

Rémoulade. French Quarter, 309 Bourbon St. (504) 523-0377.

Rene Bistrot. Warehouse District, 700 Tchoupitoulas St. (504) 613-2350.

Tujague's. French Quarter, 823 Decatur St. (504) 525-8676.

Scarlett O'Hara's. French Quarter, 329 Decatur. (504) 525-1985.

Sugar House. Warehouse District, 315 Julia St. (504) 525-1993.

Two Sisters Kitchen. Mid-City, 223 N. Derbigny St. (504) 524-0056.

DESSERT AND COFFEE

Angelo Brocato. Mid-City, 214 N. Carrollton Ave. (504) 486-1465.

Antoine's Annex. French Quarter, 513 Royal St. (504) 581-4422.

Blue Dot Donuts. Mid-City, 4301 Canal St. (504) 218-4866.

Café Beignet. French Quarter, 311 Bourbon St. (504) 525-2611.

Café Du Monde. French Quarter, 800 Decatur St. (504) 525-4544.

Creole Creamery. Uptown, 4924 Prytania St. (504) 894-8680.

Maple Street Patisserie. Carrollton, 7638 Maple St. (504) 304-1526.

Morning Call Coffee Stand. City Park Area, 56 Dreyfous Dr. (504) 300-1157.

New Orleans Cake Café and Bakery. Marigny, 2440 Chartres St. (504) 943-0010.

Orange Couch. Marigny, 2339 Royal St. (504) 267-7327.

Sucré. Uptown, 3025 Magazine St. (504) 520-8311.

FRENCH

Café Degas. Mid-City, 3127 Esplanade Ave. (504) 945-5635.

Ciro's Coté Sud. Carrollton, 7918 Maple St. (504) 866-9551.

Flaming Torch. Uptown, 737 Octavia. (504) 895-0900.

La Crêpe Nanou. Uptown, 1410 Robert St. (504) 899-2670.

La Madeleine. Riverbend, 601 S. Carrollton Ave. (504) 861-8661.

La Petite Grocery. Uptown, 4238 Magazine St. (504) 891-3377.

Le Fin Du Monde. Uptown, 2917 Magazine St. (504) 895-2500.

Le Foret. Warehouse District, 129 Camp St. (504) 553-6738.

Lilette. Uptown, 3637 Magazine St. (504) 895-1636.

Lüke. Warehouse District, 333 St. Charles Ave. (504) 378-2840.

Martinique. Uptown, 5908 Magazine St. (504) 891-8495.

Meauxbar. French Quarter, 942 N. Rampart St. (504) 569-9979.

Ste. Marie. Warehouse District, 930 Poydras St. (504) 304-6988.

Tempt. Warehouse District, 931 Canal St. (Saint Hotel). (504) 875-2600.

HAMBURGERS

Balcony Bar and Café. Uptown, 1104 Harmony St. (504) 895-1600.

Beachcorner. Mid-City, 4905 Canal St. (504) 456-7470.

Bruno's Tavern. Carrollton, 7538 Maple St. (504) 861-7615.

Bud's Broiler. Mid-City, 500 City Park Ave. (504) 486-2559.

Bud's Broiler. Uptown, 3151 Calhoun St. (504) 861-0906.

Camellia Grill. Riverbend, 626 S. Carrollton Ave. (504) 309-2679.

Camellia Grill. French Quarter, 540 Chartres St. (504) 522-1800.

Charcoal's Gourmet Burger Bar. Uptown, 2200 Magazine St. (504) 644-4311.

Clover Grill. French Quarter, 900 Bourbon St. (504) 598-1010.

Company Burger. Uptown, 4600 Freret St. (504) 267-0320.

Cowbell. Riverbend, 1200 Eagle St. (504) 866-4222.

Dino's Bar & Grill. Warehouse District, 1128 Tchoupitoulas St. (504) 558-0900.

GB's Patio Bar & Grill. Carrollton, 8117 Maple St. (504) 861-0067.

Juicy Lucy's. Mid-City, 133 N. Carrollton Ave. (504) 598-5044.

Port of Call. French Quarter, 838 Esplanade Ave. (504) 523-0120.

Ruby Red's. Warehouse District, 301 Baronne St. (504) 528-9225.

Smashburger. Garden District, 3300 Magazine St. (504) 342-2653.

TruBurger. Carrollton, 8115 Oak St. (504) 218-5416.

Yo-Mama's. French Quarter, 727 St. Peter St. (504) 522-1125.

ITALIAN

A Mano. Warehouse District, 870 Tchoupitoulas St. (504) 208-9280.

Adolfo's. Marigny, 611 Frenchmen St. (504) 948-3800.

Café Giovanni. French Quarter, 117 Decatur St. (504) 529-2154.

Cibugnu. Central Business District, 709 St. Charles St. (504) 558-8990.

Domenica. Central Business District, 123 Baronne St. (Roosevelt Hotel). (504) 648-6020.

Eleven 79. Warehouse District, 1179 Annunciation St. (504) 569-0001.

Frank's. French Quarter, 933 Decatur St. (504) 525-1602.

Il Posto Café. Uptown, 4607 Dryades St. (504) 895-2620.

Irene's Cuisine. French Quarter, 539 St. Philip St. (504) 529-8811.

Italian Barrel. French Quarter, 430 Barracks St. (504) 569-0198.

Mandina's. Mid-City, 3800 Canal St. (504) 482-9179.

Maple Street Café. Carrollton, 7623 Maple St. (504) 314-9003.

Maximo's Italian Grill. French Quarter, 1117 Decatur St. (504) 586-8883.

Mona Lisa. French Quarter, 1212 Royal St. (504) 522-6746.

Nonna Mia. Bayou St. John, 3125 Esplanade Ave. (504) 948-1717.

Pascal's Manale. Uptown, 1838 Napoleon Ave. (504) 895-4877.

Red Gravy Café. Warehouse District, 125 Camp St. (504) 561-8844.

Tommy's Cuisine. Warehouse District, 746 Tchoupitoulas St. (504) 581-1103.

Tony Moran's. French Quarter, 240 Bourbon St. (504) 523-3181.

Venezia. Mid-City, 134 N. Carrollton Ave. (504) 488-7991.

Vincent's. Carrollton, 7839 St. Charles Ave. (504) 866-9313.

JAPANESE

Chiba. Carrollton, 8312 Oak St. (504) 826-9119.

Geisha. Warehouse District, 111 Tchoupitoulas St. (504) 522-8850.

Ginger Lime. French Quarter, 200 Decatur St. (504) 525-7455.

Good Times Sushi. Gentilly, 5315 Elysian Fields Ave. (504) 265-0721.

Hana. Carrollton, 8116 Hampson St. (504) 865-1634.

Horinoya. Central Business District, 920 Poydras St. (504) 561-8914.

Kakkoii. Carrollton, 7537 Maple St. (504) 570-6440.

Kyoto. Uptown, 4920 Prytania St. (504) 891-3644.

Little Tokyo. Mid-City, 310 N. Carrollton Ave. (504) 485-5658.

Little Tokyo Noodle Bar. Carrollton, 1340 S. Carrollton Ave. (504) 861-6088.

Mikimoto. Carrollton, 3301 S. Carrollton Ave. (504) 488-1881.

Miyako. Garden District, 1403 St. Charles Ave. (504) 410-9997.

Ninja. Uptown, 8433 Oak St. (504) 866-1119.

Origami. Uptown, 5130 Freret St. (504) 891-3715.

Rock-n-Sake. Warehouse District, 823 Fulton St. (504) 581-7253.

Sake Café. Garden District, 2830 Magazine St. (504) 894-0033.

Sekisui Samurai. French Quarter, 239 Decatur St. (504) 525-9595.

Sushi Brothers. Garden District, 1612 St. Charles Ave. (504) 581-4449.

Wasabi. Marigny, 900 Frenchmen St. (504) 943-9433.

MEXICAN

Canal Street Bistro. Mid-City, 3903 Canal St. (504) 482-1225.

El Gato Negro. French Quarter, 81 French Market Place. (504) 525-9752.

El Rinconsito. Mid-City, 216 N. Carrollton Ave. (504) 484-0500.

Felipe's Taqueria. Carrollton, 6215 S. Miro St. (504) 309-2776.

Felipe's Taqueria. French Quarter, 301 N. Peters St. (504) 267-4406.

Juan's Flying Burrito. Garden District, 2018 Magazine St. (504) 569-0000.

Juan's Flying Burrito. Mid-City, 4724 S. Carrollton Ave. (504) 486-9950.

La Casita. Warehouse District, 634 Julia St. (504) 218-8043.

Santa Fe. Bayou St. John, 3201 Esplanade Ave. (504) 948-0077.

Superior Bar & Grill. Uptown, 3636 Charles Ave. (504) 899-4200.

Taqueria Corona. Uptown, 5932 Magazine St. (504) 897-3974.

Taqueria Guerrero Mexico. Mid-City, 208 N. Carrollton Ave. (504) 484-6959.

MIDDLE EASTERN

Ali Baba. French Quarter, 732 St. Peter St. (504) 412-8111.

Attiki. French Quarter, 230 Decatur St. (504) 587-3756.

Babylon Café. Carrollton, 7724 Maple St. (504) 314-0010.

Byblos. Uptown, 3218 Magazine St. (504) 894-1233.

Cleo's Mediterranean Cuisine. Central Business District, 165 University Place. (504) 522-4504.

Fatoush. Marigny, 2372 St. Claude Ave. (504) 371-5074.

Jamila's. Uptown, 7806 Maple St. (504) 866-4366.

Lebanon's Café. Carrollton, 1500 S. Carrollton Ave. (504) 862-6200.

Mona's Café. Marigny, 504 Frenchmen St. (504) 949-4115.

Mona's Café. Mid-City, 3901 Banks St. (504) 482-7743.

Mona's Café. Carrollton, 1120 S. Carrollton Ave. (504) 861-8174.

Mona's Café. Uptown, 4126 Magazine St. (504) 894-9800.

Pyramids Café. Uptown, 3149 Calhoun St. (504) 861-9602.

PIZZA

Ancora Pizzeria. Uptown, 4508 Freret St. (504) 324-1636.

Angeletto's Pizzeria. Warehouse District, 220 S. Robertson St. (504) 581-3500.

Angeli. French Quarter, 1141 Decatur St. (504) 566-0077.

Café Nino. Carrollton, 1519 S. Carrollton Ave. (504) 865-9200.

Café Roma. Uptown, 1901 Sophie Wright Place. (504) 524-2419.

Dough Bowl. Uptown, 1039 Broadway. (504) 861-2200.

Fellini's Café. Mid-City, 900 N. Carrollton Ave. (504) 488-2155.

Fresco. Uptown, 7625 Maple St. (504) 865-7046.

Italian Pie. Central Business District, 417 S. Rampart St. (504) 522-7552.

Italian Pie. Mid-City, 125 N. Carrollton Ave. (504) 483-9949.

Italian Pie. Uptown, 3706 Prytania St. (504) 266-2523.

Lazaro's Pizza. Mid-City, 4413 Banks St. (504) 483-8609.

Louisiana Pizza Kitchen. French Quarter, 95 French Market Place.
(504) 522-9500.

Louisiana Pizza Kitchen. Riverbend, 615 S. Carrollton Ave. (504) 866-5900.

Magazine Pizza. Warehouse District. 1068 Magazine St. (504) 568-0212.

Midway Pizza. Uptown, 4725 Freret St. (504) 322-2815.

New York Pizza. Uptown, 4418 Magazine. (504) 891-2376.

Pepperoni's Café. Riverbend, 8123 Hampson St. (504) 865-0336.

Phillips Restaurant and Bar. Uptown, 733 Cherokee St. (at Maple St.).
(504) 865-1155.

Pizza Delicious. Bywater, 617 Piety St. (504) 676-8482.

Pizzicare. Mid-City, 3001 Tulane Ave. (504) 301-4823.

Reginelli's Pizza. Uptown, 3244 Magazine St. (504) 895-7272.

Reginelli's Pizza. Uptown, 741 State St. (504) 899-1414.

Reginelli's Pizza. Warehouse District, 930 Poydras St. (504) 586-0068.

Roman Pizza. Uptown, 7329 Cohn St. (504) 866-1166.

Slice. Garden District, 1513 St. Charles Ave. (504) 525-7437.

Slice. Uptown, 5538 Magazine St. (504) 897-4800.

Theo's Pizza. Uptown, 4218 Magazine St. (504) 894-8554.

Theo's Pizza. Mid-City, 4024 Canal St. (504) 302-1133.

Warehouse District Pizza. Warehouse District, 325 Andrew Higgins Dr. (504) 529-1466.

SEAFOOD

Acme Oyster House. French Quarter, 724 Iberville St. (504) 522-5973.

Bourbon House. French Quarter, 144 Bourbon St. (504) 522-0111.

Bubba Gump's Shrimp Company. French Quarter, 429 Decatur St. (504) 522-5800.

Casamento's. Uptown, 4330 Magazine St. (504) 895-9761.

Corner Oyster House. French Quarter, 500 St. Peter St. (504) 522-0999.

Crazy Lobster. Warehouse District, 1 Poydras St. (504) 569-3380.

Deanie's Seafood. French Quarter, 841 Iberville St. (504) 581-1316.

Desire Oyster Bar. French Quarter, 300 Bourbon St. (504) 586-0300.

Drago's. Warehouse District, 2 Poydras St. (Hilton Hotel). (504) 584-3911.

Ernst Café. Warehouse District, 600 S. Peters St. (504) 525-8544.

French Market Restaurant. French Quarter, 1001 Decatur St. (504) 525-7879.

Grand Isle. Warehouse District, 575 Convention Center Blvd. (504) 520-8530.

Gumbo Pot. French Quarter, 600 Decatur St. (504) 522-1010.

G. W. Fins. French Quarter, 808 Bienville St. (504) 581-3467.

Jack Dempsey's. Bywater, 738 Poland Ave. (504) 943-9914.

KJean's Seafood. Mid-City, 236 N. Carrollton Ave. (504) 488-7503.

Oceana Grill. French Quarter, 739 Conti St. (504) 525-6002.

Pêche Seafood Grill. Warehouse District, 800 Magazine St. (504) 522-1744.

Pier 424. French Quarter, 424 Bourbon St. (504) 309-1574.

Ralph & Kacoo's. French Quarter, 519 Toulouse St. (504) 522-5226.

Red Fish Grill. French Quarter, 115 Bourbon St. (504) 598-1200.

Royal House. French Quarter, 441 Royal St. (504) 528-2601.

Sammy's Seafood. French Quarter, 627 Bourbon St. (504) 525-8442.

Superior Seafood. Uptown, 4338 St. Charles Ave. (504) 293-3474.

SPANISH

Barcelona Tapas. Carrollton, 720 Dublin St. (504) 861-9696.

Café Granada. Carrollton, 1506 S. Carrollton Ave. (504) 865-1612.

Galvez. French Quarter, 914 N. Peters St. (504) 595-3400.

Lola's. Bayou St. John, 3312 Esplanade Ave. (504) 488-6946.

Rio Mar. Warehouse District, 800 S. Peters St. (504) 525-3474.

Santa Fe Tapas. Garden District, 1327 St. Charles Ave. (504) 304-9915.

STEAK HOUSE

Besh Steakhouse. Central Business District, Harrah's New Orleans Casino, 8 Canal St. (504) 533-6111.

Charlie's Steak House. Uptown, 4510 Dryades St. (504) 895-9705.

Chophouse. Warehouse District, 322 Magazine St. (504) 522-7902.

Crescent City Steak House. Mid-City, 1001 N. Broad St. (504) 821-3271.

Delmonico. Garden District, 1300 St. Charles Ave. (504) 525-4937.

Desi Vega's. Warehouse District, 628 St. Charles Ave. (504) 523-7600.

Dickie Brennan's Steakhouse. French Quarter, 716 Iberville St. (504) 522-2467.

Embers Steak House. French Quarter, 700 Bourbon St. (504) 523-1485.

La Boca. Warehouse District & Center City, 857 Fulton St. (504) 525-8205.

Morton's The Steakhouse. Central Business District, 365 Canal St. (Canal Place Mall). (504) 566-0221.

Mr. John's Steakhouse. Uptown, 2111 St. Charles Ave. (504) 679-7697.

Ruth's Chris Steak House. Warehouse District, 525 Fulton St. (504) 587-7099.

Star Steak & Lobster. French Quarter, 237 Decatur St. (504) 525-6151.

THAI

Bangkok Thai. Riverbend, 513 S. Carrollton Ave. (504) 861-3932.

Basil Leaf. Carrollton, 1438 S. Carrollton Ave. (504) 862-9001.

Chill Out Café. Carrollton, 729 Burdette St. (504) 872-9628.

La Thai Cuisine. Uptown, 4938 Prytania St. (504) 899-8886.

Sukho Thai. Marigny, 1913 Royal St. (504) 948-9309.

Sukho Thai. Uptown, 4519 Magazine St. (504) 373-6471.

VIETNAMESE

Ba Chi Canteen. Carrollton, 7900 Maple St. (504) 373-5628.

Café Minh. Mid-City, 4139 Canal St. (504) 482-6266.

Doson's Noodle House. Mid-City, 135 N. Carrollton Ave. (504) 309-7283.

Jazmine Café. Riverbend, 614 S. Carrollton Ave. (504) 866-9301.

Lilly's Café. Garden District, 1813 Magazine St. (504) 599-9999.

Magasin Vietnamese Café. Uptown, 4201 Magazine St. (504) 896-7611.

Pho Noi Viet. Garden District, 2005 Magazine St. (504) 522-3399.

Viet Orleans Bistro. Warehouse District, 300 Baronne St. (504) 333-6917.

CULINARY TOURS AND COOKING CLASSES

CLASSES

Cleaver & Co.

3917 Baronne St. • (504) 227-3830
Old-world butcher offers limited
schedule of classes for meat cutting and
sausage making.

Creole Delicacies

533 St. Ann St. • (504) 525-9508
Specialty shop known for creamy
pralines; gives lessons on how to make
local essentials like a roux.

Crescent City Cooks

201 Chartres St. • (504) 529-1600
Shelley Ross and Nita Duhe teach
classes featuring local dishes—shrimp
étouffée, red beans and rice, Bananas
Foster.

Langlois Culinary Crossroads

184 N. Rampart St. • (504) 934-1010
Classes taught by author and radio
host Amy Cyrex-Sins in a turn-of-
the-century Italian market. Langlois
is named after Governor Bienville's
housekeeper, who taught a fusion of
French and Creole culinary traditions.

New Orleans Cooking Experiences

1519 Carondelet St. • (504) 430-5274
More upscale classes (crawfish
shortcake, baked oysters, white-
chocolate bread pudding) taught by
noted chefs and cookbook authors
(Frank Brigsten, Poppy Tooker, Gerard
Maras). Unlike most, these are not
demonstration classes. You'll get your
hands dirty.

New Orleans School of Cooking

524 St. Louis St. • (800) 237-4841
Located in an old molasses warehouse,
twice-a-day classes feature local classics
like gumbo, jambalaya, or pralines.

Vonn Fass

5725 Magazine St. • (504) 302-1455
Upscale store selling oils, vinegars, wine,
and spirits has chef-run cooking classes
for local and seasonal dishes.

TOURS

Clandestine New Orleans

5300 Freret St. • (504) 301-2991
Clandestine creates totally unique New
Orleans events. They specialize in small
to mid-sized events (one guest to five
hundred) for intrepid adventurers who
are looking to go beyond "cookie cutter"
experiences. They'll set up crawfish
boils, boucheries, and private dinners in
unique locations, often with a renowned
chef on hand.

Destination Kitchen

910 Dublin St. • (855) 353-6634
Choose to be a "foodie for a day"

or "foodie for a half day." On these culinary and cultural tours, dine in New Orleans's best restaurants and meet some of New Orleans's finest individuals that care about this city's food culture.

Langlois Culinary Crossroads

1841 N. Rampart St. • (504) 934-1010 On the tour, you'll meander through our streets with a local guide who will unwind the history of good eating in New Orleans and the importance of these neighborhoods and establishments in forming the city's unique cuisine.

New Orleans Culinary Bike Tour

634 Elysian Fields • (504) 400-5468 Confederacy of Cruisers had the city's first neighborhood culinary tours. These tours will give you an understanding of the joy it is to spend a life in one of America's food meccas. You'll bike through the Creole side of town stopping at a few personally picked spots that will let you sample local cuisine.

New Orleans Culinary History Tours

(504) 875-6570 New Orleans Culinary History Tours has been offering tours since 2004. Founder Kelly Hamilton holds an MA in history and is a former instructor at Xavier University of Louisiana.

Tastebud Tours

2649 Desoto St. • (219) 929-664 Culinary walking tours. Savor NOLA's favorites on a Taste of New Orleans food tour. Enjoy a muffuletta at Serio's, winners of the Food Network's *Throwdown with Bobby Flay*. Savor jambalaya at the Old Coffee Shop, featured on Guy Fieri's *Diners, Drive-ins and Dives*.

ACKNOWLEDGMENTS

First I must thank my editor, Ann Triestman. Over the years, we have worked together in almost every capacity. When I was William Morrow's publisher, Ann worked for me as an editor. We worked together when, as a literary agent, I sold her the book *My Parachute Is Beige*, a humorous career guide for slackers. Now, I work for her. As an editor at Countryman, a division of W. W. Norton, and knowing my love for New Orleans, Ann approached me to do this book.

Ann and everyone at W. W. Norton and Countryman Press have been extremely attentive and responsive to my every quiver and quibble for this admittedly "midlist" book. I even got the cover I wanted! For an author to get the cover they want is practically unheard of in the annals of publishing history. I need to thank Stacie Herndon, my long time e-mail friend (we've never met) who designed my website nearly ten years ago and now has designed my book cover. You may see her work (and hire her!) at Heelgrinder.com. Anne Ricketts is likewise a BFF I have only met online. She's an exceptional sculptor, has written an incredible memoir I completely failed to sell as her literary agent, and is an amazingly soulful person who served as an early reader. She suggested the $$$ price codes shown by each restaurant and encouraged me to reveal more personality over factoids. I must give a huge thanks to Rick Olivier. I first met Rick in 2000 when he photographed my wedding, and now he has contributed his photos to bring this book to life. You can view his work at www.rickolivier.com. When you come to New Orleans, in addition to eating our food, you should take in a performance by Rick's Grammy-nominated band, the Creole String Beans. I want to personally acknowledge Kermit Hummel, Countryman's director; Lisa Sacks, managing editor (who diligently and brilliantly tried to teach an old dog like me dropbox, ftp, and how to disable tracking. She failed. Great teachers need great students.); Norton's VP of sales, Bill Rusin (who liked my title); and Tom Haushalter, publicity manager and published poet. I also thank every salesperson nationwide, copy editor, designer, and warehouse packer and shipper in Scranton, PA, whose names I'll never know but all of whom contributed to the book.

I have to give a big, spilling-off-the-plate thank-you to all the judges who jumped in to create the "Best of" appendix. Marcelle Bienvenu, Lolis Eric Elie, Gwendolyn Knapp, Ian McNulty, Sara Roahen, Amy Cyrex Sins, Judy Walker, and Liz Williams are an A-list of New Orleans food experts. A special nod to the effervescent Poppy Tooker, who more than serving as a judge, served as my ride out to the region's book distributor, forty-five minutes outside the city, and who let me into her home to lather me with food stories and allow me to love on her three pugs. (I'm a pug person.) All nine judges responded to me with an enthusiastic "yes" within one day of my e-mail request. Their quick replies reminded me of one of the many reasons I love New Orleans. The people here are remarkably friendly, open, and ever ready for the next adventure. Unlike most cities (and you know who you are), in New Orleans choosing to participate is rarely about making money nor advancing your "brand," but "sounds like fun, let's do it." The spirit of New Orleans is even better than her food.

I need a special thank-you for my daughter, Ella, for letting me hog our one home computer for the late nights and long hours writing this book. Having thanked my daughter, I should thank my son, Austin, even though he lives 1,304 miles away in New York and had little to do with this book. He was a great student at Vassar and Columbia and now is a great teacher.

Finally, I must thank my wife, Marnie Carmichael. Living in New York at the time, we chose a destination wedding in New Orleans. It was the best wedding ever. Kermit Ruffins was our wedding band. Rockin Dopsie had been our Friday night band. The food was a cochon de lait, oyster-shucking station, and Southern sides like spoon bread. We had so much fun that when our wedding started to wind down, we grabbed half the attending friends and family and headed out to the Mid-City Rock 'n' Bowl. Nathan and the Zydeco Cha-Chas were playing that night. I bowled a beer-impaired sixty-three. On our wedding day, I'm sure Marnie, when she said "for better or worse," had no idea how worse the worse could be. We've been through deaths, destitution, lawsuits, betrayals (by family members and business partners—not each other), and the breaking of every dish we owned when the kitchen cabinet fell off the wall. Marnie and I stood dumbfounded, looking at tiny shards of porcelain spread across our kitchen floor. We had just moved to New Orleans. I finally said, "I think that's New Orleans saying, 'hello.'" About the only thing we haven't lost over the years is our commitment to each other. Marnie is involved in every aspect of my life and you can thank her for the REASON TO GO and WHAT TO GET entries accompanying most restaurant listings.

Oh, and thank you for being the type of reader who reads acknowledgments.

NEWS & NOTES

Every day since finishing the manuscript for *Eat Dat New Orleans*, I think of someplace I left out.

That's just the nature of trying to write a comprehensive book on something so massive as New Orleans' food culture. I thought of Kitchen Witch, a culinary bookshop, and Tamarind, the restaurant at Tivoli & Lee Hotel, literally as the book was going to press.

To right these wrongs, and to update any new or closed restaurants (hopefully to announce the re-opening of Brennan's on Royal), there is a website: www.eatdatnola.com.

The website will have new and updated words and images. There will also be the opportunity to go all Urbanspoon and Yelp on me, telling me how ridiculous my comments are, or suggesting a favorite joint not mentioned in my book. Maybe the site will even offer items to buy, like autographed Mr. Okra photographs or chef toques embroidered with *Eat Dat New Orleans*. Probably not. But do come visit www.eatdatnola.com.

ALPHABETICAL INDEX

NEIGHBORHOOD INDEX